MORAL RULES

BY
JOHN LEE

© Copyright 1999
First published 1999

Abacus Educational Services
424 Birmingham Road
Marlbrook
Bromsgrove
Worcestershire
B61 OHL

ISBN 1 898653 15 1

Other titles available in the series:
1. Ethical Theory and Language
3. Christian Ethics (in preparation)
4. Homosexuality

Also available:

Philosophy of Religion series:
1. Religious Language
2. The Problem of Evil
3. Faith and Reason
4. God and Proof
5. Revelation and Religious Experience
6. Life after Death
7. Miracles

Other titles on the Synoptic Gospels and the Fourth Gospel are also available.

CONTENTS

INTRODUCTION

This booklet has been written specifically to cater for the needs of A/AS students of Philosophy and Religious Studies. However, it may equally be used as an introduction to ethics by the interested lay person or by first year undergraduates.

The style of the booklet is similar to the style employed in other booklets in other series. It is structured around key questions that have developed from classroom experience. It also contains a section that deals with exam questions and should therefore be useful for both teaching and revision.

Philosophy, of which ethics is a part, can be great fun to both study and to teach. It is a subject that both staff and students can become fully engaged in. It is therefore hoped that learning about ethics will prove to be an enjoyable experience.

WHAT IS ETHICS?

As was mentioned in the first booklet in this series, Ethics is a wide-ranging subject. There are many questions that could be considered ethical: what ought we to do? Are animal experiments right? What is the meaning of the word "good"? Indeed ethics is often divided into three main areas:

Metaethics—the study of the nature of morality.

Normative ethics—the examination of whether there are any moral rules.

Practical ethics—the area of ethics that applies ethical theory to different moral problems.

A more detailed description of these different areas of ethics can be found in the first booklet in this series. This first booklet also looked in detail at the meaning of moral terms i.e. it examined Metaethics. This booklet is concerned with normative ethics. In other words the discussion focuses on whether there are any rules that should be followed.

ARE THERE ANY MORAL RULES?

Another way of putting the question as to whether there are any moral rules is to ask whether it can be worked out what we ought to do i.e. are there any principles that we need to follow when deciding what is right or wrong. This question is at the heart of normative ethics.

In order to understand the different responses to this question it is important to recognize that moral rules could be about more than one thing. As was mentioned in the first booklet in this series morality could be about either means or ends. The means are the method you use to do something; whereas the ends are the outcome or what you achieve. It is therefore possible to have a moral rule about means (i.e. the moral rule tells you how to do something) or you could have a moral rule about ends (i.e. the moral rule tells you what outcome you should aim for).

Please note that the debate as to whether there are moral rules is different to the one about whether morality is to do with ends or means. This is because it is possible, for example, to reject the whole idea of moral rules whether you believe that it is the outcome or the method that is important. (Someone could, for example, argue that moral language was meaningless and therefore there are no rules at all.)

It is also important to remember that philosophers have used other words to describe theories based on ends and means. These words are "deontological" (literally meaning "concerned with duty") which is used to describe theories that are based on means; and "teleological" (literally meaning "concerned with ends") which is used to describe theories based on ends. Teleological theories are also sometimes known as *Consequentialism* because it is the consequences that are important.

Three major ethical theories will be considered. One centres on the idea that there is a moral rule we should follow that it based on ends; another is deontological; the third is also based on ends and is a very important theory in the discussion about Christian ethics. The first theory is called Utilitarianism, the second is based on the work of the philosopher Kant and the third is known as Situation ethics.

UTILITARIANISM

The idea of utility can be found in the work of the Scottish philosopher David Hume (1711-1776). However, Utilitarianism as a theory was first developed by the British philosopher Jeremy Bentham (1748-1832). Bentham's ideas were later worked on by his one time pupil John Stuart Mill (1806-1873), who is perhaps the most famous Utilitarian.

It is important to note that whilst Utilitarianism is an ethical theory, it was also conceived as a political measure. Bentham, for example, thought that he had developed a means by which governments and individuals could work out what the correct course of action was.

As has already been mentioned Utilitarianism is a teleological theory i.e. it is interested in ends not the means by which those ends are achieved. However, the theory suggests that there is one rule that everyone should follow in order to determine what is right and wrong.

What is this rule all about? Put simply, and perhaps obviously, Utilitarianism is based on the idea of "utility". "Utility" means "usefulness". What Utilitarians suggest is that everyone should do the most "useful" thing. However, there seems to be an immediate problem with this idea in that it is not obvious what "useful" means. The answer to this problem, according to Utilitarians, is that "useful" means "happiness": it is useful (i.e. good to you) to be happy. This is, in fact, a development of another ethical theory known as Hedonism. Hedonism is the theory that what is good is pleasure (see the first booklet in this series). Utilitarians also define good in terms of happiness. Indeed for a Utilitarian the only thing that is good in itself is happiness.

So what is the rule? Utilitarianism is all about attempting to determine the "most useful" course of action. The most useful action will be the one that brings about the greatest happiness. This is usually called the **Principle of Utility** (see below).

Another key feature of Utilitarianism is that it attempts to be "scientific" in that Utilitarians believe that the amount of happiness can be calculated. To examine what this means the work of Bentham will first be looked at. Then how and why Mill revised Bentham will be discussed.

▶BENTHAM.

Essentially what Bentham attempted to do, in terms of ethics, was to answer three questions:

> How can we judge what is right and wrong?
> How can we measure happiness?
> How can people be made to follow what is right?

▷How can we judge what is right and wrong? (The principle of utility.)

Bentham believed that it was possible to work out what is right and wrong by following one rule: what he called the Principle of Utility. This Principle of Utility is often summed up by the slogan "the greatest happiness of the greatest number". What this means, according to Bentham, is that we should approve of actions that bring about the greatest happiness and disapprove of those actions that do not. As has already been mentioned, the Utilitarian aim is to follow the most useful course of action i.e. the one that brings about the most happiness. (This is often expressed as what is right is what "maximizes" happiness.) This is the principle (rule) that everyone should follow.

It should be noted that this Principle of Utility does *not* simply mean the happiness of the majority. To illustrate this point imagine that you have been given the task of distributing 4 bars of chocolate to you and 3 friends. What is the Utilitarian course of action? The obvious answer seems to be to have one bar of chocolate each (assuming that you all like chocolate) as you would all be happy. However, this may *not* actually be the Utilitarian action. You could, for example, absolutely adore chocolate. You could, in fact, be 20 times as happy than your friends if you were given all the chocolate. In this case the *right* course of action, according to Utilitarianism, would be to give you all the chocolate! This would actually create more happiness than if they were distributed evenly.

A good way of summing up the Principle of Utility is to say that "it is not the happiness of the majority, it is the majority of happiness."

▷How can we measure happiness? (The Felicific Calculus.)

Bentham believed that it was possible to calculate the amount of happiness in a similar way to the way that calculations are made in science and maths. He called the means for doing this the **Felicific Calculus** (if something is 'felicific' it brings about happiness; calculus is a means of working something out.) The felicific calculus is also sometimes referred to as the 'hedonistic calculus' or the 'pleasure calculus".

It is obviously crucial for Bentham to be able to work out the amount of happiness so that the greatest happiness can be calculated and thus what is right can be determined. Bentham thought that there were 7 different elements that need to be taken into account when working out happiness. These 7 parts of the Felicific Calculus are:

1. The Intensity of the pleasure.
2. The Duration of the pleasure i.e. how long it lasts (the longer the better).
3. The Certainty of the pleasure: some actions are better because pleasure will definitely follow; whereas with other actions the outcome might not be guaranteed.
4. The Fecundity of the pleasure: fecundity means 'productive". What Bentham means by this is how likely the action will result in other pleasures or the repeat of pleasure.
5. The Propinquity of the pleasure: this means how near the pleasure is to you.
6. The Purity of the pleasure: some pleasures may involve a certain amount of pain; these are not as desirable as those that do not.
7. The Extent of the pleasure: the more people who experience the pleasure the better.

Bentham believed that when all these elements were looked at it was possible to determine the amount of pleasure and consequently what the right course of action is.

▷How can people be made to follow what is right? (Sanctions.)

Bentham also tried to establish a reason why people should follow the Principle of Utility. The reason he gave was that people should be punished if they do not follow the rules and laws determined by the Principle of Utility. Another word for punishment is sanction and this is the word that Bentham preferred. These sanctions could be physical (e.g. pain being inflicted), political (e.g. having your freedom taken away from you) or moral (e.g. being made to feel guilty).

▶MILL.

It was John Stuart Mill's aim to revise and adapt Bentham's ideas. Mill felt that this revision was necessary because Bentham's work had been criticized by many other writers. Indeed Mill agreed with the criticisms that had been made and perhaps part of Mill's response can be seen as an intellectual rebellion against his one time teacher.

Mill attempted to adapt Bentham's thoughts by introducing a number of different ideas and distinctions. These included:

> A distinction between higher and lower pleasures.
> A proof of the Principle of Utility.
> A wider understanding of human nature.
> A distinction between Act and Rule Utilitarianism.
> A wider view of sanctions and of justice.

▷Higher and Lower pleasures.

One of the criticisms of Bentham's philosophy was that it was a 'swine' (pig) philosophy. The accusation was that, with its emphasis on pleasure, Utilitarianism made human beings no better than pigs: if our only interests are sex, eating and sleeping, then we are exactly the same as pigs.

Mill responded to this criticism by claiming that humans can have better quality pleasures than pigs. Some pleasures, according to Mill, might be better because of quantity (e.g. 5 cheeseburgers may be better than 1). However, there may be other pleasures that are better because of their quality (e.g. there may be something about the nature of discussing philosophy that makes it a better pleasure than eating cheeseburgers). Those pleasures that are better due to their quality are described by Mill as 'higher' pleasures.

For Mill the 'higher' pleasures are those that stimulate the mind (i.e. those that pigs cannot have). The 'lower' pleasures are the physical ones (such as eating). The higher pleasures, according to Mill, are the ones that should be more desirable and are therefore better. Mill expressed this by stating

> 'It is better to be a human being dissatisfied than a pig satisfied; better to be Socrates [famous Greek philosopher] dissatisfied than a fool satisfied. And if the fool, or the pig, are a different opinion, it is because they only know their own side of the question.' (*Utilitarianism*, J.S. Mill.)

Mill did recognize that, in reality, some people do not always opt for the higher pleasures. According to Mill this may be due to such things as ignorance or other personal circumstances. What everyone ought to do is to look at the experiences of those people who have experienced both. Mill believed that those who have had experience of higher and lower pleasures will always say that it is the higher pleasures that are better.

▷ Proof of the Principle of Utility.

Bentham believed that an actual proof of the Principle of Utility was not possible. Mill argued that some sort of proof was possible. Mill's proof falls into 3 parts and he attempted to establish 3 things: that happiness is desirable; that happiness is the only thing that is desirable; and that the general happiness of all is desirable.

The only evidence that Mill thought was necessary to show that happiness is desirable is that it is actually desired. Mill made the comparison to visibility and the proof that something is visible is that it can be seen.

Secondly, Mill attempted to show that happiness is the only thing that is desirable as an end. The proof of this, for Mill, is that whilst other things seem to be desirable (such as my football team winning the cup), they are only desirable because they bring about happiness.

Lastly, Mill attempts to show that the general happiness of all is desirable. The proof of this is that if you increase the general happiness (i.e. the happiness of everyone), then your own happiness will also be increased.

Thus the proof falls into 3 stages. Mill believes that in order to establish that happiness is the only thing that is desirable, it is first necessary to show that happiness is desirable. Having done this Mill believes that it follows that everyone should desire the general happiness (the Principle of Utility) because it will increase the only thing that we should desire (happiness).

This proof of the Principle of Utility has been criticized by many philosophers and there is some general agreement that it does not work. Each of the three parts of the proof can be criticized. For example, the first part of the argument may not be a proof as there is an important difference between the ideas of visibility and desirability. The fact that something is desired does not necessarily make it desirable because 'desirable' implies some sort of moral judgement. In other words to describe something as 'desirable' is to say that it *should be* desired not that it is desired. I might, for example, desire the death of everyone I don't like but this doesn't make this course of action desirable because it is not a good thing. Similarly the third part of Mill's argument could be criticized by saying that increasing the general happiness may not increase my happiness and therefore may not be desirable.

▷ **Human nature.**

Bentham was a strict hedonist that is he believed that everything that everyone did was in her/his own interest. Mill, however, had a slightly wider view and recognized that humans do sometimes act to help other people. However, this did not effect Utilitarianism for Mill because generally humans act in their own interests i.e. even though it is not always true, as a rule humans will act egoistically.

▷ **Act and Rule Utilitarianism.**

Mill also attempted to respond to the problem as to how we are meant to go about making moral decisions. There does not always seem to be time to work out which is the most Utilitarian course of action i.e. it is difficult to see how the greatest amount of happiness can be calculated in a short space of time. Imagine you are in the situation in which there are two people trapped in a burning building and you have the chance to save either one of them: if you sit down and work out which person's rescue would bring about the greatest happiness, then they both may die.

Mill's response to this problem was to suggest that there has been enough time to calculate what the right course of action would be. Everyone has had all their previous experiences to help them. Indeed humans have developed rules about what is right and wrong. These rules may not always be true (i.e. they may not always bring about the greatest happiness) but they are useful tools for deciding what should be done. One common example of a possible rule is the idea that it is wrong to kill innocent people.

This has led to a distinction being made between two types of Utilitarian: **Act Utilitarians** (such as Bentham) who believe that previous experience does not count and that the principle of utility should be applied anew to every moral situation; and **Rule Utilitarians** (such as Mill) who believe that previous experience does count and that rules can be developed from the principle of Utility. Since the time of Mill much of the debate within Utilitarianism has been about which of these positions is correct.

▷A wider view of sanctions and justice.

Another area in which Mill attempted to revise Bentham's ideas was in respect to sanctions. Bentham believed that external sanctions, such as the law and public opinion, were the only things that could make people do things. In other words what Bentham did not explain was why people should be moral in the absence of sanctions. Mill thus introduced the idea of 'internal sanctions' to combat this problem. What Mill meant by internal sanctions was the idea of conscience or guilt that give us a reason to be moral even if we are not going to be punished by others.

In a similar way Mill attempted to show that Utilitarianism allowed for some concept of justice in that, as a rule, our concept of justice (fairness) will lead to the greatest happiness of the greatest number.

▶CRITICISMS OF UTILITARIANISM.

- *What is pleasure?* As has already been noted Utilitarianism is based on the idea of Hedonism. Indeed this is what led many philosophers to suggest that Utilitarianism was a 'swine philosophy' as it was simply based on pleasure. Mill did attempt to respond to this accusation by suggesting a distinction between higher and lower pleasures. However, other problems remain: isn't pleasure different for all of us? Can't pain sometimes lead to pleasure and isn't this a contradiction? (For example, having my nose rebroken may cause a lot of pain but may lead to long term benefits.) Indeed is Mill right to suggest that 'higher' pleasures are in fact better? Many people would argue that things like sex and eating are better than discussing philosophy.

- *Is Human nature egoistic?* Another problem that has already been noted is the idea that humans do not always seem to act in their own interest. For example, there are many examples of individuals risking their lives in order to save others. This is clearly a problem for Bentham's version of Utilitarianism although it is one of the things that Mill recognized. Mill argued that, whist it may not always be in your interest to follow the principle of utility, it was sensible to do so.

- *How do we go about making moral decisions?* As has already been noted there may not always be enough time to work out what most utilitarian course of action might be. Once again Mill responded to this problem and claimed that humans develop shorthand rules which help them make moral decisions. However, other philosophers have questioned whether the Felicific Calculus is realistic. It is difficult to see, for example, whether you should choose the most intense pleasure or the one that lasts the longer. How can you decide between the two? Similarly, it could be argued that it is very difficult to predict the consequences of any action, and therefore difficult to predict the greatest good of the greatest number, especially if someone is trying to take a long term view.

- *Utilitarianism and Justice.* Imagine the following situation. You live in a small town and there has been a murder. No one really knows who did it but the council decides to charge you with the crime. They find you guilty and you are sentenced to death. As a consequence of this everyone decides that it is not a good idea to do anything wrong again. In other words your punishment has brought about the greatest happiness of the greatest number and therefore, according to Utilitarianism, is right. However, most people (especially you) would argue that your punishment is not fair and goes against the idea of justice. Thus it is difficult to see how Utilitarianism can include a concept of justice because it is not important to how decisions about what is right and wrong should be made.

- *Is the principle of utility what we mean by morality?* For a Utilitarian, an action is good if, and only if, it brings about the greatest good of the greatest number. In other words it does not matter what an individual's motives are or indeed how the greatest good of the greatest number is achieved. This goes against the idea that it is intentions, such as love and care, that are the important parts of morality.

- *Is happiness the only thing that is important?* Essentially this is another way of seeing the above problem. For a Utilitarian, the only thing that is important is the idea of happiness. Thus anything that brings about happiness is right. However, consider the situation in which the government decides to put a happiness-producing drug into the water supply. Everyone becomes wonderfully happy but many people would not consider this to be right. (The writer Aldous Huxley parodied the idea of Utilitarianism in his novel *Brave New World*.)

- *The naturalistic fallacy.* As was mentioned in the first booklet in this series, Utilitarianism can be seen as a form of Naturalism. Naturalism is any theory that attempts to reduce ethics to something natural. In the case of Utilitarianism, the theory reduces morality to the idea of pleasure i.e. something natural about human beings. As a form of Naturalism, Utilitarianism is open to the same sorts of criticisms that are levelled at Naturalism. One of these was famously made by the philosopher G.E.Moore who argued that it was a mistake in reasoning (a fallacy) to try to reduce ethics to something natural because ethics cannot be analysed in this way. Moore's criticism is known as the naturalistic fallacy. (For a fuller discussion of the naturalistic fallacy and the idea of Naturalism, see the first booklet in this series.)

- *Why be a Utilitarian?* The answer to this question given by Bentham and Mill was that it is in our own interest to be a Utilitarian. Mill has a 'proof' of this, although it is generally agreed that this proof does not work. However, there is perhaps an even more fundamental problem. If the principle of utility is the only ethical principle, what reasons could there be for adopting it? It could be argued that it brings about the greatest good of the greatest number but this is an example of a circular argument. (The reason for doing X cannot be X.) It is difficult to see, however, how else a Utilitarian could argue that everyone should follow the principle of utility.

KANT

Immanuel Kant (1724-1804) is one of the most historically significant philosophers of all time. He was a German Protestant who wrote on a number of philosophical issues. Indeed Kant's ethical theory is only a fraction of his philosophy.

In terms of ethics, Kant attempted to provide a means by which what we ought to do can be known i.e. he attempted to provide a rule that should be followed. Kant's rule is often likened to the Roman Catholic idea of Natural Law. (This is discussed in the third booklet in this series.) In order to understand Kant's ethics it is important to recognize some ideas that underlie what he believed.

▶ UNDERLYING THEMES.

▷ How do we solve moral problems?

For Kant the answer to this question is that we use reason. Human beings, according to Kant, are rational and can work out what is right and wrong.

▷ Imperatives

An imperative is something that must be done. For example, it could be said that it is imperative for you to eat. This means that you must eat, it is something that you have to do.

Kant thought that there are two types of imperative and it is important to understand them in order to understand his ethical theory. Another way of saying that there are two types of imperative is to say that there are two types of answer to the question 'What ought we do?' The first is an instruction if you want to achieve a goal; the second is things that we should do in all situations whether we want to achieve something or not.

Consider the question: what ought I do in order to get to Manchester? Here my goal (aim) is to get to Manchester and, for Kant, it would be an example of the first type of imperative. The answer to the question will be an instruction (e.g. take the M6 or get off at Manchester

Piccadilly Station). Kant called these types of imperatives **Hypothetical Imperatives**. An hypothetical is something that is assumed to be. Thus a hypothetical imperative is one that tells you what to do if you want to achieve something.

Kant believed that morality is different. It is not about hypothetical imperatives because it is not about achieving things; it is not about goals. Morality, for Kant, has **Categorical Imperatives**. If something is categorical, it is true without condition. Thus the imperatives (things that ought to be done) of morality are things that should be done without condition; they should not be done because something needs to be achieved. For Kant, the categorical imperative is the one moral rule to follow.

▷**Deontological**.

Kant's idea of the categorical imperative implies that it is not the ends that are important for morality, it is the means; morality is not interested in consequences. For example, morality is not about things like happiness. (Kant's views are, therefore, very different to Utilitarianism.)

▷**Universalisability.**

Kant believed that moral rules and ideas are true for all people in all situations i.e. they are objective and absolute. They are objective, according to Kant, because they are based on rationality (reason) and everyone is rational (i.e. rationality is also objective). Kant called this idea **Universalisability**. If something is 'universalisable", then it can be true for all people at all times.

▷**The 'good will'.**

Kant also argued that actions are good if, and only if, they are done because they are morally right. In other words it is our intention that is important. Kant used the word 'will' to describe intention and he argued that it is the 'good will' that morality is about. A good will, for Kant, is one that intends to obey what is right not one that intends to satisfy its own desires.

The will is important to Kant because he believed that there is a distinction between good behaviour and good will. Kant used the example of the shopkeeper to illustrate this point. The shopkeeper might be very kind and pleasant to you. This is good behaviour, what she/he does is good. However, it may not show a good will because she/he may only be being nice to you in order to make a profit. A good will is one that does the right thing with the right intention (unlike the shopkeeper) and it is the good will, according to Kant, that is morally right.

▶THE CATEGORICAL IMPERATIVE.

As has already been mentioned, Kant believed that there is one rule that should be followed in order to decide what is right and wrong. This rule he called the categorical imperative. Kant believed that all other moral rules are really instances of this one general rule. Kant also suggested that there are a number of ways of expressing the categorical imperative. The 2 most important are:

▷Universalisabilty.

> "Always act according to that maxim whose universality as a law you can at the same time will...such an imperative is categorical." *(Foundations of the Metaphysics of Morals, Kant.)*

What Kant suggested is that anything that is morally right should be able to be done by all people in all situations i.e. what is right should be universalisable. In other words anything that cannot be universal (true for everyone) cannot be morally right.

Thus, for Kant, whenever anyone tries to decide whether something is right, she/he should ask the question 'What if everyone did that?' This question actually subdivides into two further questions: is it logically possible for everyone to do it? Do you rationally want everyone to do it?

To illustrate his point Kant provided some examples of moral rules. For example, Kant argued that it was morally wrong to break promises because, logically, it would not make sense if everyone did it. If it were universal that everyone could break promises, then there would actually be no point in making them because there would be no reason for anyone to believe any promise that had been made. (A very similar argument could be made against lying.) Thus breaking promises goes against the first question. However, what about laziness? It is logically possible for everyone to be lazy. However, Kant argued that this is something that we would not want everyone to do and is therefore wrong (i.e. not universal) for that reason.

▷Humans are ends in themselves.

> "Act in such a way that you always treat humanity, whether your own person or in the person of any other, never simply as a means but always at the same time as an end." (Ibid.)

What Kant meant by this is that human beings are valuable and should therefore be respected. They are not respected if they are treated as means. You could treat objects, such as a piece of wool, as a means (e.g. to make a jumper) but it is wrong just to use people in order to get something. It would be wrong, for example, for me to lie to you in order to con you out of money as I would be treating you as a means (to get money) and not as an end. It is important to note that Kant does recognize that it is possible to use people for means (for example, to get tomatoes from the greengrocer) what is wrong is to treat people only as a means.

To understand what Kant means by these two formulations of the categorical imperative, consider the example of stealing. Kant would have argued that stealing is wrong. It is wrong because it does not involve treating people as ends (they are just means to get money); it is also wrong because it is not something that could be universal (we would not want everyone to steal).

▶CRITICISMS OF KANT'S ETHICS.

- *Are we rational?* Kant assumes that everyone is a rational human being and should act rationally. However, this could be questioned and indeed many people do not always act rationally. For example, what about the fanatic who is totally convinced of her position? Anything you say to her will not convince her that she is wrong. Further, it could be argued that being rational does not lead to the categorical imperative. Indeed one of the arguments for Egoism (the theory that we should put ourselves first) is the idea of rationality and that being rational leads to self-interest.

- *Motives.* Kant argued that the only reason to be moral is that you should. However, this effectively rules out other motives for action, such as love and compassion. For example, according to Kant, I should help my grandmother because it is the right thing to do not because I care about her. If my motivation is some sort of end (such as the happiness of my grandma), this is wrong according to Kant's ethics even though most people would seem to think that it is a good thing.

- *Is the categorical imperative too general?* It is perhaps difficult to see how the categorical imperative, as it is so broad, can be applied to specific moral issues. Consider the example of telling lies. This is obviously wrong according to the categorical imperative. However, it is possible that telling lies in order to save a life could be ruled in by the categorical imperative. Similarly, Kant does not provide any solution to the problem of what to do if there is a clash of instructions deduced from the categorical imperative.

- *What is Kant trying to do?* Kant seems to give a way of determining what is and what is not morally right. However, even if this is successful, it is an assumption to say that we are morally obliged to follow what Kant concludes.

SITUATION ETHICS

Religion has for a long time been a source of moral rules for many people. Indeed probably the most famous western set of rules is the 10 Commandments. The idea that God is the author of morality is discussed in the first booklet in this series. However, within particular religions there has been much discussion as to what rules should be followed. Kant's ethics, for example, in one sense can be seen as a defence of the traditional view of Christian ethics.

A wider discussion of Christian ethics can be found in the third booklet in this series. However, there is an important approach that provides an alternative view of moral rules. It is known as 'Situation ethics' or alternatively as 'Situationism' and whilst this theory is part of the Christian tradition it could be applied more widely.

Situation ethics is an idea that was first developed by Joseph Fletcher in a book published in 1966 entitled *Situation Ethics*. Essentially what Fletcher attempted to do was to create a compromise between having too many rules and no rules at all. Fletcher rejected the idea that everyone should follow a whole series of rules because, he felt, this puts the law first and makes the law the most important thing. He also rejected the idea that there are no rules because he felt that if there are not any rules, then there was no basis for making moral decisions.

Instead of a whole number of rules or no rules at all, Fletcher suggested that there is only one rule that everyone should follow. This rule is about love and Fletcher called it the 'Law of Love.' Indeed Fletcher defined what people should do in terms of love: the right course of action is to do the most loving thing.

How do we know what the most loving thing to do is? As the name 'Situation ethics' suggests, for Fletcher, it is the *situation* that is important for determining what should be done. There is, therefore, no way of knowing beforehand what is right and wrong because each situation is different and particular circumstances will have to be taken into account. All anyone should do in any situation is to determine what the most loving course of action would be: that is what is right.

Thus Fletcher's view of ethics is a form of relativism: there are no hard and fast rules about what is right and wrong, except to say that the Law of Love should be followed. An immediate clarification is perhaps needed, however: what is love? Is Fletcher suggesting that everyone should stare vacantly into each other's eyes whist holding hands in every situation? This sort of love, however, is not what Fletcher meant.

Traditionally there are a number of different ways in which love can be defined. Indeed the word 'love' can be used in a variety of different ways and in a variety of different contexts. The Ancient Greeks had different words for the different types of love and these are often used to refer to the different meanings of 'love'. There is the sort of love that someone can have for objects or places; for example 'I love whisky' or 'I love Scotland'. The Greek word for this is 'storge'. There is the sort of love you can have for other people. This is often called 'brotherly love' and the Greek for this is 'philos'. Further, there is the sort of physical love associated with sex and lust. The word for this is 'eros' (from which the English word 'erotic' comes). In addition to these, however, is perhaps a more profound sort of love that is associated with religious belief and often with the idea of sacrifice; this sort of love is known as 'agape'. It is this sort of love that the Law of Love is about, according to Fletcher.

To understand and develop what Fletcher's ethics is about, six basic ideas can be identified in his book. They are:

▶ **"Only love is intrinsically good; nothing else."**

What this means is that there is no thing or action that is good in itself. Something is only good if, and only if, it brings about love. (This is similar to the Utilitarian idea that something is only good if it produces happiness.) To love, for Fletcher, is to try to be like God. Indeed the opposite of love is indifference not hate.

▶ **"The ruling norm of Christian ethics is love; nothing else."**

As has already been mentioned 'norm' means rule. For Fletcher,

Christian ethics is based on this one idea. Fletcher refers to Jesus' idea as to what the most important commandment is, which is 'to love God and love your neighbour as yourself.' [Mark 12:33] However, Fletcher does recognize that some rules might prove to be useful. For example, Fletcher states that generally the Ten Commandments ought to be followed unless there is some sort of conflict. In the case where there is some sort of dispute what should be followed is the most loving course of action.

▶"Love and Justice are the same. Justice is love distributed."

This is an important idea for Fletcher. Justice, for Fletcher, is giving to people what is due to them. Fletcher argued that what is due to them is love: everyone is entitled to love. Thus justice is all about loving people. Fletcher argued that love does not exist in some emotional vacuum i.e. humans should be able to use their heads and calculate what is the right thing to do. For Fletcher, this is what justice is: 'love using its head'.

▶"Love wills the neighbour's good whether we like the neighbour or not."

This is another idea that Fletcher developed form Jesus' teaching to 'love your neighbour'. [Mark 12:33] It is important here to remember Fletcher's understanding of what love is. It is about the idea of sacrifice and thus people should give love without expecting anything in return. This does not imply that everyone should like or please her/his neighbour. For example, forcing someone to take an unpleasant exam may not please her/him but may be the most loving course of action.

▶"Only the end justifies the means; nothing else."

Fletcher's Situation ethics is another example of a teleological theory i.e. it is the ends that are important and not the means. In other words anything can be done if it brings about the most loving thing.

▶"Love's decisions are made situationally, not prescriptively."

For Fletcher there is no way of knowing beforehand whether something is right or wrong because each situation is different. Moral choices are made whilst in a situation not before. This means that ultimately there are no correct or incorrect answers to any general moral questions because it is the situation that is all-important. For example, Fletcher would have argued that it is meaningless to discuss whether things like euthanasia are right; moral decisions can only be discussed when a real situation is known.

▶ SOME EXAMPLES.

Fletcher also provided some examples to illustrate his ethical philosophy. He described a series of possible situations and whilst he does not always come out and say that they are right, they illustrate the sort of thinking that needs to take place in order to determine what the most loving thing to do is.

▷ Sacrificial adultery.

Adultery is when someone sleeps with someone who is not his/her spouse. Many people might argue that adultery is wrong; indeed not to commit adultery is one of the 10 Commandments. However, Fletcher suggested that it is conceivable that in some circumstances it could be the most loving thing to do. Fletcher gave the example of a woman in a prison camp who becomes pregnant in order to be released: to obtain her release is the only reason that she gets pregnant. Therefore it may be the right thing to do.

▷ The lying spy.

Telling untruths is another thing that many people think is wrong. However, what about the situation in which someone is a spy? If she/he lies, then many lives may be saved. Thus the most loving thing, in this situation, might be to lie.

▷ Sacrificial suicide.

Fletcher indicated that suicide could be done out of love and as the most loving thing. In other words, according to Situation ethics it might sometimes be right. Fletcher himself mentioned the true story of Mother Maria who took someone's place in a Nazi gas chamber: she gave up her life so someone else could be saved.

At the end of the day Fletcher's approach to ethics could be summed up by saying that there is no real answer to any general question about what is right and wrong. In other words it is no use, for example, asking whether something like abortion is right. What is needed is a real situation.

▶**CRITICISMS OF SITUATION ETHICS.**

- *Is one rule too general?* It has been argued that Fletcher does not really give any real instructions about what morally ought to be done. If ethics can be reduced to one moral rule, which Fletcher believes that it can, then this rule must be very general. The rule must be able to cover every eventuality. However, it is difficult to see how such a wide rule can be applied. In other words what does 'do the loving thing' mean? What are we being asked to do by such a general statement? Fletcher's rule might be seen to be very vague. Fletcher argued that the loving course of action cannot be known until a real situation i.e. the one moral rule is by necessity vague. However, in any situation how do you know what the loving thing to do is? Surely you need more instruction than the simple suggestion to be loving.

- *There could be more than one rule.* Fletcher's main argument against having more than one rule was that this would put the law first. However, this argument may be flawed. It is possible to conceive, for example, of a system of one rule that does put the law first e.g. to have the rule 'follow the government'. Alternatively, there seem no reason why, logically, there could not be more than one rule.

- *There could be a different rule.* Fletcher reduces the whole of normative ethics to one idea, love. However, why does this one rule have to be love? Other religions, for example, might suggest other rules e.g. Buddhism contains the idea of compassion. How do you decide between these rules? In a sense Fletcher's ethics is very much an interpretation of Christian ethics. It is perhaps difficult to see how Fletcher might be right if someone is not a Christian.

- *Before or after?* There also seems to be some ambiguity in the way that Fletcher believes what is right ought to be determined. He argued that it is the consequences of our actions that are important i.e. it is by looking at the results of our actions we determine whether we have done the loving thing. However, there is no way of knowing before hand what those consequences might be. Therefore, there is no way of knowing what the most loving thing to do is. Consequently it could be argued that Fletcher did not really provide any sort of rule at all, only a means of judging something after the event.

- *What about God?* The traditional Christian view is whatever God does is love and essentially humans should try to follow this. However, Fletcher goes against this idea because, for Fletcher, it is the situation that determines what love is i.e. love is dependent upon the particular circumstances.

- *Fletcher and Utilitarianism.* In many ways Fletcher's idea of ethics is very similar to that of Utilitarianism. Fletcher agreed with this. He argued that it is love that is the foundation of the principle of utility. However, as such his ethics is open to the same sort of criticisms that have been levelled against Utilitarianism e.g. how do we know that the end justifies the means?

DO THESE THEORIES SHOW THAT THERE ARE MORAL RULES?

Three major theories have been examined. All three considered that there is one rule that ought to be followed. For Utilitarianism and Situation ethics the rule was based on either happiness or love. Happiness and love were considered to be consequences of actions. Thus for both these theories, the rule was concerned with ends i.e. it is the outcomes that need to be examined in order to judge whether an action is right or not. Suppose, for example, that we have to decide whether going to war with country X is the right thing to do. The theories of Utilitarianism and Situation ethics would inform us to look at the consequences: will it bring about the greatest happiness? Or, will it be the most loving course of action?

However, this idea of consequences is an area in which both theories have been criticized. For example, neither theory gives an adequate response to the problem that future consequences can never be known. Indeed there are major problems with each theory (see above sections).

Is there, however, a more general idea that underlies the theories of Utilitarianism and Situation ethics? In many ways the two theories are very similar. Indeed this was one of the things that Fletcher recognized about his theory. Both theories are often described as formulations of one ancient rule called the **golden rule**. The golden rule is 'treat others as you would like to be treated.' Whilst this phrase is a direct teaching of Jesus [Matthew 7:12] it does have echoes and equivalents in many cultures and religions.

Kant's ideas, in contrast to Utilitarianism and Situation ethics, are based on means. Again, however, there are major criticisms of Kant's particular theory. For example, Kant assumes that we are rational and this may not always be true.

Thus, in other words, none of the ethical theories mentioned are entirely successful. However, there are further criticisms of the whole approach. These criticisms may also apply to the idea of the golden rule. Firstly, why do we need only one rule? It seems somehow strange that many philosophers have attempted to reduce ethics to one rule. Many systems require more than rule. It seems inconceivable, for example, that any government could run the country with just one rule. Indeed it might seem quite easy to accept a many ruled ethical theory. There seems to be no contradiction in having a whole series of rules, such as, for example, the Ten Commandments. Another similar criticism of having one moral rule is that such a rule must be very general. It is difficult to see how any such rule could apply to every situation. Indeed this is a criticism made of the three theories that have been examined.

However, there is perhaps a more fundamental problem whether there is one rule or many. What basis is there for having moral rules anyway? Mill and Kant thought that they could prove their respective theories but these proofs were not successful. There may be no reason for accepting any moral rules. Indeed the idea of moral rules assumes that the very idea of morality makes sense. Some philosophers have questioned this. It has been argued, for example, that morals are simply expressions of personal opinion. If this is the case, then the idea that there are moral rules for everyone does not make sense.

WORKSHEET

1. i Make a list of things that give you happiness.

    ii Try to put them in order. (Is this an easy task?)

    iii Compare your list with others. How similar or different are your lists?

    iv Does this pose any problems for Utilitarianism? If so, why?

2. Look back at the Felicific Calculus on page 9. Give an example of a pleasure that would be greater for each of the 7 parts. (For example, a tub of ice cream might last longer than a roller coaster ride.)

3. Try to apply the Categorical Imperative to the following. (I.e. would Kant have thought the following are right?) Give reasons for your answer.

    i Abortion
    ii Treat everyone the same
    iii Stealing
    iv Lying
    v Kindness
    vi Abortion if the mother's life is in danger
    vii Voluntary Euthanasia
    viii Suicide
    ix Lying to save a life
    x Helping my Grandmother.

    Are there any assumptions that you need to make?

    Hint: consider whether these things can be universal (i.e. whether it is logical possible for them to be universal and whether we would want them to be universal); and consider whether they involve treating people as ends.

4. Imagine the situation in which your old and beloved Philosophy teacher is very ill and has lost his/her mind.

   i How might you go about determining what the most loving thing to do for your teacher is?

   ii How can you decide whether the decision you have made is right?

   iii Try to imagine one situation in which you think that Fletcher would have thought Euthanasia might be right and one situation in which you think that he would have thought that it is wrong.

5.   i Make a list of rules that you would have if you were stranded with other people on a desert island.

   ii Can you think of any instances in which you would want these rules to be broken?

   iii What would you do about people who didn't want to follow your rules?

   iv Do you think that different ethical philosophers (e.g. Kant, Fletcher and Utilitarians) would agree or differ with your rules? Give reasons.

EXAM QUESTIONS

Exam questions on ethics tend to focus on one particular area, such as Utilitarianism or Situation ethics. It sounds obvious but the most important thing to do is to answer the question. One way of attempting to do this is at the end of writing each paragraph ask the question, 'What has this got to do with the title?". Once you have thought about this write it at the end of the paragraph, so that the examiner is clear how the question has been answered.

It is also very important to plan your essay. This will help give you the necessary structure in order to answer the question. Consider the following examples:

How does Mill's version of Utilitarianism differ from Bentham's? Is either right?

This is an interesting question in that it has an important rider (extra) question. It is important to remember to answer this part as it can easily be missed.

INTRODUCTION	What is Utilitarianism?
	What was Bentham's view?
	    the principle of utility
	    the felicific calculus
	    sanctions

MILL	Why did Mill differ? (Because of criticisms etc.)
	How?
	    higher/lower pleasures
	    proof of the principle
	    human nature
	    act and rule
	    sanctions

IS EITHER RIGHT?	What problems are there with Utilitarianism? e.g. Justice
CONCLUSION	Is Utilitarianism in some form still possible?

Compare and contrast the ethics of Kant and Fletcher.

INTRODUCTION   Perhaps a mention of historical perspective:
Kant 18th Century, Fletcher 20th Century.
Both commenting on normative ethics.

COMPARE   Both attempt to provide one rule
Both can be seen as versions of Christian ethics
Both see humans as valuable things.

CONTRAST   Kant's ideas based on categorical imperative;
Fletcher's on love.
Kant's based on means; Fletcher's on consequences.
Kant has absolutes; for Fletcher nothing is
absolute.
Kant's ideas may lead to more than one rule;
Fletcher's do not.
For Kant reason is central; for Fletcher emotion
(love) is central.

CONCLUSION   Is either theory convincing?

FURTHER READING

Many general introductions to philosophy, some of which are listed here, contain a chapter or chapters on ethical theory and are worth having a look at. Another useful source can be dictionaries of philosophy, which often have some very good articles about different ethical theories. Do be careful, however, when looking at books on ethics as many do tend to focus on practical ethics (moral problems) rather than ethical theory. It can also be worthwhile reading the original works of many of the philosophers mentioned in this booklet: many, such as J.S. Mill, are very readable.

Philosophy: the basics.
By Nigel Warburton (Routledge 1992)
Readability: *** Content: ###
Provides a good outline of the main ideas and theories found in ethics.

Mastering Philosophy.

By Anthony Harrison-Barbet (MacMillan 1990)
Readability: * Content: ###
Contains a very detailed discussion of particular philosopher's ethical theories. These discussions are very usefully based on the original texts of those philosophers.

Philosophy.
Mel Thompson (Teach Yourself Books 1995)
Readability: *** Content: #
Provides some good examples of different ethical theories as well as a good summary of some of the main ethical ideas.

Ethics.
By Peter K. McInerney and George W. Rainbolt (Harper Collins 1994)
Readability: **** Content: ###
A very readable account which covers most of the topics in ethics very well.

The Puzzle of Ethics.
By Peter Vardy and Paul Grosch (Fount 1994)
Readability: * * * Content: ###
A good introduction with some interesting perspectives. Particularly good on Utilitarianism and Kant.

Moral Maze.
By David Cook (SPCK 1983)
Readability: * * * Content: ##
Whist this book is mostly about Christian ethics, the early general sections are very good and provide a good introduction to ethical theory.

An Introduction to Ethics.
By J.D. Mabbot (Hutchinson and Co. 1966)
Readability: * Content: ####
A classic introduction which contains a good detailed discussion of most ethical theories.

KEY   Readability   * manageable;   * * good;
                     * * * very good;   * * * * excellent.

         Content   # adequate;   ## good;
                     ### very good;   #### excellent.

GLOSSARY

Absolute—always, unquestionably true.

Categorical—unconditional.

Consequentialism—another word for teleological.

Deontological—literally 'concerned with duty"; based on means.

Descriptive—something that indicates what's there.

Egoism—theory that humans are self-interested i.e. work for their own ends.

Emotivism—theory that morals are based on emotions.

Ends—the outcomes.

Hedonism—theory that states that what is right is happiness.

Imperative—something that should be done.

Intuitionism—theory that states that morals are based on our intuitions.

Means—how something is achieved.

Naturalism—theory that states that morals are based on some aspect of nature.

Objective—true, factual.

Prescriptive—something that gives an instruction.

Relative—dependent upon something else.

Situation ethics—theory developed by Fletcher that states that we should do the most loving thing in any situation.

Subjective—internal, personal, based on opinion.

Teleological—literally 'concerned with ends".

Universalisability—capable of being true for everyone.

Utilitarianism—theory that states that what is right is the greatest happiness of the greatest number.

Discovery Guide to
Vietnam

Kim Naylor

IMMEL
Publishing

ACKNOWLEDGEMENTS

I would like to thank Leon Bartlett and Thi Bei Nguyen - my travelling companions in Vietnam - and their family in Ho Chi Minh City and Can Tho for all the assistance, kindness, adventure and fun they provided me during my stay in their country. The publisher Eland Books kindly allowed permission to use extracts from 'A Dragon Apparent' by Norman Lewis.

Discovery Guide to Vietnam, first edition

Published by Immel Publishing Ltd.,
20 Berkeley St., London W1X 5AE.
Tel: 071 491 1799; fax: 071 493 5524

Text copyright © 1994 Kim Naylor
Photographs © 1994 Kim Naylor

Layout and cover design by Jane Stark
Typesetting by Johan Hofsteenge
Printed in Great Britain by The Bath Press, Avon

A CIP catalogue record for this book is available from the British Library

ISBN 0 907151 71 X

To help with the next edition, the reader is asked to send information and comments to the General Editor, *Discovery Guide to Vietnam*, Immel Publishing Ltd., 20 Berkeley St., London W1X 5AE.

CONTENTS

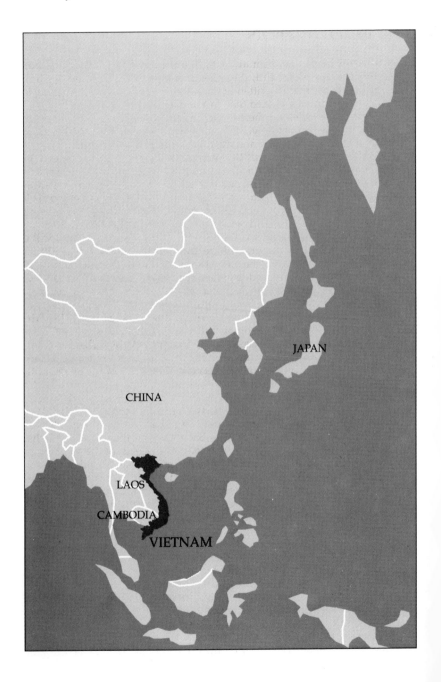

INTRODUCTION

Two movements, Colonialism and Communism, did much to shape our world this century. One dead, the other dying, their history and the link from the first to the next is written in the soil of many countries. Nowhere is this more graphically illustrated than in Vietnam. The Vietnamese defeat of their French rulers at Dien Bien Phu is one of the most celebrated victories over Colonialism anywhere. The rise of Ho Chi Minh, their charismatic leader and liberator, clothed as a Communist, led to America's invasion of Vietnam. The country became the West's most bloody battlefield in its universal fight against Communism.

War followed by a period of purdah, imposed from within and from without, has rendered Vietnam virtually out of bounds to tourists for well over a generation. Now the veil is slowly lifting, revealing a tantalising beauty. A long slender land with a 3000 km coast overlooking the shimmering turquoise South China Sea, the abundant rice flats of the Mekong and the Red, the luxuriously verdant hills of the interior; a culture traditionally associated with the Chinese but rich in its own identity; and character, fiery in its will for independence but ready to embrace friends. As for business, *'No country in the East, and perhaps none in the world, produces richer or a greater variety of articles proper for carrying on an advantageous commerce.'* So wrote Charles Chapman who visited Vietnam in 1778. Two hundred years on and this land of the Orient is as seductive as ever.

This book comprises three sections. The first provides a background and practical information about Vietnam, giving an account of Vietnam's history and of Vietnam's peoples. While the Viets constitute 85 % of the inhabitants, the remainder of the population are from the "Ethnic Minorities', as the country's many tribes and minority groups are collectively called. The second is divided into three further parts - Vietnam's regions of Bac Phan (the north), Trung Phan (the centre) and Nam Phan (the south), and serves as the guide to the country. Starting in Bac Phan and the Red River Delta, the cradle of the ethnic Viets, the guide follows the path of the Viets' Nam Tien - their centuries long southward expansion. During this migration the Viets slowly colonised what is present Vietnam, including the once brilliant Kingdom of Champa which dominated the central coastal plains. In defeat, a 16th century Cham king put a curse on the Vietnamese, a damnation which - some say - manifested itself in the later colonisation of Vietnam by the French, followed by civil war and the invasion by the Americans.

Vietnam is going through a transitory stage. Travel regulations and facilities - visa requirements, accommodation, internal travel permits, transport and the like - are bound to change and so this book provides general information about these matters rather than specific details which are liable to date very quickly. Anyway, most of the present visitors to Vietnam are either tourists on organised tours or businessmen whose travel needs will have been attended to by tour operators or sponsors. The independent traveller has yet to penetrate Vietnam. At present those wishing to go it alone , especially on the cheap, are faced with the tiresome task of gaining permission to travel the country freely. But regulations will relax and such travellers should get up to date information on current travel trends in Vietnam; the addresses of sources of advice are on page 25.

SECTION 1:
BACKGROUND

Travel Facts

Country File

Cyclists on a bridge over the Red River.

TRAVEL FACTS

TRAVELLING TO VIETNAM

By Air
An increasing number of airlines - both European and Far Eastern carriers - are operating services to Vietnam. Bangkok, 80 minutes by air from Ho Chi Minh City, has become the hub for flights in and out of Vietnam. Flights from Europe service various *en route* destinations in the Middle East and Asia.

AIRLINES

EUROPEAN CARRIERS:
Air France: Twice a week from Paris to Ho Chi Minh City.
Aeroflot: Twice a week from Moscow to Ho Chi Minh City and five times a week from Moscow to Hanoi.
Czechoslovak Airlines: Once a week from Prague to Ho Chi Minh City.
Lufthansa: Twice a week from Frankfurt to Ho Chi Minh City.
KLM: Once a week from Amsterdam to Ho Chi Minh City.

FAR EASTERN CARRIERS:
Thai Airways: Four times a week from Bangkok to Ho Chi Minh City and three times a week from Bangkok to Hanoi.
Vietnam Airlines: (Hang Khong Viet Nam): Three times a week from Bangkok to Ho Chi Minh City and twice a week from Bangkok to Hanoi; once a week from Manila to Ho Chi Minh City; once a week from Singapore to Ho Chi Minh City; once a week from Vientiane to both Hanoi and Ho Chi Minh City; four time a week from Phnom Penh to Ho Chi Minh City and twice a week from Phnom Penh to Hanoi (in conjunction with Kampuchean Airlines).
Philippine Airlines: Once a week from Manila to Ho Chi Minh City.
Cathay Pacific: Three flights a week from Hong Kong to Ho Chi Minh City.
Cassidy Airlines (Charter Company): Once a week from Singapore to Ho Chi Minh City.
Garuda: Twice a week from Denpasar (Bali), Djakarta and Batam (convenient to Singapore) to Ho Chi Minh City.
Malaysian Airline System: Twice a week from Kuala Lumpur to Ho Chi Minh City.

Airports
Noi Bai Airport is 48 kms north - west of Hanoi City Centre; **Tan Son Nhat Airport** is 8 kms north - west of downtown Ho Chi Minh City. There are taxis to the airports and they charge a set tariff - payable in U.S. dollars - for a ride into town.

Overland
The Vietnam-Cambodia border is open and there is a daily bus service between Phnom Penh and Ho Chi Minh City via the Moc Bai border crossing. There is also the daily Mekong ferry from Phnom Penh to river ports in Vietnam's western province of An Giang. Less frequent or non-

existent is any form of public transport service across the Vietnam-Cambodia border crossings further north. The Vietnam-Laos borders are closed at present. The Vietnam-China border was opened in late 1991; how easy it is for foreigners to cross this frontier is unknown.

TRAVELLING WITHIN VIETNAM

By Road

Highway One runs along the coastal plain from Hanoi via Hue, Da Nang, Nha Trang to Ho Chi Minh City and serves as the main transport route through the country. This was the course taken by the Viets during their Nam Tien - southward migration. In the 19th century, after the Nguyen Emperors had established Hue as their capital, the highway became known as 'The Mandarins' Road'. During the Vietnam War it was bombed and sabotaged by both sides and, in spring 1975, the Northern army pushed southwards down this path - by now dubbed '**The Highway of Hell**' or 'The Highway of Terror' - capturing all that was along the way and causing tens of thousands to flee ahead of them. The highway is, for the most part, only two lane and there are many stretches and bridges, particularly in the north, which are desperately in need of repair. While Highway One is open throughout the year, heavy rains and typhoons during the monsoon season can render it temporarily impassable.

Travelling the length of Highway One and ideally taking excursions off the route - is an excellent itinerary. It covers ten latitudes along an historic path, it incorporates Vietnam's main centres of interest and it touches on some of the country's finest beaches. Allow a minimum of three to five days to complete the full 1710 km.

Highway 14 - another war torn route - runs from north to south through the forested mountains of the Central Highlands, west-east roads link it to Highway One.

In the north, roads radiate in all directions from Hanoi - the most important being the **Hanoi-Haiphong route** - and some head deep into the mountain provinces. In the south, the southbound road out of Ho Chi Minh City branches into the provinces of **Mekong Delta**.

Many roads are currently under repair, nevertheless many - often marked boldly in red on maps - are in poor condition and are hardly passable in a normal vehicle, particularly in the monsoon season. Up to date information on road conditions should be sought before embarking on remoter routes.

Before 1975 the roads in the South were commonly known as 'Routes', now they tend to be called 'Highways'. Some of the numbers have also changed.

Buses

Express Buses, mini-buses and the more basic local buses - you still come across archaic charcoal-burning contraptions - ply the roads. In theory there is nothing to stop tourists travelling by public bus, however, buses have yet to become a mode of tourist transport. Both **Hanoi** and **Ho Chi Minh City** have several **bus depots** and the Tourist Offices can give relevant advice.

The express service between Hanoi and Ho Chi Minh City takes two days and two nights.

Cars can be hired - this is usually done through the Tourist Office - though you will be required to employ a driver and possibly a guide/interpreter. You are charged a **daily dollar rate**, including or excluding petrol. You will be expected to pay for the driver's and guide's lodgings, though this will be at the lower 'Vietnamese Rate'.

By Rail
The main railway is between **Hanoi and Ho Chi Minh City** (1726 km) and, for the most part, follows Highway One. Sometimes the two routes even share the same path across bridges. Built by the French, who laid most of the present communications infrastructure, this railway, like Highway One, was severed at the 17th parallel when Vietnam was divided in 1954. The link between the former two nations was re-established after 1975.

There are several other rail roads, mainly heading out of Hanoi. The cog and wheel Phan Rang-Da Lat line joined the coast to the Central Highlands. Opened in 1935, the railway became the target of Viet Cong terrorism and was closed in the late 1960s. Old track was taken from here and used in the rebuilding of the Hanoi-Ho Chi Minh City line.

International tour operators, in conjunction with *Vietnamtourism*, are now running **train tours** along the **Hanoi-Ho Chi Minh City route**. Special carriages - modified to cater for tourists - are attached to scheduled trains. While the normal direct service takes 52 hours, the rail tour allows time for the tourists to see the sights along the way and lasts about **nine days in total**. Some foreigners do travel this route independently, but they are expected to pay the 'Tourist Rate' for their fare.

Diesel locomotives are used on the main passenger services; steam engines tend to operate on the freight services. Old steam engines can be seen in depots along the rail routes.

By Water
Rivers flow from the mountains in the north and feed into the **Red River** and its delta. In central Vietnam rivers run from the Central highlands eastwards down onto the coastal plain and to the South China Sea. In the south a vast area of flat plains is criss-crossed by the rivers and canals of the **Mekong Delta**. These waterways provide important avenues of transport for the locals. At present tourists rarely travel these routes, aside from taking **short river boat excursions** from the main centres. There are always boats, however, ranging from sampans to rusty ferries, for the more adventurous. To secure a vessel or find out about a timetable, ask down at the wharfside.

By Air
Hang Khong Vietnam operate several daily flights between Hanoi and Ho Chi Minh City. There are also internal services to the main provincial towns. Whilst these flights are often heavily booked, the dollar paying foreigner is often given preference to locals when it comes to buying tickets.

TRAVELLING WITHIN TOWNS
Transport
There are **bus** services in the main towns and in Hanoi there are also ancient **trams** rattling along the older streets. **Taxis** are available at the hotels or through the Tourist Office and they will probably charge a set dollar fare - a rate worth establishing before the journey. However, the most common way of getting around is aboard a *cyclo* - a manually operated tricycle with the passenger seat in the front - which can be picked up at any street corner; it is wisest to negotiate the fare - which is paid in *dong* - before the ride. Alternatively, join the crowds and hop on a **bike**; the Tourist Office can advise you where to hire your bike.

NAMES

New names are given at the start of **new historical eras**. In Vietnam there have been several of these historical periods in recent times and the re-naming rituals - following in quick succession - can lead to confusion. For example, the French called Saigon's main downtown street *Rue Catinat*, this was re-named *Tu Do* by the Vietnamese after the colonial era and then *Dong Khoi* (Uprising) when the North liberated Saigon in 1975.

Streets, buildings, hotels, shops and the like are commonly named after Vietnam's past heroes, or major events such as *Liberation* and *Reunification*, or important dates such as 30th April. Less prosaic are names like *Ascending Dragon* or the *Flowering Lotus*.

The different names taken by the erstwhile **emperors** can be a bit muddling. A regal name - *Nien Hien* as it was called - was traditionally adopted by the emperor at his coronation. For example, *Nguyen Anh* took the name *Gia Long* on ascending the throne. Sometimes a posthumous name was also given.

In Vietnam, **peoples' names** start with the surname. For example, in the name *Nguyen Thi Bey*, *Nguyen* is the surname and *Thi* and *Bey* are the forenames.

Accommodation
The planned - and part materialised - hotel boom in Vietnam is an indication of the country's emergence into the real world. Some of Ho Chi Minh City's better pre-1975 hotels, notably the *Continental*, have been recently refurbished, and at great cost, to an international standard, but most continue to show all-the cracks of many years of neglect. The likes of the *Hilton, Holiday Inn* and *Sheraton* will doubtless arrive but for the present the glitzy symbol of ostentatious high living is the *Saigon Floating Hotel* which suddenly appeared from across the ocean, like the coming of the capitalists' Ark, as soon as the hard years of socialism seemed to be easing.

The best hotels and the widest range of accommodation are in **Ho Chi Minh City**. There is markedly less on offer in **Hanoi**. Elsewhere in the country accommodation is found in the larger towns, the old beach and hill resorts and provincial capitals. Standards vary, but are generally better in the former South than in the North. However, everything tends to be fairly decrepit unless touched by the magic wand of modernisation. Behind the charm of a colonial or a sixties facade will probably be the original bathrooms, fixtures and fittings now in various states of malfunction. Some places are squalid with cockroaches and even less welcome bed fellows.

Westerners are expected to stay in 'Tourist Hotels', which are better and more expensive than 'Vietnamese Hotels'. Going native is not always easy. A foreigner arriving at a locals' hotel will be redirected to appropriate accommodation; if there is no choice he will more than likely have to pay the inflated 'Tourist Rate'. Indeed, foreigners must pay their bills in hard currency - preferably dollars - and room rates range from about $25 to $150 (the latter is the rate at the *Saigon Floating Hotel*) a night. They are also required to leave their passports with the hotelier during their stay so they can be registered with the local authorities. Alternative lodging, such as rooms in private homes, hostels and camp sites, is not really part of the accommodation scene as yet.

MONEY

Currency
The *dong* is the Vietnamese unit of currency, 1, 2, 5, 10, 20, 30, 50, 100, 200, 500, 1000, 2000 and 5000 dong bills are in circulation, however, the 500 Dong bill is currently the lowest value now being printed.

Hawkers and souvenir shops in Ho Chi Minh city sell the **old currency** of the Republic of Vietnam. Aware of a market in numismatological hardware the vendors now present **war medals** and **badges** along with their coins.

Exchange
The **US dollar** is the currency to take to Vietnam. $1 = 11,000 dong (d) is the approximate rate often quoted, but this may well be meaningless. Dollars can be exchanged at banks, hotels or authorised exchange bureaux in some shops. The rate varies by about 10% between these establishments, with the banks offering the best deal, though with the inconvenience of a long wait. There is a black market, though the rate may not be much better than the official exchange. **Travellers' cheques** - in US dollars - tend only to be accepted at some banks, while **credit cards** are virtually redundant. Increased exposure to the outside world will doubtless ease the flow of money in all its forms, but at the moment hard cash is the way to pay for almost everything.

Banking hours are usually : *7.30-11.30 and 13.30 to 15.30, Monday to Friday, and Saturday mornings.*

There seems little option to carrying around large amounts of money when travelling in Vietnam. **Street crime** - pickpocketing and mugging - is apparently on the increase and so it is probably wiser to leave valuables in the safety of the hotel when based in any one place.

There is no limit to the amount of money foreigners may bring into Vietnam, but they will be expected to fill in a **currency declaration form** on entering the country. **Receipts of exchange transactions** should be retained and may be requested by officials on departure.

Appreciation of Services Rendered
Tips (10%) are sometimes added to the bill in the Tourist Hotels. Otherwise it is a matter of personal choice. Where prices are negotiated, such as for a *cyclo* ride, they are probably inclusive of 'tips', but a barman or waiter, not in a position to wheel and deal, greatly appreciates a **10% gratuity**. While the dollar is much loved, foreigners often express their 'Thank You' less brashly with a gift of a cigarette, denominations being a single smoke, a packet and a carton. The **cigarette** is money and the *State 555* brand - available in Duty Free, government 'Dollar Shops' and in the market - is the most favoured currency. Beware of cheap imitations, such as State 333, which is sold in similar packets. A bottle of **whisky** or **wine** is an alternative for a special 'Thanks'. As for kids, their 'currency' is sticks or packets of **chewing gum** or similar. This is also locally available.

PAPERWORK
Any attempt to unravel the rules behind the paperwork would be futile and would probably put most people off going to Vietnam. Visas, declaration forms, police registration, internal travel permits and much more are all part and parcel of the trip and coping with all the regulations and red tape without letting them get you down is part of the secret of a success. To keep abreast of **current requirements** and the easiest ways to deal with them it is advisable to contact **tour operators** specialising in Vietnam, **Vietnamese embassies** and, once in Vietnam, *Vietnamtourism* (see 'Tourism' on page 22) who try and control tourists' movements and have the power to ease or aggravate paperwork.

Bureaucracy can not be condemned as a product of socialism. The Vietnamese penchant for paperwork has deeper roots:

'We were boarded this morning, while under sail, by a large covered boat containing a number of mandarins, one of which the linguist told us was a commissary of marine. He was furnished with a bundle of papers, and requested to be informed of the name of the ship, to what country belonging, what was our armament, what cargo we brought, what articles of commerce we were in pursuit of, and, finally, the name, age, and personal description, of every individual on board? Our answers to all which questions were committed to paper by a secretary in attendance, and thirteen copies were taken by other writers in the train. To each of these papers my signature was requested; and after proper explanations from the linguist, who urged me to be very careful in returning correct answers to all the questions, I complied. Four of these papers, we were told, were to be sent to the king. One of the viceroy, and the rest to be distributed among different official mandarins in Saigon.'

(John White, American sailor, 1819)

The situation today:

Visas
Entry visas are required by all foreigners travelling to Vietnam and are obtainable from Vietnamese embassies and consuls around the world. Prices vary but are not too exorbitant. Visitors tend to fall into two categories, the Tourist and the Businessman.

Tourist Visas
Tourists are usually expected to visit Vietnam as part of an **organised group**. If this is the case, the tour operators will take care of the visa requirement. Be prepared to release your **passport** to the embassy several weeks in advance, fill in the **application form** in triplicate and supply three **passport photos** of yourself. Tourists wishing to travel independently may find it easier to tag onto a tour and come to some agreement with the operator who can then cater for individual requirements but still take care of the paperwork. In **Bangkok**, a springboard for many a prospective Vietnam tourist, the **delegation** issue visas relatively quickly and with minimal formality. Furthermore, you will find a fair choice of tour operators servicing Vietnam here.Visas may only be valid for a week or two; **extensions** are available in Hanoi and Ho Chi Minh City (contact the **Immigration Police** or *Vietnamtourism*).

Business Visas
Businessmen should be invited by an official organisation in Vietnam - a ministry, company or the like - and have an **authorised letter** of invitation from their **sponsor**. Once this has been approved by the embassy the visa is issued. Again, allow time for the bureaucracy to function. **Multiple entry visas** lasting six months or longer may be available to businessmen.

Immigration
Two immigration forms have to be completed on arrival. You retain one of them and this must be submitted on departure.

Customs
Two customs forms - on which you must declare any valuables in your possession - have to be completed on arrival. The one you keep has to be submitted on departure.

DAY TO DAY

Electricity
Vietnam uses twin voltages **110 and 220 volts**. Hotels usually have both. Electric sockets tend to have the standard two pin plugs.

Time
GMT +7

Discovery Guide to Vietnam

EMBASSIES

SELECTED VIETNAMESE EMBASSIES WORLDWIDE

Australia
6 Timbarra Crescent
O'Malley
ACT 2603
Tel: (062) 866059

Britain
12-14 Victoria Road
London W8 5RD
Tel: (71) 937 1912

Cambodia
Achar Mean Boulevard
Phnom Penh
Tel: 23142

France
62 rue de Boileau
75016 Paris
Tel: 45 24 50 63

Germany
Konstantinstr. 37
5300 Bonn 2
Tel: (0228) 357022

Italy
Piazza Barberini 12
00187 Rome
Tel: (06) 475 4098

Lacs
Thanon That Luang
Tel: 5578

Sweden
Orby Slottsväg 26
125 36 Älvsjbü
Tel: (8) 861 218

Thailand
83/1 Wireless Road
Bangkok
Tel: (02) 251 7201

USA
Vietnamese Mission to
the United Nations
20 Waterside Plaza
New York
NY10010
Tel: 212 685 8001

There are no embassies
in Canada or New
Zealand

SELECTED FOREIGN EMBASSIES IN HANOI

British Embassy
16 Ly Thuong Kiet
Tel: 52510, 52349
Telex: 411405, BRITEM-V
Cable: BRITISH
EMBASSY - PRODOME
- HANOI - VIETNAM

Australia
66 Ly Thuong Kie
Tel: 252763

Cambodia
71 Tran Hung Dao
Tel: 253788

France
49 Ba Trieu
Tel: 252719

Germany
25 Phan Boi Chau
Tel: 253663

Italy
9 Le Phung Hieu
Tel: 256246

Laos
22 Tran Binh Trong
Tel: 254576

Sweden
So 2, Duong 358
Khu Van Phuc
Quan Ba Dinh
Tel: 254824

Thailand
Khu Trung Tu
Tel: 256043

The USA, Canada and
New Zealand do not
have embassies here.

At present there is no British Consulate in the Ho Chi Minh City or anywhere else in the country.
The British Embassy compiles the useful *Vietnam: A Guide for British Businessmen*, which provides businessmen with up to date information about travel and business conduct in Vietnam. The booklet - including a list of Vietnamese corporations - is available from the Department of Trade and Industry, 1-19 Victoria Street, London SW1H DET; Tel: 071-215 5000.

Communications
International calls via the operator can be made at the Central Post Offices in Hanoi and Ho Chi Minh City and from the main hotels; telexes can also be made at these places. Phoning is quite expensive. International communication links are rapidly improving due to assistance from Australia's OTC International, and direct and cheaper calls are on the way. **Fax lines** are now being set up in Vietnam. **Air mail post** can still take several weeks to reach the West, however.

Health
There are no mandatory vaccination requirements for entry into Vietnam, however, it is recommended that visitors are vaccinated against *Cholera, Polio, Typhoid* and *Tetanus. Malaria* is prevalent in parts of the country and the relevant tablets - seek professional advice - should be taken as prophylactic.

Contact London's Hospital for Tropical Diseases on 071-387 4411 (they also have a direct 'Healthline' with recorded details, tel: 0898 345081, code 77 for Vietnam or the School of Hygiene and Tropical Medicine on 071-636 8636 for current advice on the necessary health measures). Your local doctor should also have the required information.

Doctors and hospitals in Vietnam are short of facilities and medicines and in event of a **serious illness** the patient would be wise to travel to Bangkok or elsewhere for treatment. Make sure you have **full medical insurance** to cover the cost of an air ambulance, as well as treatment, if necessary. If you need any **medicines** regularly, be sure to take a plentiful supply with you.

Water - unless boiled - should not be drunk. Bottled water, sodas and beers are safe alternatives and are readily found in the towns. Ice in drinks should be avoided.

Clothing
Light weight tropical clothing is worn throughout the country for most of the year. However, in the north and in the hills it can get chilly in winter and it is worth carrying a **jumper** during these cooler months. Some sort of **waterproof garment** or **umbrella** is useful during the rainy season.

Vietnamese seem quite casual about dress codes and **white shirt-sleeves** or a **safari suit** is generally the acceptable wear for **businessmen**; a **jacket and tie** is worn on formal occasions in the winter months in the north.

As yet, Westerners wearing flip flops, shorts and singlets are not a common sight on the city streets.

No religious or other laws require women to cover their arms and heads or wear long skirts. A certain level of conservatism in dress is wise, and respectful when visiting temples.

Opening Hours
Most places - **offices, museums,** and **shops** open around **8am** and close around **5pm** and take a **lunch break** for an hour or two around midday; some shops remain open in the evenings.

Crimes

Westerners may be the target for **pickpockets**, but they do not seem to be the prey of the more serious criminals. It is probably worth notifying the police - who seem quite approachable - of any theft, but the chances of retrieving a snatched wallet are as hopeless in Vietnam as anywhere else.

As for committing crimes, involvement with **drugs** is illegal. What happens to Westerners caught in the act is uncertain. There does not seem to be a precedent - if there has been, he has not been heard of since.

What to Buy

Vietnam's handicraft speciality is **black lacquerware** inlaid with mother of pearl. Other souvenirs include **jewellery**, **silk** and **ornaments** - made of ivory, bone, tortoise shell, jade, bronze, teak and mahogany - in a variety of forms such as the popular Buddhas, birds and boxes. Unique to Vietnam is the elegant *ao dai*, the women's traditional dress, and the *non la*, a conical hat that is a particular speciality from **Hue**.

HANDICRAFTS

An envoy despatched to China by Emperor Le Thanh Tong in the mid-15th century returned home having learnt the art of **lacquerware**. The lacquer is a cream-coloured resin collected from the *rhus succedanea* or *rhus vernicifera*. This is boiled for 40 hours in an iron pot - to give it the black colour - and mixed with a pine resin - to give it the texture. The object to be lacquered - traditionally teak - has to be carefully prepared before the actual lacquer is laid. The spreading of the many coats of the lacquer is interrupted by long intervals of drying. The whole process is long and laborious. Mother of pearl, gold, nacre and egg shell are inlaid as decoration. Vietnamese lacquerware is widely regarded as the finest in the world.

The making of **ceramics** is also an ancient tradition learnt from the Chinese and the **elephant stools** seen in the craft shops are copied from a style introduced from China during the '1000 years of domination'.

Basketry, embroidery, weaving, hat making, wood and stone carving are practised throughout the country, with marked differences in the styles of the crafts of the various ethnic groups. **Ivory** - from the tusks of elephants which have died naturally (so they say) - is carved and sold as handicrafts, as are **bone** and **tortoise shell**.

Day by day the variety of consumer spoils on offer in downtown Ho Chi Minh City increases. They range from the latest lines in T-shirts and imitation and genuine brand names to radios and videos from Japan and South Korea. The place is not as flush with flash gadgetry as other South East Asian cities, but is heading in that direction. Elsewhere it is a very different story, though there should be no problem finding basic necessities, such as toiletries. It is the same pattern with **food** - greater variety and availability in Ho Chi Minh City, less choice and quality elsewhere.

Personal medicaments - including the likes of aspirin and malaria tablets - should be brought from home. Similarly, **quality slide film** is absent even in Ho Chi Minh City.

The shopping centres for food and most other goods tend to be the **markets** although the former colonial downtown shops of Ho Chi Minh City, dusty since 1975, are now preparing themselves for a lucrative future. Hanoi and the rest of the country will follow suit in due course.

As for prices, they tend to be low though they may well be inflated for the foreigner. Haggling is the norm.

Vietnamese Diet

Light in frame, scrawny in physique, tough in muscle, the Vietnamese body is nurtured on a low-fat, high-protein diet. **Beef, pork, chicken** and **duck** are the most popular meats - though there are local specialities such as **dog** in Haiphong and **snake, frog** and **snail** elsewhere; **fish,** as one would expect in a country with such a long coastline, also features prominently. The delicious dishes tend not be elaborate in preparation; and while the influences from old colonists China and France have crept into the cuisine, the Vietnamese cooking is distinct in character. When ordering - and indeed when choosing a restaurant - it is best to be advised by the locals who know the specialities and where best to get them.

There is an abundance of **vegetables** and **tropical fruits** - longan, banana, mangosteen, citrus fruits, melon, custard apples, jack fruit, pineapple, papaya, sapodilla - and the orchards are heavy with them in the summer.

Noodles and **rice** are the base for most dishes. **Tea** and **coffee** - both home grown - are the main beverages. Locally brewed **beer** is sold under different labels and bottles of Chinese beer and cans of familiar Western lager are also available. Vietnamese will cool their beers by drinking it on the rocks: Ice, however, harbours disease and should be avoided.

SOME VIETNAMESE DISHES

Pho - pronounced fur - is a noodle soup with, most commonly, shreds of beef, chicken, or pork and seasoning. Sometimes referred to as *Hanoi pho* - because of its place of origin - it is eaten throughout the country at any meal, though it is most typically a breakfast dish.

Nuoc man is the pungent-smelling fermented fish sauce for which Vietnam is famed.

Nem (north) or *cha gio* (south) are rice pancakes - spring rolls - filled with meat and vegetables.

Mien luon is noodle and eel soup to which an assortment of vegetables and seasonings are added.

Bun cha is a popular pork dish served with noodles.

Banh chung are sticky, square rice cakes - filled with pork and mung beans - which are traditionally eaten at Tet.

Ech tam bot ran is a dish made from plump field frogs.

Sea swallows' nests - a mass of strands secreted by swallows to shape their homes - are a delicacy and are collected from caves in off-shore islands.

Bo bay mon is a dish comprising 'beef cooked seven ways'.

Bun thang is noodles with chicken, pork and prawns and covered with the stock of the ingredients.

TOURISM

Though tourists have been coming to Vietnam since the late 1970s their numbers have been small and have been predominantly from the Soviet Block countries. In announcing '1990 - The Year of Tourism', the Vietnamese government revealed its intention to encourage foreigners to visit the country. It was a bold and premature proclamation, given that Vietnam does not have the infrastructure, as yet, to cope with the hoped influx of tourists. But at least it has told the West that the door is open and that everybody is welcome.

The majority of 'Westerners' visiting Vietnam are *Viet Kieu* - overseas Vietnamese - many of whom were supporters of the old Southern regime or 'Boat People', who fled for fear of persecution under the Communists or because they hoped for a better life elsewhere. They now return from all over the West - very often on special *Viet Kieu* package tours - to visit the motherland, to see family and pay respects to the ancestral graves. Their conspicuous consumer wealth - and plumper waistlines - contrast starkly with the lot of their brothers and sisters who stayed behind, and they are tantalising advertisements for those thinking about skipping the country. Nevertheless, the increasingly easy-going government welcomes the *Viet Kieu*, because with them they bring dollars.

Dollars are definitely the motivating force behind this open door policy to tourism. While the *Viet Kieu* invariably stay with families, other tourists are expected to conduct all travel affairs through *Vietnamtourism* - the official government Tourist Office - or one of its regional equivalents. And everything they provide comes at inflated prices - the 'Tourist Rate' compared to the 'Vietnamese Rate' - and must be paid for in U.S. dollars.

The mark-up is variable, a few hundred *dong* extra because you look rich or 400% more than the locals' price in the case of the train ticket from Hanoi to Ho Chi Minh City. Haggle if this discrimination gets extreme.

The visitor has some options, though they are limited:

• Join a **tour organised by a foreign based tour operator** (see below) who probably in conjunction with *Vietnamtourism* - will take care of visa, itineraries, transport, hotel, travel permits and all other travel necessities. This is the easiest, headache-free and probably the most cost effective way of seeing the country. Such operators can also arrange individual **custom-made tours**.

• If you have obtained a visa and arrived in Vietnam **under your own steam** you can arrange a **tour programme** with *Vietnamtourism*, who offer a variety of itineraries lasting anything from a day to three weeks (see page 25). Alternatively they can arrange a personal tour, though they will expect you to use one of their cars/minibuses and drivers, plus a guide interpreter. This can be expensive - less so if there are several of you.

• The **'low budget' independent traveller** has not really appeared in Vietnam as yet, partly because visas are usually difficult to obtain unless you are 'officially invited' (see 'visas' on page 17). In theory you can travel on **public transport** around the country as you will, though relatively few Westerners have done so. There is a Catch 22: **permits** are needed to visit the different regions and these are only obtained if you have 'authorised' (i.e., *Vietnamtourism*) transport arrangements. In these early days of tourism such travellers fall into a grey area. It is not that the authorities want necessarily to curtail their freedom, rather they want to keep a control on the tourist industry, not least because of the revenue it earns. Once tourism is better established restrictions are bound to be relaxed. For the moment, however, the independent traveller should seek the advice of the Tourist Office before embarking on a solo trip and should be prepared to pay the 'Tourist Rate' for hotel rooms, train tickets and the like.

• The **Western businessman** travelling to Vietnam will invariably be **'sponsored'** by his business colleagues in Vietnam, who will have taken care of all the bureaucratic formalities as well as accommodation and any necessary transport.

The whole scene is changing so rapidly in Vietnam and it is strongly advised that you seek up to date information on the current tourist trends.

The best up-to-date and non-official information is, of course, from recent visitors to Vietnam and current publications. Tour operators specialising in Vietnam can be useful sources, some are mentioned below (see page 25).

Museums
In 1899 the *Ecole Française d'Extreme Orient* embarked on the study of Indo-chinese culture as part of a larger task of documenting the cultures of the French colonies. In doing so it laid the foundations of Vietnam's most important museums, the **History Museum** in **Hanoi** and the **National Museum** in **Ho Chi Minh City**.

Other museums document the cultures of Ethnic Minorities - these include the famous **Cham Museum** in **Da Nang** - and the lives of Ho Chi Minh and other heroes. But most conspicuous are the **Revolutionary Museums** which give accounts of the fight of the *Viet Minh* against the French and the **War Museums** - the 'Atrocities Museums' - which graphically relate the horrors of the Vietnam War.

Museum **opening times** are usually **7.30 to 11.00 am** and **1.30 to 4pm daily except Mondays**. There may be some regional differences.

Entertainment
There has been a recent revival in the traditional arts. Tourists are sometimes taken to see *Hat Boi Choi* - a **Vietnamese opera** with much singing of romantic ballads and moral parables, or to other forms of **theatre**. The Vietnamese are great poets and **poetry recitals** are often held, though foreigners, able to appreciate the emotions, are not likely to understand the full story line. **Water puppetry**, a type of theatre unique to Vietnam, is mainly enacted in the north. The **ceremonies** and **rituals** of the *montagnards* are sometimes performed specially for the tourists visiting the **Ethnic Minority villages**. **Circus** is popular family entertainment and can be seen

at the main towns. **Folk dances** and the like are regularly staged at several of the major Tourist Hotels. There are **cinemas**, although **video parlours** have now appeared - usually showing Kung Fu imports from Hong Kong; apparently the Rambos have also done the rounds.

WATER PUPPETRY

Puppetry is very much part of he Vietnamese art scene, as it is in various places elsewhere in this part of the world. Water puppetry *(Mua Roi Nuoc)*, though, is unique to Vietnam. According to folklore it originated centuries ago, during a seasonal Red River flood, when the puppeteers were short of dry land and took to the water to continue their performances. The shows subsequently won a growing audience around the country and the puppeteers found they were able to carve a new art for themselves. They used the surface of the water as the stage and hung a screen to serve as the backdrop. They would hide themselves behind the screen, standing waist-deep in the river or pond, and dangling their puppets on the end of bamboos, would skilfully enact their play at their watery theatre.

The **weekend dances** held at some of the hotels in the cities and towns around Vietnam are fun and attract the local hip crowd. Music is often provided by a live band as well as a disco and the repertoire ranges from traditional folksongs to dated Western chart toppers and, possibly the latest jazz/rock/pop. The style of dancing does not necessarily co-ordinate with the type of music.

Prostitution, once so common in pre-1975 Saigon, is increasingly evident in present Ho Chi Minh City. The young girls hang around the lobbies of some of the less salubrious hotels but there is by no means the blatant sex scene that is now for sale in Bangkok and Manila or used to be on offer in this city in the olden days.

Local Tours

Normally *Vietnamtourism* and the provincial Tourist Offices show Vietnam to visitors through a choice of some 20 or so **set touring programmes**, ranging from **one day city tours** to **three week nationwide tours**. Full, up to date information about these programmes - which incorporate the country's main sights - should be available from the international tour companies operating to Vietnam or from *Vietnamtourism* or the provincial Tourist Office. There are fixed dollar rates for these tours, though there is some flexibility in price depending on the numbers in the group.

TOURIST INFORMATION

Vietnamtourism, Vietnam's state Tourist Office, has its headquarters in Hanoi:

Its representation in Ho Chi Minh City is at:

54 Nguyen Du
Hanoi
Socialist Republic of Vietnam
Tel: 54674; 52986; 55963
Telex: 4269 TOURISM VT
4552 TOURISM VT

71 Nguyen Hue
Ho Chi Minh City
Socialist Republic of Vietnam
Tel: 90772; 90775; 90776
Telex: 295 DULIVINA SG

While *Vietnamtourism* is the overall body in charge of he country's tourism, there is also the **provincial** Tourist Offices, which are usually based at the provincial capital in or near the main Tourist Hotel.

The headquarters for the **Hanoi** Tourist Office is at: 18 Ly Thuong Kiet, Hanoi; tel: 54239, 57885; telex: 4537 CTDL HN HVT. The main *Ho Chi Minh City* or Saigon Tourist Office is at: 1 Dong Khoi, Ho Chi Minh City; tel: 95515, 95517; telex: 275 SG, 276 SG.

VIETNAM TOURIST INFORMATION WORLDWIDE

Australia

16 Railway Street
Lidcombe
2141 Sydney
Tel: 6432099

Orbit Tours
C 29 Mlc Centre
Castlereagh Street
(Box 3484)
2001 Sydney
NSW 2001
Tel: 2333288

Britain

* *TBN (Vietnam)*
7 Palmerston Close
Chester
Cheshire CH1 5DA
Tel: 0244 374915
Fax: 0244 314635

Regent Holidays
13 Small Street
Bristol BS1 1DE
Tel: 0272 211711

France

Hit Voyages
21 rue des Bernardins
75005 Paris
Tel: 43 54 17 17

International Tourisme
26 Boulevard St.
Marcel
75005 Paris
Tel: 45 87 07 70

Germany

Indoculture Tours
Bismarckplatz 1
7000 Stuttgart
Tel: 0711 61 7057

Saratours
Sallstr 21
3000 Hanover
Tel: 0511 282353

New Zealand

Destinations
Premier Building
4 Durham Street
Auckland
Tel: 390 464

USA

Indochina Consulting Group
844 Elda Lane
Westbury
NY 11590
Tel: 51 633 36662

Viet Tours
8907 Westminster Avenue
Garden Grove
CA 92644
Tel: 714 895 2588

* TBN are both an independent tour operator - with a personal and in depth knowledge of all matters Vietnamese - as well as *Vietnamtourism's* representatives in Britain.

COUNTRY FILE

EARLY TRAVELLERS

Early Western travellers to Vietnam returned home with vivid accounts of the country's magnificent Nature:

'The innudations have the same effect here as the periodical overflowings of the Nile in Egypt, and render the country one of the most fruitful in the world. In many parts the land produces three crops of grain in the year. All the fruits of India are found here in the greatest perfection, with many of those of China.

No country in the East, and perhaps none in the world, produces, richer or a greater variety of articles proper for carrying on an advantageous commerce, cinnamon, pepper, cardamoms, silk, cotton, sugar, aguila wood, sapan wood and ivory, are the principal.' Charles Chapman (1778)

American John White was equally enthusiastic, when he wrote, some forty year later:

'The climate of Cochin China is as fine as that of any other country within the torrid zone; the periodical winds passing over, and refreshing every part of it. The winters are unusually cool for the latitude in which it is situated, and the keen breezes from the mountains are favourable to health and vigour. The numerous streams and springs with which it abounds, are extremely valuable as means of facilitating agriculture and internal commerce. Its abundance of fine bays, harbours, and rivers, and the safety and facility of navigation on its coasts, give it a decided superiority over many other countries, for the purpose of maritime commerce; and in respect of the natural productions of the soil and adjacent sea, both as regards quantity and quality, no country in the East can excel it. The mountains produce gold, silver, copper, iron and other metals. The forests, besides the various kinds of odoriferous woods, such as the eagle, the rose, the sappan, and others, afford iron-wood, several species of the varnish-tree, the sammer or pitch tree, the gambooge, the bamboo, and the rattan, besides a great variety of woods useful in dying, in construction, and the mechanic arts. The country produces also cinnamon, honey, wax, plenty of various kinds, areka, betel, tobacco, cotton, raw silk, sugar, musk, cassia, cardamoms, some petter, indigo, sago, ivory, gold dust, rhinoceroses' horns, and rice of six different kinds. The four latter articles are regal monopolies. The mulberry tree, the food of the silk-worm, grows spontaneously, and in great abundance and luxuriance. Great quantities of silk might consequently be raised. Many medicinal plants and roots are also produced. Specimens of several kinds were bought me by the missionaries, among which was galangal of an excellent

Greatest riches of the Orient

American enthusiasm for Vietnam

quality . . . The sugar-cane grows in great luxuriance. There are two kinds. One is large, high, and abounding with juice; great quantities of this is exposed in the bazaars, and eaten in the raw state. The smaller kind produces most of the saccharine salt, and from this most of the sugar is made . . . The indigo-plant grows in great profusion and its produce is brought to the market in a liquid state, the natives not being acquainted with the art of proceeding any farther in the manufacture of it.'

Colonials create cash crops

The French, too, appreciated Vietnam's natural wealth and, having colonised the country, they set about exploiting its resources. In the 1930s Vietnam was amongst the top three rice-producing countries in the world, while rubber, tea, coffee, timber and coal were the country's main revenue earners.

GEOGRAPHY

Covering many latitudes

Long, slender S-shaped Vietnam, covering an area of 329,566 sq km - roughly one and a third times the size of the United Kingdom, lies between 23 degrees 22' and 8 degrees 30' North latitudes and the 102 degrees 10' and 109 degrees 29' East longitudes. The country is at its widest - 530 km - in the far north, but it narrows sharply, with the long central region tapering to 50 km in breadth, before gradually fanning out again in the south where the maximum width is 475 km. The distance between the northern most and southern most points is 1650 km. Vietnam is bordered by China to the north, Laos and Cambodia and the Gulf of Thailand to the west, and South China Sea to the east and south and has a coastline some 3260 km long. Beyond the seas, Thailand and Malaysia - 400 km to the west and south-west - and the Philippines (Manila) - 1250 km to the east - are the nearest substantial land masses.

Borders

Vietnam's present borders have evolved over many centuries and tend to correspond with geographical and/or ethnic boundaries. Its northern border with China has been acknowledged for hundreds of years, but was only ratified formally by a Franco-Chinese pact in the late 19th century. Migrating southwards in their **Nam Tien movement**, the Vietnamese people gradually extended their southern and eastern borders, reaching their present limits in the late 18th century.

In the late 19th century, the French carved Vietnam into three regions - **Tonkin** (north), **Annam** (central) and **Cochin China** (south) - which then became part of

```
┌─ PROVINCES AND CAPITALS OF VIETNAM ──────────────────┐
```

Province   **Capital**
Ho Chi Minh City *(9)*   *Ho Chi Minh City*
Haiphong *(5)*   *Haiphong*
An Giang *(14)*   *Long Xuyen*
Bac Thai   *Thai Nguyen*
Ben Tre *(15)*   *Ben Tre*
Binh Tri Thien   *Hue*
Cao Bang   *Cao Bang*
Cuu Long *(16)*   *Vinh Long*
Gia Lai – Contum   *Pleiku*
Dac Lac   *Buon Ma Thuot*
Dong Nai   *Bien Hoa*
Dong Thap *(13)*   *Sadec*
Ha Bac *(2)*   *Bac Giang*
Ha Tuyen   *Tuyen Quang*
Ha Nam Ninh *(8)*   *Nam Dinh*
Ha Son Binh *(7)*   *Ha Dong*
Hai Hung *(4)*   *Hai Duong*
Hau Giang *(17)*   *Can Tho*
Hoang Lien Son   *Yen Bai*
Kien Giang *(18)*   *Rach Gia*
Lai Chau   *Lai Chau*
Lam Dong   *Da Lat*
Lang Son   *Lang Son*
Long An *(11)*   *Tan An*
Minh Hai *(19)*   *Ca Mau*
Nghe Tinh   *Vinh*
Nghia Binh   *Qui Nhon*
Phu Khanh   *Nha Trang*
Quang Ninh *(3)*   *Hon Gai*
Quang Nam – Da Nang   *Da Nang*
Son La   *Son La*
Song Be   *Thu Dau Mot*
Tay Ninh *(10)*   *Tay Ninh*
Thai Binh *(6)*   *Thai Binh*
Thanh Hoa   *Thanh Hoa*
Thuan Hai   *Phan Thiet*
Tien Giang *(12)*   *My Tho*
Vinh Phu *(1)*   *Viet Tri*
Vung Tau – Con Dao Special Zone   *Vung Tau*

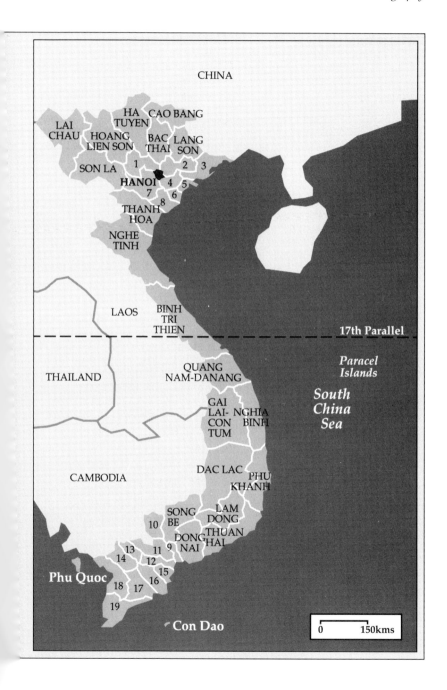

France's eastern estate

French Indo-china, along with **Cambodia** and **Laos**. The country was briefly re-united by Ho Chi Minh as the **Democratic Republic of Vietnam** following the initial overthrow of the French in 1945.

After World War II however, the Allies monitored the surrender of the Japanese in Vietnam and, for administrative purposes, divided the country at the **16th parallel**.

Though victorious over the French at **Dien Bien Phu**, Ho Chi Minh and the Viet Minh agreed to the **1954 Geneva Accords** which stipulated that Vietnam should be temporarily divided at the **17th parallel** - along the River Ben Hai, up to the village of Bo Ho Su and then west to the Laos border - pending general elections. The elections were never held and this demarcation line continued to divide the Democratic Republic of Vietnam - 157,781 sq km - from the Republic of Vietnam (as the State of Vietnam was re-named in 1955) - 171,785 sq km - until 1975.

Geographical Regions

Four-fifths of Vietnam is mountain or hill, with the **Truong Son range** running much the length of the country. In the north and south are the flat rice plains of the **Red River Delta** and the **Mekong River Delta** respectively. Viewed on a map from the South China Sea, Vietnam is graphically described as looking like 'a long bamboo pole with baskets of rice hanging at either end.'

Mountains, rivers and paddies

Vietnam's wide variety of topography can be divided into five main geographical regions.

The Mekong Delta

Rising in the high plateau of Tibet the 4180 km long **Mekong River** - also known as the Song Cuu Long, the River of Nine Dragons - flows south-eastwards through Tibet and China before serving as the border, first between Burma and Laos and then Thailand and Laos. It continues into Cambodia and splits at Phnom Penh. The two streams cross into Vietnam, the smaller, lower branch - the **Hau Giang** - flows a more direct path to the South China Sea dividing only once, just before the coast. The upper - the **Tien Giang** - splits into four main channels some 80 km inland before emptying into the sea at seven places. Hence the Mekong has a total of eight mouths - as can be seen on most moderately detailed maps. But eight is an inauspicious number and so a tiny insignificant outlet of the river was 'discovered' and

Nine mouths of the Mekong

honoured as the ninth mouth of the great Mekong - thus the River of Nine Dragons.

The waters of the Mekong start to rise in late May and reach their highest level in September; they then subside and are at their lowest in April. The delta region has been formed over eons by the sediment deposits washed down by the river; indeed, this silt continued to advance the coastline up to 80 metres a year. The Mekong Delta region covers 67,340 sq km, however this area also embraces the Van Co, Sai Gon and Dong Nai river systems which lie just to the north. The delta proper starts 50 km south of Saigon. The soil is extremely rich and is heavily farmed, with 23,000 km under cultivation.

Rich earth

Rice is by far the major crop. Along with the main rivers, numerous small streams and canals serve as essential paths of travel around the Mekong Delta, though the shallowness of the waterways caused by silting precludes larger vessels.

Truong Son Mountain Range (Chaine Annamitique)
The 1200 km Truong Son range is the southern extension of the mountains which separate the sources of the Mekong and the Yangtse. The range originates in Laos and enters northern Vietnam around the upper reaches of the **River Ca**. It continues south eastwards, forming Vietnam's border with Laos and then Cambodia, and ends at the Mekong Delta, 80 km north of Saigon. In the north, the Truong Son is narrow and rugged, but further south, it broadens into the **Central Highlands** plateau. The steep eastern slopes give way to the narrow coastal plain, while the less severe western slopes lead down the Mekong valley. The peaks of the Truong Son are mainly above 1525 metres, the highest, *Ngoc Linh* in **Gia Lai – Contum Province**, reaching 2598 metres.

Central Highlands
The Central Highlands - 320 km long and 160 km wide (an area of almost 52,000 sq km) - are mainly covered by

Mountain plantations

tropical forest, though **tea, coffee, rubber, fruits** and **vegetables** are all grown commercially.

Central Lowlands
The Central Lowlands, the narrow strip of plains sandwiched between the **Truong Son range** and the **South China Sea**, stretches from the Mekong Delta in the south to the Red River Delta in the north. Its breadth varies. At its maximum it is 64 km wide, in other places,

between Da Nang and Hue for example, the mountains extend right to the coast pinching out the plains completely. In the past these have served as natural ethnic and political boundaries.

Pristine beaches

Long beaches of fine white sand stretch along much of the coast and around the off-shore islands. While the plains are not as fertile as either the Mekong or Red River delta regions, they are extensively farmed - especially between Mui Dai and Da Nang and from around Dong Hoi northwards - with **rice**, once again, being the main crop.

Red River Delta

The Red river (Song Hong) rises in China - where it is know as the River Yuan - and flows south-east, entering Vietnam at **Lao Cai** in the **Northern Highlands**. It is joined by two main tributaries, the **Da (Black)** and **Lo (Clear) Rivers**, and continues in the same direction, splitting into channels which themselves branch into smaller streams. These finally carry the Red River's waters into the **Gulf of Tonkin**.

Waterways of the north

Like the Mekong the Red has carried an enormous quantity of silt over time and this deposit has formed the delta region, an area of 15,000 sq km which also includes the smaller **Thai Binh River Delta**. The river continues to wash 80 million cubic metres of alluvium into the sea each year, expanding the shore faster than the Mekong. The land is particularly low, mostly between 1 and 3 metres above sea level, and this, coupled with the Red's huge flow of water - 2275 cubic metres per second in the rainy season, which is twice that of the Nile's - has left the delta exposed to catastrophic floods. The high water level can be as much as 7.5 metres above the land and so a network of **dikes** and **drainage canals** has been built to protect life, home and crop.

Fear of floods

Despite the risk of death through flood, the Red River Delta is the most densely populated region of Vietnam - indeed this is the cradle of Vietnamese civilisation (see page 87) - and one of the most fertile, with **rice** being the predominant crop.

Northern Highlands

The Northern Highlands rise above the northern flatlands of the **Red River Delta**. They are lowest where they form the border with China and are highest and most rugged in the north and north-east where they form a **continuation of the Truong Son range**. The region,

River rather than road covering 105,000 sq km, is forested and sparsely populated. The Red and its tributaries are the main rivers cutting their paths through the highlands, which is characterised by deep gorges and valleys, and, while some of the streams are navigable by small vessels, there are few roads, leaving this area one of the most isolated in Vietnam.

GEOGRAPHICAL TERMS

Cua: River mouth	*Ho:* Lake
Dao: Island	*Mui:* Cape
Deo: Pass	*Nui:* Mount
	Song: River

The Paracel and Sprately Islands
The Paracel Islands (the **Hoang Xa archipelago**) and the Sprately Islands (the **Truong Xa archipelago**) are 300 km east of **Da Nang** and 550 km south east of **Vung Tau** respectively. These groups of islands once had a fearful reputation amongst mariners of the South China Seas. John White, the early 19th American sailor, repudiated the myth:

'The Paracels . . . were formerly, and indeed till very recently, dreaded by navigators, being represented as one continued chain of low islands, coral reefs, and sand banks . . . forming a fancied resemblance to the human foot. This archipelago, once so formidable from its great imaginary extent and terrific character, is now ascertained to be a group of island and reefs, of no great extent, with good safe channels between them, and in many places good anchorage.'

Islands under dispute Vietnam's claim to the archipelagos has traditionally been contested by the Chinese. The main resources of both groups are **phosphates** and **tortoise shells**.

Fauna
'The sportman may in half an hour fill his game-bag (with birds) to overflowing. The woods and mountains abound with wild beasts, such as elephants, tigers, rhinoceroses, &c, ', noted John White. Vietnam was indeed a hunter's paradise - one of the greatest in the world from all accounts - and hunting was traditionally the emperors' favourite pastime. In the 1930s a keen shot called Archibald Harrison listed the main animal and bird species of interest in his book *'Indo China, A Sportman's Opportunity'*.

A hunter's list

Animals: elephant, rhinoceros, sladang (3 varieties), wild cattle (2), tiger, panther (2), bear (3), wild dog (2), sambar, brown antlered deer, wild hog (2), spotted deer, goat antelope, hare, badger, porcupine, civet cat (2), marten, ant eater, flying squirrel (3), lizard (2), tortoise (4), python, cobra, alligator, otter (2) monkey (8), wild cat, mongoose.

Birds: peacock, crane, marabou, stork, horn bill (2), water hen (6), teal, wild duck, snipe, heron (2), plover, pheasant (3), partridge (2), quail (2), parakeet, pigeon (8), vulture, eagle, falcon (3), crow, 'Grand Duke', screech owl.

Certain Ethnic Minorities still hunt, however, big game hunting as a sport is now prohibited. Some species are nearly extinct and, by designating tracts of land as **game reserves**, the Vietnamese wildlife body hopes to revive the numbers of these threatened animals.

The abundant variety of animals and birds - the above lists by no means include all the species - is well matched by the numerous types of **fish**, of which there are over 300 in Vietnam's coastal waters alone; the **Nha Trang Oceanographic Institute** has many examples on display.

Climate

Vietnam's climate - sub-tropical in the north and tropical in the south - varies according to region. Taking the country as a whole, the best time to visit Vietnam is between November-December and April - the **dry season**, especially in the south - when the temperatures are at their most clement.

Best season

The **winter monsoon** in the north arrives around mid-September, lasts until April and is characterised by fog and drizzle - the *crachin* - which is particularly common in February and March. In the south it comes around November, though it is not such a feature and does not bring much rain inland.

The main rain - the **summer monsoons** - hit Vietnam in late spring. In the north they fall between April and October with the heaviest downpours being in July and August, while in the south they fall between May and November with the greatest precipitation in June to September.

Heavy rains

The **average annual rainfall** in Hanoi is 180 cm and in Ho Chi Minh City it is 200 cm. Hue's yearly rainfall of 300 cm is the highest in the country (Phan Rang with 70 cm per annum has the lowest). Here, the monsoonal season runs from September to February with the highest falls from November to February. Central Vietnam, in particular, is affected by flooding.

Generally **temperatures** and **humidity** are high. In Hanoi temperatures range from 42°F to 105°F with the lowest mean monthly average being 63°F in January and the highest being 85°F in June. In Ho Chi Minh City the range is not as great, varying from 75°F to 85°F with December - the coolest month - having an average of 78°F and April - the warmest - recording a mean of 83°F.

Coastal typhoons are common in Vietnam - especially in the north and central regions. There are normally about ten a year, between July to November. They can cause substantial damage.

Hot winds

Strong, dry, hot winds - the *Gio Lao* (**Winds of Laos**) - blow across the Central Highlands in summer. There is occasional **snow** on the higher mountains of northern Vietnam.

Economy

Seventy percent of Vietnam's population is involved in **agriculture**, with **rice** as the main crop. Intrinsically a highly productive country, Vietnam has had its problems; 10 million hectares of fertile land were rendered barren

Devastation

during the **Vietnam War** as a result of American bombing; mismanagement in the wake of the war led to poor yields; unusually **adverse weather** destroyed harvests in the 1980s. Recently, though, outputs have been high and Vietnam is once again exporting rice. With its long coastline Vietnam has also always had an affinity with the sea and enjoyed its booty of **fish**; there are plans to develop the export market of fish.

Vietnam's other natural resources are **timber** and various minerals such as **coal**, **iron ore**, **manganese**, **bauxite** and **titanium**. A joint Vietnamese-Soviet enterprise began drilling **oil** off the Vung Tau coast in the 1980s. Now the Western oil companies are bidding for tenders to exploit these rich reserves. With the recent decentralisation of the economy, private enterprise has been allowed greater freedom and the manufacturing industry, and textiles in particular, has expanded at a fair pace.

In 1988 40,000 **tourists** visited Vietnam. This figure increased by 20,000 the following year and in 1990, the official **Year of Tourism**, it was hoped 150,000 would spend their holidays in Vietnam. The number of tourists

The rise of tourism

is one thing, the colour of their money is another. 'Non-spending' holiday-makers from the former Eastern block used to constitute the bulk of guests; more recently the *Viet Kieu* (overseas Vietnamese) have been allowed home to visit the families they left behind and with them they bring much wanted dollars. Now it is hoped there will be an increase in the hard currency foreign tourists.

With the break up of the Soviet family Vietnam is out in the open market. It has the potential to do well once the Americans drop their trade embargo.

Politics

The **Socialist Republic of Vietnam** (*Cong Hoa Xa Hoi Chu Nghia Viet Nam*) came into being in July 1976 after the unification of the **Democratic Republic of Vietnam** (the North) and the **Republic of Vietnam** (the South).

The ruling party, the Vietnamese Communist Party (*Dan Cong San Viet*), was founded by **Ho Chi Minh** in 1931 and it created a socialist state on the Marxist-Leninist lines, though an element of Confucian thinking retains a respect for the past. The government is centralised and comprises a bicameral legislature of a **National Assembly** whose 495 members represent the people and elect the **Council of State** and the **Council of Ministers** (the cabinet) who exercise executive powers. At the top of the hierarchy are the **General Secretary**, currently Nguyen Van Linh, the **Prime Minster** and the **President of the Council.** The post of **Chairman** has remained vacant since the death of Ho Chi Minh.

Legacy of Ho Chi Minh's communism

Population

Vietnam's population is 54.25 million (1989), but is estimated to rise to 88 million by 2000 with 2.5% population growth. Some 40% of today's population has been born since the end of the Vietnam War.

Life expectancy is 66 years, though a 1989 census revealed that Vietnam had 2,432 people (1,728 women and 704 men) over the age of 100, with Mrs Ngan Thi Guang from Nghe Tinh Province, aged 142 years, being the oldest.

Old Mrs Ngan

Population density is 195 people per sq km; **Thai Binh** is the most heavily populated province with 1,105 people per sq km.

Twenty one percent of the population are urban dwellers. **City populations** (1989): Hanoi 2.7 million; Ho Chi Minh 4 million; Haiphong 1.5 million; Da Nang 0.5 million; Hue 0.2 million.

Over one million Vietnamese have fled the country since 1976. Most live in the USA and, in particular, in California. Vietnamese who are living overseas are known as *Viet Kieu*.

Exodus to the west

Language and Literacy

Vietnamese is the **Lingua franca**. Chinese is spoken by the Chinese and the various Ethnic Minorities converse amongst themselves in their own dialects. Some of the educated older generation have a knowledge of French, though, surprisingly, the language of the ex-Colonials is not more widespread.

Russian was the compulsory second language taught in schools between 1975 and the late 1980s and Vietnamese students were able to study in the Soviet Union. Now, however, students can choose the language they wish to study and the overwhelming majority plump for English.

The young choose English

Vietnamese is written in *Quoc Ngu* - the national Romanised script. In the 17th century Catholic missionaries developed *Quoc Ngu* and in 1649 Father Alexander de Rhodes, a Jesuit scholar living in the Far East, translated the catechism into this script; two years later he published a Latin-Portuguese-Vietnamese (*Quoc Ngu*) dictionary.

Chu Nho - the traditional Chinese-type characters - continued to be used by Vietnamese scholars, however, the ending of the long established triennial exam system, early this century, meant that *Quoc Ngu* gained greater prominence. The French also promoted *Quoc Ngu* and the relative simplicity of the script has helped minimalise the level of illiteracy in Vietnam. According to a 1979 survey, 16% of the population are literate.

'Hay Noi Tieng Viet' - 'Speak Vietnamese' - a Vietnamese-Russian-English-French phrasebook is available from bookshops and street vendors in Vietnam; it is published by the Foreign Languages Publishing House, Hanoi.

THE PEOPLES OF VIETNAM

Austro-Asian Language Family

Comprising the *Viet-Muong, Mon-Khmer, Tay-Thai, Kadai* and *Meo-Zao* language groups. Peoples of southern mongoloid stock who are believed to have originated along the Mekong Valley, in Yunan province in South China, from where they migrated in various directions including southwards into Vietnam.

Movement of a people

Viet-Muong:

Viet: 85% of Vietnam's population; from their heartland in the **Red River Delta**, they spread southwards to colonise the **coastal plains** and the **Mekong Delta** (see page 44).

37

Muong: 500,000, inhabiting hills south-west of the Red River in **Thanh Hoa, Ha Son Binh, Vinh Phu** and **Son La** provinces. These may be 'pre-Chinese Viets', descendants of Viets who migrated to these homelands in response to the first Chinese invasion of Vietnam.

Chut: Small group, traditionally **cave dwellers** (*chut* means cave) living in the hills of northern **Binh Tri Thien** province.

Mon-Khmer:

Bahnar: 100,000, living mainly in the **Central Highland** province of **Gia Lai-Contum**; they had to resist Cham and Viet incursions in the 15th century, but were annexed by the Laotians in the 18th century. Many were converted to Christianity by missionaries and, in 1887, Father Guerlach deployed 1200 of their tribesmen as his force against the Jarai.

Sharp toothed Brau

Brau: Some inhabit **Gia Long-Contum** province though they live mainly in Laos and Cambodia. They achieve beauty by tattooing their faces and bodies, filing their teeth and stretching their earlobes with heavy ornaments.

Bru Van-Kieu: 35,000 in Vietnam, living in the hills of **Binh Tri Thien** province bordering Laos. They maintained the **Ho Chi Minh Trail** and suffered badly under American fire at **Khe Sanh** in 1968.

Cua (Chor): 15,000 living in the hills and valleys of **Quang Nam-Da Nang** and **Nghia** provinces. Lighter in colour to most Mon-Khmers, revealing traces of mongoloid ancestry, they served as **trackers** for the Viet Cong.

Cho Ro: 7,000 living in **Dong Nai** province around **Xuan Loc**, they have long had contact with mainstream Vietnam. Traditionally they would burn their houses and move on after a family death.

Star gazers on the hills

Co Tu: 25,000 living in hills of north **Quang Nam-Da Nang** and south **Binh Tri Thien** provinces. They have an acute **knowledge of astronomy** and names of days correspond with the shape of the moon.

Gie-Trieng: 15,000 living in the hills of **Quang Nam-Da** and **Gia Lai-Contum** provinces. They believe that the soul lives in the ear and on death is embodied in the *te* bird which takes it to the ancestral cave.

Halang: 50,000 living in the **dense forests of western Gia Lai-Contum** province and Laos and Cambodia. A branch of the *Sedang* (*halang* means mixed blood) they also **pan gold**. Apparently the large gap between big and second toes is caused by holding craft instruments there.

Hre: 70,000 live in the valleys and hills (lowland and

highland Hre respectively) of **Nghia Binh** province; they traditionally trade with the Chams and Viets along the coast.

Hroi: Inhabiting the borderlines of **Quang Nam, Nghia Binh** and **Gia Lai-Contum** provinces; these are a **hybrid** of the neighbouring *Bahnar* and *Cham* peoples famous for a **poison** which they concoct from cong tree sap and red peppers. A worm, a frog or chicken droppings are eaten as an antidote.

Drastic antidotes

Jeh (Die): 20,000 in **Gia Lai-Contum** and **Quang Nam-Da Nang** provinces. Unwarlike, they suffered because of *Sedang* expansionism. Out of a great respect for Nature, they wash their houses only once a year for fear of dirtying water.

Katu: 25,000, divided into the lowland and highland *Katu* living on the plains and hills of **Quang Nam-Da Nang** province. Traditionally they would hunt **human sacrifices** to appease the spirits; their name means 'savage'.

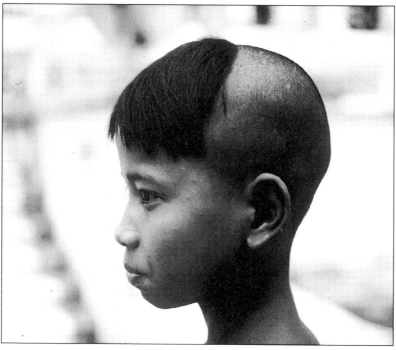

Khmer boy.

Khang: 2000 living in the hills of **Son La** and **Lai Chau** provinces of north west Vietnam; they have close associations with the Thai who traditionally treat them with contempt.

Khmer: Cambodia's predominant tribe whose ancient homeland included the **Mekong Delta**. Many fled here during the *Khmer Rouge* genocide of the 1970s and they now number over 1 million in Vietnam (see page 45).

Kho Mu: 23,000 hill peoples of north **Nghe Tinh**, **Son La**, **Lai Chau** and **Hoang Lien Son** provinces; slash and burn **cotton growers**, they traditionally served as cheap labour for the Thai.

Koho: Generic term for a group of tribes, including the *Sre* and *Kil*, numbering 70,000, living mainly in **Lam Dong** province. They are masters of oblique talk: 'The bamboo is ready to cut, slice it' actually means 'The rice wine has fermented, come and drink it.'

Ma: 20,000 in **Lam Dong** province. Fierce to man, kind to nature, hostile to outsiders (pork liver served by the chief indicates acceptance), they **do not cut trees** as they are the source of the Earth's fertility.

The eco Ma

Mang: 2000 living between the Da and Na rivers in **Lai Chau** province. Traditionally semi-nomadic they, like other small tribes, fell under the sway of the Thai.

M'ong: 50,000 living in **Dac Lac** and **Lam Dong** provinces. They killed French explorer-ethnographer Henri Matre and French administrators. Though they are famous for their **white feather headdresses**, berets, worn inside out to reveal the designer label, became *de rigeur* under French rule.

O Du: Small tribe numbering hundreds living in **Nghe Tinh** province; **hunter gatherers**, they traditionally served the Thai.

Rengao: 15,000 living in **Gia Lai-Contum** province, they are closely associated with neighbouring *Sedang* and *Bahnar* tribes. They were part of Father Guerlack's *Bahnar* force against the *Jarai* as well as David Mayrena's *Sedang* nation.

Sedang: 50,000 living in **Gia Lai-Contum** province. In 1888 French soldier-adventurer David Mayrena created a confederation of *Sedang* tribes with himself as King Marie I of the Sedang, but his kingdom was shortlived and he died in Singapore soon after coronation. The first to be trained by the US Special Forces, they once fought the Viet Cong with crossbows.

Vietnam's French king

Stieng: 50,000 around the central and northern **Son Be** province. French rubber planters in the 1920s-30s pushed

Victims of the
French
rubbermen

them deeper in to the hills; they rose against the French in 1933, but were crushed after 3 months.

Ta Oi: 20,000 live around **Khe Sanh** in **Binh Tri Thien** province and in Laos. Slash and burn **rice farmers**, they are skilled in taming elephants.

Kinh Mun: 10,000 in **Lai Chau** and **Son La** provinces and Laos; they fell under Thai domination. During the Vietnam war they fought alongside the communists and were commended for downing 2 US planes.

Thai-Tay:

Bo Y: Numbering little more than 1000. Oppressed, they migrated within the past 250 years from China into the borderlands of **Lai Chau** and **Hoang Lien Son** provinces. Women are known for their **silver jewellery**.

Giay: 30,000 living in **Lai Chau** and **Hoang Lien Son** provinces near the Chinese border. Related to the *Tay*, *Thai* and *Nung*, their women have pink threads in their hair and stars on their cloth bags.

Lao: 7000 living in **Son La** and **Lai Chau** provinces near Laos. They **fish** (salting and pickling their catch) and **grow rice**. They have close contact with the neighbouring *Black Thai*.

Lu: 3000 in northern **Lai Chau** province. In medieval times they inhabited the **Dien Bien Phu** and **Tuan Giao** districts and had a significant citadel; in the 18th century they were pushed north to their present homeland.

Pushed by the
Chinese

Nung: 500,000 in the **northern provinces** bordering China. Entering Vietnam at different periods to escape Imperial Chinese oppression they settled as **maize hill farmers**; many still speak **Cantonese**.

San Chay: 75,000 living in **Ha Tuyen** and **Bac Thai** provinces, they fled China in the 17th century and are divided into the *Cao Lan* and *San Chi* group. They have close ties with their *Tay* neighbours.

Tay (Tho): Numbering around 800,000 these form the largest *montagnard* ethnic minority. One group lives in **Cao Bang** and **Lang Son**, another in **Bac Thai** and **Ha Tuyen** provinces. Generally they had close relations with the Viets and fought alongside them against the Chinese and French. They are associated with the *Thai*.

Thai: Not to be confused with the Thai of Thailand though of the same large group, they number 700,000 and live mainly in **Lai Chau**, **Hoang Lien Son** and **Son La** provinces. An influential people divided into *Black*, *White* and *Red Thai*, their names derive from the colour of the blouses worn by the women. The *Thai-Tay* peoples originally migrated **from China** in the 4th century AD, though they arrived in greater numbers in the 11th-12th centuries, with the *Thai* entering Vietnam from the west and occupying the north-west and the *Tay* arriving from the east and settling in north-east Vietnam; traditionally they dominated the smaller tribes of the area.

Kadai:

Usually regarded as a sub-group of the *Thai-Tay*, the *Kadai* tongue also shows characteristics of the *Viet-Muong*, *Mon-Khmer* and *Malayo-Polynesian* languages. There are four small Kadai tribes: the *Co Lao, La Chi* and *Pu Peo* inhabit northern **Ha Tuyen** province, while the *La Ha* live by rivers in **Hoang Lien Son** and **Son La** provinces.

Meo-Zao:

Meo (Miao): 150,00 spread throughout the northern highland provinces, especially near the Chinese border, and divided into the *White Meo, Black Meo, Red Meo, flowering Meo* and the *Meo Mung-Sao.* They arrived **from China** in the past 200 years, with a great influx coming after the T'ai Ping Revolution in 1860; they once rose against the French who tried to impose heavy taxes.

Pa Then: 2000 living in **Ha Tuyen** province, mainly on the left bank of the Gam; they migrated **from China** at the turn of the 19th century; traditionally divided into 8 families (*pa then*),

Zao (Yan Man): 300,000 living in the **Hoang Lien Son, Vinh Phu, Ha Tuyen, Cao Bang, Lang Son** and **Bac Thai** provinces, they have been arriving **from China** over the past 700 years. They are well known for their **paper made from bark** which enabled them to pass down literature.

Austronesian (Malayo-Polynesian) Language Family

Peoples from this group are found throughout the East Indies; they are said to have originated from Indonesia, the Indian sub-continent or China's Kwantung region.

Cham: 75,000 living along the **central coastal provinces** as well as **An Giang** and **Tay Ninh** provinces, these are the descendants of the once splendid **Champa Kingdom.** Now fishermen, farmers and makers of **excellent ox carts**, they also serve as **traders** between the Viets and the *montagnards.*

Chu Ru: 8000 living in **Lam Dong** province. Pushed inland by *Chams* expansionism, they were named *Cru*, 'land eaters' by the hill peoples they displaced.

A rich ancient
culture

Jarai (Giarai): 200,000 living in the southern part of **Gia Lai-Contum** and northern **Dac Lac** provinces these form the largest ethnic minority in the Central Highlands. They co-habited with the *Chams* on the coast before moving up here 2000 years ago. Their **King of Fire** in Pleiku and **King of Water** in Cheo Reo were famous way beyond their borders, while their attack on missionary supply convoys led Father Guerlach to form a force of *Bahnar* tribesmen to fight the *Jarai*.

Rhade: 150,000 living in **Dac Lac** (around **Ban Me Thuot**) and western **Phu Khanh** provinces. The *Rhade* believe that their forefathers migrated from a South China Sea island to the Vietnam coast before returning to these highlands, their spiritual-ancestral homeland. They lost land when French acquirement of the fertile Dac Lac plateau intensified in 1925; the French regarded them as the most intelligent of the *montagnards*.

Smart tribe

Roglai: 55,000 living in **Thuan Hai** and **Phu Khanh** provinces. These were coastal dwellers who pushed inland until further migration was prevented by the mountains, which also served to keep them isolated from the *Koho* to the west. In the past they helped the *Chams* fight the *Viets*; the *Viets* later exacted tribute of ivory and rhino horn. Traditionally they would **trade** goods from the interior, **travelling by river** to the coast.

Sino-Tibetan Language Family
Comprising the Chinese and Tibeto-Burmese language groups which trace their origins to China.

Chinese:
Hoa (Chinese): Vietnam's ethnic Chinese number between 1 and 2 million and tend to live in the cities, **Cholon** being their main centre (see page 226).

Ngai and their fish sauce

Ngai: 2000 living mainly on the coast and islands of **Quang Ninh** and **Haiphong** provinces, they fled China at different periods. Traditionally **fishermen** with houseboats, they are famous for their **Cat Hai fish sauce**.

San Ziu: 65,000 living in the **north eastern provinces**, mainly at the foot of hills, and known for efficiently **restoring eroded land**. They arrived from China in the 1600s; some are **saltmakers** and **fishermen**.

Tibeto-Burmese:
A group of half a dozen small tribes, the *Coong, Ha Nhi, La Hu, Lo Lo, Phu La* and *Sila,* who arrived from China over the past 600 years (the Sila came from Laos) and

SPREAD OF A CULTURE

Eighty five percent of Vietnamese are *Viet* (*Kinh*), an ethnic group from the Red River Delta which gradually pushed southwards in a migration which is know as the *Nam Tien* ('The March to the South').

The *Nam Tien* probably began before the time of Christ, though 939 AD, the year the Vietnamese gained independence from China, is normally regarded as the official starting date. An expanding population in need of new land, suitable for cultivating rice, and the constant military threat from China generated the migration, and with sea to the east, mountains to the west and the Chinese to the north, southwards was the only direction in which to head.

To a great extent *Nam Tien* was organised. The government promoted **Nong Trai**, the homesteading of new territories, by offering citizens incentives to extend the southern frontier and settle and farm the occupied land. Under the **Lao Trai** scheme prisoners who took part in *Nong Trai* were pardoned and, in times of peace, soldiers built their own bases along the way under the **Don Dien** programme.

The southward colonisation ate away the **Champa Kingdom** and by the end of the 17th century the Viets had absorbed their territories, culture and population, leaving only a few scattered communities intact. Beyond, the Champa Kingdom was the **Khmer Mekong Delta**. By the late 18th century this too had been overwhelmed by the Viets, the *Nam Tien* was complete and the borders of present Vietnam were established.

THE CHAMS AND THE KHMER

The *Viets* successful southward colonisation from the Red River delta was at the expense of two groups of peoples, the *Chams*, whose ancient kingdom stretched along the central coastal plain, and the *Khmers*, who had long occupied the Mekong Delta region.

Today the remnants of the *Chams* number about 70,000 and live mainly in the **central coastal province**, especially around **Phan Rang, Phan Ri Cu** and **Phan Thiet**; other groups settled in the provinces of **An Giang** and **Tay Ninh** near the Cambodian border.

The *Chams* were influenced by **Hinduism** and later by **Islam**, both brought over from India, and today there are still the *Kaphir* (Hindu) and the *Bani* (Muslim) *Chams*. Both groups live at peace with each other and even share the same God, *Ovloh* or *Allah*, which the *Kaphir* claim the *Bani* found in their Hindu pantheon.

There are few legacies of the splendid Indianised **Champa Kingdom**, which flourished between the 2nd and 15th centuries AD, except for some decaying **brown brick towers** along the central coastal plain and **sculptures and other relics** in the **Da Nang museum**.

The *Khmers* had inhabited the **Mekong Delta** since they had overthrown the Hindu Funan kings in 535. The result of this victory was the evolution of the **Kambuja-Khmer Kingdom**, which became one of Asia's great empires during the Angkor period between 802 and 1432. There was rivalry with the neighbouring *Chams* who, in 1177, sent a fleet up the Mekong and ransacked the capital of **Angkor**; but by 1190 the *Khmers* controlled most of south-east Asia and annexed the Champa kingdom.

With the decline of the Khmer kingdom, the *Khmers* of the Mekong became vulnerable to the *Viets'* southward-drive and they were finally absorbed into Vietnam on the completion of the **Nguyen Lords' colonisation** in 1758. In the 1970s *Khmers* fled Pol Pot's genocide in Cambodia and have settled in Vietnam, raising the Mekong region's *Khmer* population to over one million.

The *Khmers* are **Theravada Buddhists** (most Vietnamese are **Mahayana Buddhists**) and they have many **pagodas** around the Mekong. Aspects of their Funienese-Hindu past can still be traced in some of their customs.

THE CHINESE

The largest ethnic group amongst the non-Viets is the Chinese, the **Hoa Ch'iao** (Chinese living abroad), numbering over 1 million in Vietnam. Chinese have been migrating into Vietnam since the 3rd century BC, sometimes as invaders at other times to escape persecution.

A wave of **Ming** supporters arrived in Vietnam in 1644 after the rise of the **Manchu** in China and they were encouraged by the **Nguyen Lord** to settle in the newly colonised **Mekong Delta**; the **Opium Wars** (1839-42) generated an exodus and French offered jobs to migrant Chinese in the rice trade in Cochin China; 400,000 fled into Vietnam when Japan invaded China in 1937; and a further influx arrived in 1945 after the Second World War.

Most come from south China and belong to five main dialect groups: *Cantonese, Teochiu* - by far the largest two - *Hakka, Fukienese* and *Hainanese*. They established societies based on these groups, named *bangs* by Emperor Gia Long but later called *Chinese Regional Administrative Groups*, which serve as powerful community organisations.

The Chinese have never really integrated with the rest of the population. Many, especially the *Teochiu* and *Fukienese*, are traditionally **occupied in commerce** and by the mid 1950s 85% of Vietnam's trade passed through their hands.

In 1956 **President Ngo Dinh Diem** issued **Ordinance No. 48** which required all 0.5 million Chinese born in Vietnam to take Vietnamese citizenship and **Ordinance No. 53** which prohibited foreigners, essentially Chinese, to engage in certain professions. The Chinese reacted by disrupting the economy until a compromise was reached with Diem. More Chinese than Vietnamese, they fear reprisals when relations between China and Vietnam are strained and many fled the country after China invaded the border town of Lang Son in 1979.

settled in the north western provinces of **Lai Chau** and **Hoang Lien Son**.

Montagnards

The land of the Viets, the Red and Mekong deltas and the coastal plains, constitute only 20% of the country's area. The rest of Vietnam is forested hills and mountains, sparsely populated by the *Nguoi thieu-so* (minority people) or, as the French called them the *'montagnards'*. The old perjorative *'moi'*, meaning 'savage' in Vietnamese, is no longer used.

In search of savages with tails

'In the early part of the last century the Mois seem to have been regarded as articulate animals rather than human beings. Europeans did their best, but without success, to acquire specimens for zoological collections in Europe. In 1819, Captain Rey of Bordeaux, who carried a cargo of fire-arms to the Emperor of Annam, was assured by no less a dignitary than the Mandarin of Strangers, of the existence of 'Moys, or wild men' . . . They had tails, he said, and he had managed to capture one and bring it back with him to the capital as a present for the Emperor.

Lost tribe of Israel?

Before the end of the century, these opinions had to be modified. The explorer Mouhot - discoverer of Angkor Vat - had published an account of his visit to the Stieng tribe. The Mois were officially conceded souls and some theorists even began to raise the matter of the lost tribes of Israel. However, until the colonial era with its census-taking, and head-taxes, these newly promoted human beings remained inaccessible, and still fairly mysterious, in their forests.'

From **'A Dragon Apparent'** by Norman Lewis.

Common Customs

Much of Vietnam's interior is remote and fairly inaccessible and many of the *montagnard* tribes are rarely visited by outsiders. The population of tribes may number a few hundred or several hundred thousand and though each has its own distinct culture they share some common customs.

All the tribes farm. The large majority grow **rice** as the main crop - although the type of rice and method of cultivation depend on the location. The **slash and burn** technique, which clears a patch of land, farms it until the soil is exhausted of nutrients and then moves on, is common.

Many tribes hunt for additional food with a **wide variety of prey** including lizards, snakes, rats, boars, monkeys and larger animals of the jungle. **Tigers** are generally treated with great awe, **elephants** are tamed and harnessed for work, and **buffaloes** are the prime sacrificial beast. **Rhinos**, once killed for their horn which was traded as an aphrodisiac, are now very scarce. Riverain tribes fish, and **forest flora** is gathered both for **food** and as **medicine** or **poison**.

Animal's role

Kinship systems amongst the ethnic minorities are usually **patrilineal**, though peoples of the **Austronesian** group tend to be **matrilineal**.

Houses are frequently **built on stilts** with bamboo, wood, wattle or grasses used for the walls and some sort of thatch for the roofs. They are usually clustered in family, clan or village **compounds** with the **'long house'**, up to 100 metres long amongst the *Rhade*, serving as a communal building. Different parts of the house are designated to specific family members. Objects, such as a buffalo skull on the wall or a carved wooden statue by the doorway, have a tutelary purpose, while the hearth is respected as it is home to the kitchen spirit. There is normally a **shrine to the ancestors. Graves** or **tombs** are on the edge of the settlement and may be **highly elaborate** affairs with all the fancy designs and ornaments having **symbolic meaning**.

Animism

Living so close to nature, the tribes have very strong animistic beliefs. Everything around them - animals, trees, streams, the sky, thunder, stones - embody spirits which must be respected. **Taboos** enshroud all these things; it may be taboo, for example, to touch a particular rock or to cross a stream after dark, or, according to the

Don't scrape the pot

M'nong, for a person to scrape rice from a pot with a knife as this tempts a tiger to attack. If these taboos are violated a **sacrifice** is necessary to avert disaster. French colonial administrators who unwittingly contravened tribal taboos on their rounds of duty were sometimes ceremoniously put to death. There is also deep reverence for Nature. The *Lo Lo* regard the large trees as guardians of the springs and home of the Spirit of the Earth and will not fell them.

Superstitions are rife and a **code of omens** controls the *montagnard's* life. For example, the *M'nong* believe that a dog stepping over a baby must be killed and eaten by all those who attended the child's birth; several tribes give

Unfortunate names

newly borns' names such as 'dung', or 'urine' so as not to attract the spirits of evil (i.e. disease) and only when the child is older, and stronger, is the name changed; a bird singing on the left of the farmer may portend a good harvest, heard from the right it signifies a poor yield; if a mouse is seen running across a forest track, then abandon the hunt.

Outside religions have has some impact. French missionaries won converts, for example amongst the Bahnar, though Christianity was usually practised in tandem with animism. Up in the north, tribes with Chinese origins often believed in a mixture of Buddhism, Confucianism, Taoism and animism. The *Lao* **tattoo** their wrists with a Buddhist swastika and their thighs with images of animals.

Aspects from outside culture are rationally interpreted. According to *Hre* logic, for example, an aeroplane was seen as a half-man, half-animal which ate no rice, but drank (petrol); the pilot was the father and only he could command the beast. And when war came, some tribes viewed planes and helicopters as symbols of benevolence if they off loaded food supplies, or harbingers of destruction if they dropped bombs.

Local's view of the plane

The **belief that a person's soul survives death** and becomes a protector of the family line is common amongst nearly all peoples of Vietnam. Homage must therefore be paid to the dead. Families have **shrines** to their ancestors in their homes and it is imperative to visit relatives' graves, especially on the death anniversary and festive days when they may hold a picnic, bringing with them the dead person's favourite food and drink. It is a happy occasion.

Happy about death

A dead *Bahnar* tribesman, for example, is wrapped in mats and taken to the burial ground at nightfall where he is placed in a wooden coffin. Valuable symbols of this world such as gongs, jars, and statues may be put in the grave to provide decoration, company or protection. There follows a **long period of mourning**, possibly lasting several years, during which time the wife observes various social restrictions. Finally, the **abandonment of the tomb ceremony** is held, with partying, and animals are sacrificed. The deceased has at last quit the land of the living; the mourning is over and the wife is free.

Animals are sacrificed to encourage the spirits to provide a **good harvest** or to placate them in the event of a **taboo violation**. In the past there were **human sacrifices**. A *Katu* man would hunt and kill a victim and smear his blood on his face before returning home to an orgy of feasting; such a man was a prize husband. Animal sacrifices are also performed on special occasions and a **person's wealth** may be measured by the number of sacrifices he notches up. Chickens and pigs are common ceremonial offerings, though the supreme sacrificial beast is the buffalo.

The **traditional buffalo sacrifice** is a brutal ritual. The creature is tethered to a special pole and tribesmen stab it with spears and slash into its flesh with axes, severing tendons and ligaments. Death is protracted, its very slowness is seen, perversely, as an honour to the buffalo. The banging of ceremonial gongs and the consumption of potent rice wine accompanies many of these special rituals.

Slow death by axe

As for **tribal hospitality**, *Hre* guests are greeted with **rice wine** which they are expected to drink until rendered literally 'legless'. A good guest is a drunk guest lying flat on his back. Their **enemies** were likely to be **attacked by arrows** dipped in a potion including centipedes' and serpents' teeth which could kill within 10 minutes of entering the blood system.

Modern Changes

How many of the old customs still exist amongst the *montagnards* is uncertain as there has been a dearth of anthropological studies in recent years. The **tattooing** *(xam minh)* of faces and bodies amongst some tribes is not as common as in the past; nor is the **puberty ritual** of filing teeth to sharp points - or right down to the gum - or the **lacquering** *(nhuom rang)* of the teeth black. **Earlobes** weighted by heavy objects and hanging down to the

---

DRESS

The wide variety of traditional dress - individual tribal versions of a cotton skirt, blouse, shawl and headgear for women and a loin cloth and shirt for men - is slowly being replaced amongst some peoples by the Western-styled shirt and trousers. Down on the plains, the majority of Viets still wear the old fashioned pyjama suits and *ao dais* (the long blouses and flared trousers worn by women), but here too Western modes are having an impact. Conical hats, *non bai tho*, primarily for women, and the green Viet Cong *sola topis*, mainly sported by men in the north, are still classic headgear, but some of the old men wear berets, and baseball caps are particularly popular with youngsters. The Viets' *guoc*, a wooden or bamboo root shoe, is worn in the rainy season. The lower *guoc Saigon* design was an instant hit when it came on the market in 1910 and has remained in vogue ever since.

shoulders enhance a woman's beauty; however, fewer young women than before follow this fashion, most preferring to limit their adornment to wearing **elaborate jewellery**.

The making of **handicrafts** is a subsidiary occupation to farming for many tribes. **Basketry** is very common, as is **wood carving**. The *Ataouat* group of the *Katu* are famous for their **macabre wooden statues** which ward off evil outside the homes. Some of the more isolated peoples make their clothes from the bark of trees, others weave their own cotton, often dying it a rich indigo and embroidering it with designs.

Bartering was once the exclusive means of trade amongst *montagnards*. Now paper money is common currency and it buys an growing variety of novel goods offered by itinerant merchants or found on sale in the markets. The new world will soon eclipse the old.

Maintaining rights for minorities

An organisation, the *Front Unifié de Lutte des Races Opprimés* (the **United Front for the Struggle of Oppressed Races**, or FULRO has been set up by the *montagnards* to promote the rights of the ethnic minorities in Vietnam.

RELIGION

Vietnam's ancient religions

Buddhism, *Confucianism* and *Taoism* - collectively known as *Tam Giao* - are Vietnam's three traditional religions. Initially they were introduced from China and later the Ly emperors combined and developed them as the basis of the faith, morals and philosophy of Vietnam.

Buddhism, the predominant religion, was brought to Vietnam by both the Indians (*Theravada* branch) and the Chinese (*Mahayana* branch) around the same time, at the end of the 2nd century AD. It took a while for the religion to permeate through society and it was not until **Emperor Dinh Tien Hoang** gave *Mahayana Buddhism* his royal patronage in the late 10th century that it became a widely accepted faith. It increased in popularity during the **Ly Dynasty** (1010-1225) when it was decreed to be the state religion.

During the **Tran Dynasty** (1225-1400) *Buddhism* was replaced by *Confucianism* as the official faith and when the Chinese invaded in 1414 they further pushed Buddhism into obscurity, destroying its temples and literature. In the 17th century, the **Nguyen Lords** adopted Buddhism for various political motives, however it was not until 1920 that the faith underwent a more pure and religious revival.

In the early 1960s **President Diem**, a staunch Catholic, discriminated against Buddhism and this provoked strong reactions from Buddhists, including **public self immolation by monks**.

Confucianism, more a philosophy of secular ethics than a religion, was introduced into Vietnam by the Chinese during their **'1000 years of domination'** (111 BC to 938 AD) and has been instrumental in moulding Vietnamese society. It established a pattern, a way of life, an order headed by the divinely proscribed emperor and a powerful elite of mandarins. Reverence was to the emperor and, on a more personal level, to one's ancestors, who, as a matter of duty, had to be venerated.

The **French**, through introducing their colonial administration, undermined the mandarin class and thus caused the decline of Confucianism. Nevertheless, Confucianism is still a deeply entrenched way of thinking and Vietnamese still conduct their life according to the philosophy's codes.

Taoism - the teachings of **Lao Tze** which proclaimed Man's affinity with the Universe, was not adopted by Vietnamese in the same way as either Buddhism or Confucianism. It was however a significant ingredient in the *Tam Giao*, adding **mysticism** to the Vietnameses' mélange of beliefs.

The *Cult of Ancestors* - ancestral worship - is prevalent throughout Vietnam. This is based on the notion that when a person dies he is not lost to the world, rather his spirit survives and must be respected and honoured. On auspicious days, such as the **death anniversary**, the family will organise a celebration by the place of burial. The deceased without relations or someone to pray for him or to attend his grave will be destined to wander for eternity in the spirit world. It is a horrific thought and one can imagine the anguish the French caused when they desecrated Vietnamese family graves. A shrine to a dead relative is a feature in Vietnamese sitting rooms and a place of homage where prayers are said, asking for the protection of the ancestors, whose role in this world takes on an important new dimension.

Animism is followed mainly by the ethnic minorities, who believe aspects of Nature are embodied in spirits which must be respected and revered. The spirits are enshrouded in a host of **taboos** which have to be observed and these virtually control the life of the person. Spirits upset by a violation of a taboo can inflict disasters and should be appeased by a suitable **sacrifice**.

Buddhist suicide by fire

Party at the grave

Power of the taboo

Catholicism was introduced by European missionaries in the 16th century, with the **Portuguese Dominicans** and **French Jesuits** becoming the main teachers of the faith in the succeeding centuries. By the late 17th century there were 800,000 Christian converts in Vietnam. Such fervent proselytisation did not impress the Confucian indoctrinated rulers and as early as 1533, **Emperor Trang Tong** banned a missionary because of his subversive teachings. **Imperial-Christian conflict** was inevitable and the emperors periodically purged the followers of Dato - as they called Christ - and, in the mid 19th century, the French used this persecution as their excuse to invade, and ultimately colonise, Vietnam.

Once in power, the **French promoted Christianity** and discriminated in favour of Christians - and hence they won converts, a total of 1.6 million during their colonial rule. There evolved an elite of Catholics (Protestantism has never featured prominently in Vietnam) which

Catholic elite included **President Diem** and his family. The antagonism of his brother **Monseigneur Ngo Dinh Thuc**, Bishop of Hue, towards Buddhists led to the **Buddhist Riots** of the 1960s. Despite such clashes there has not been a history of intercommunal sectarian fighting between any religions in Vietnam. Many Christians, fearing persecution at the hands of the **Communists** after the division of Vietnam in 1954, fled from the North to the South and then quit the

Southbound Christians country altogether when the North's 1975 victory looked inevitable. Today, 5-10% of Vietnam's population are Christian.

Cao Daism and *Hoa Hao* are two 20th century, home grown, religious sects which became significant **socio-political parties** down in the Mekong Delta during the latter colonial years and the Vietnam War years (see page 234).

FESTIVALS

Tet

Of Vietnam's many festivals *Tet* - the celebration of the beginning of spring and the New Year - is the greatest and most universally followed. *Tet Nguyen Dan* - 'Tet's'

Celebrations of the year full name meaning **'The First Day'** - is on the 1st of the first lunar month, some time in January-February. It is a time when families get together (flights to Vietnam are over booked in the days leading up to Tet), have a party, exchange presents, clean the house, buy new clothes, pay outstanding debts, and settle differences. It is a start of a

Cao Dai Temple.

PLACES OF WORSHIP

Pagoda (Chua): Buddhist temple
Dinh: Communial house including shrine to village saint
Den: Temple in honour of hero
Mieu: Small altar in honour of spirits
Ban Tho Gia Tien: Family altar
Ban Tho Ho: Ancestral altar
Church: They still stand, though they seem closed more often than open.

new era and the way you begin it will indicate how you will spend it. The custom of *Giao Thua* heralds in the **New Year** and also the **new spirit of the hearth** - the all important household spirit. Various other rituals are also observed including *Ta Nien* when the **ancestors** are invited back to join in the family festivities. It is a time of great happiness and rejoicing at home and in the streets, which are strewn with **flowers** and loud with the din of **firecrackers** and **percussion instruments**. The festival lasts a week, of which the first three days are the most important, and ends with *Le Khai Ha,* the tradition of taking down the *Cay Neu* - the **lucky bamboo** hung with red paper and betel nuts - which are kept in the house during Tet to frighten off the evil spirits. Ideally a visit to Vietnam should coincide with Tet, however accommodation is likely to be heavily booked.

There are **numerous other festivals** throughout Vietnam. Some are celebrated nationally, others are just local affairs. The remembrance of battles, saints, ancestors - family members, heroes, emperors - is very important and festivals are held in their honour. The traditional *Khao Vong* celebrates an achievement accomplished by a fellow villager. **Regional Tourist Offices** can provide information about some of the events in their areas, otherwise you are likely to just stumble across them. Below are some of the better known national festivals and their dates:

Buddha' Birthday - 15th day of the fourth lunar month.

Buddha's Enlightenment - 8th day of the twelfth lunar month.

Hung Vuong Festival - 10th day of the third lunar month. This celebrates the legendary Hung Vuong emperors.

Honouring the young

Childrens' Festival or mid Autumn Festival - 15th day of the 8th lunar month. Presents are given to children, ancestors are worshipped and their burial places cleaned.

Le Vu Lan - 15th day of the 7th lunar month. This pays respects to the wandering souls - the spirits which have no family to pray for them.

Le Tran Nguyen - 15th day of the first lunar month. The Festival of the Learned.

Le Thanh Minh - 15 days after the first day of spring. Families decorate ancestral graves.

No fixed date	**LUNAR CALENDAR** The lunar calendar has 29 or 30 days per month and 355 days a year, but every fourth year an extra month is added to keep it synchroised with the solar calendar. Therefore days on the lunar calendar do not correspond from one year to the next with the dates on solar calendar.

8th March - National Women's Day

30th April - Liberation Day

1st May - Labour Day

1st June - Children's Day

27th June - War Veterans' Day

2nd September - Independence Day

20th November - Teachers' Day

HISTORY

'If there were a World Cup for war the Vietnamese would be clear winners. They have taken on all the top war teams and thrashed them (even though they did have home advantage)'.
Messrs. Smith and Jones.

For over 2000 years Vietnam has suffered a succession of invasions, right up until the mid 1970s when the Americans, like many before them, returned home as losers.

For centuries **China**, Vietnam's powerful northern neighbour, had been the frequent intruder, marching into northern Vietnam with monotonous regularity. Often repelled, they did, however, sometimes stay, most notably from the **second century BC to the tenth century AD**, a period known as Vietnam's **'1000 years of domination'**.

Vietnam's legendary **Tran Hung Deo**, conqueror of the Chinese in the late 18th century, gave his opinion: *'The enemy relies on numbers. To oppose the long with the short - there lies our skill. If the enemy makes a violent rush, like fire and tempest. It is easy to defeat him. But if he shows patience, like a silkworm nibbling at a mulberry leaf. If he proceeds without haste, refrains from pillaging the population, and does not seek a quick victory, then we must choose the best generals and elaborate adequate tactics, as in a chess game. The army must be united and of one mind, like father and son'.*

Tenacity, patience and, most importantly, the utter resolution of the people to gain victory at any cost, were always Vietnam's war winning tactics. The enemies'

In the shadow of China

Never succumb

55

failure to realise these strengths was the reason for their defeats. Even the highly destructive war waged by the Americans was doomed to failure against a people who were prepared to sacrifice everything for their land.

The Viet Myth

The ancient history of Vietnam is often thought of as a history of the Viet peoples rather than a history of the country's present geographical area.

Viets trace their origins to the legendary **Hong Bang Dynasty** which ruled **Van Lang** - the kingdom stretching from China's Yangste River southwards to the middle of present Vietnam - between 2879 and 258 BC.

Traditionally it is believed that **King Duong Vuong**, son of a king and a fairy, married a dragon's daughter who gave birth to **Lac Long Quan**, who in turn married a fairy named **Au Co**. This union resulted in the production of 100 eggs which hatched a 100 sons. As the offspring of a dragon, Lac Long Quan could not remain with his fairy mate however, and the couple separated. Lac Long Quan settled on the coast and plains, while Au Co remained in the hills. Each took 50 sons who became the respective procreators of Vietnam's lowland and highland ethnic groups. The eldest son founded the **Hong Bang Dynasty** in 2879 BC and a line of **18 kings**, all called **Hung Vuong**, reigned over Van Lang for the following 2600 years.

A fairy and her 100 sons

War broke out between the *Lac Viet*, the lowland tribes, and the *Au Viet* (or *Tay Au*), the highland tribes of north Vietnam, at the end of the 3rd century BC. **Thuc Phan**, leader of the *Au Viet*, defeated the last of the *Hong* in 258 BC and united the two groups of tribes, assuming the regal title of An Duong Vuong and creating his own **Thuc Dynasty** to rule the kingdom of **Au Lac** which covered most of northern Vietnam down to the Ngang Pass. He built his citadel capital at **Co Loa**, 20 km north of present Hanoi, the remains of which can still be seen today.

The Thuc Dynasty began and ended with An Duong however. His success had been due to a fairy bow which enabled him to kill thousands of his opponents with each arrow he fired. The Chinese general, **Trieu Da**, sent his son to marry An Duong Vuong's daughter and the boy managed to steal the magical weapon and deliver it to his father who, in 207 BC, used it on the Vietnamese causing their defeat.

Victory through a magical bow

Trieu Da took Trieu Vu Vuong as his royal name and created a new kingdom, **Nam Viet**, comprising parts of

northern Vietnam and southern China, with its capital at
Phien Ngu (Canton). Under the **Trieu Dynasty** Nam Viet
remained an autonomous state, though at the same time
the Vietnamese were introduced to their first real taste of
the Chinese civilisation.

1000 Years of Chinese Domination

In 111 BC the **Han Chinese** pushed southwards,
absorbing the Red River delta as their province of **Giao
Chi**. They left the Vietnamese social order reasonably
intact and their benign colonialism was accepted until 30
AD when Chinese functionaries killed a local lord in their
bid to gain direct control of the land. His widow, **Trung
Trac**, and her sister, **Trung Nhi**, gathered widespread
support from around the province and overthrew the
Chinese.

Queens for a brief moment

For three years the Vietnamese enjoyed independence.
The **Trung sisters** (the *Hai Ba Trung*) ruled as queens with
their capital at the town of **Ma Linh**, north of present
Hanoi. Independence, though, was shortlived; three years
later the Chinese returned under the leadership of Ma
Vien and quashed the popular insurrection. In defeat the
Hai Ba Trung drowned themselves in the River Hat
Giang. Today the sisters are honoured with a festival on
the fifteenth of the first lunar month of each year at their
native village of **Ha Loi, near Me Linh**.

Chinese control was now tighter, with Chinese
mandarins and officials serving in all but the most minor
bureaucratic post, and Confucianism, the Chinese
language, education system, trading methods, and arts
and crafts all being imposed from above.

Chinese influence

Under the *Han*, **Giao Chi**, whose name was changed to
Gaio Chau in 203, enjoyed stability and prosperity. An
educated, Chinese-influenced class of Vietnamese
emerged. At the same time expatriate Chinese became
increasingly 'Vietnamised' during their long terms of
office. The result was the evolution of a **Sino-Vietnamese
elite** which was partly Chinese in character but
Vietnamese in spirit and loyalty.

Passionate Amazon

A weakening Han dynasty inspired Vietnamese
freedom fighters to come to the fore. Amongst them was
the wild **Trieu Au** who in 220 rallied an army of 1000
men with impassioned oratory: *'I'd like to ride storms, kill
the sharks in the open sea, drive out the aggressors, reconquer
the country, undo the ties of serfdom, and never bend my back
to be the concubine of whatever man'*. Decked in gold
armour and atop an elephant, Trieu Au led her men into

a battle which none of them survived. All the more glorious for her recklessness, Trieu Au became a national heroine and her shrine built by an admiring emperor in the 6th century at **Phu Dien** in Thanh Hoa province, is still a place of pilgrimage.

A more promising revolt was led by **Le Bon**, descendant of a well established expatriate Chinese family, who overthrew the colonial regime and established his own government in 544. He renamed his kingdom *Van-Xuan* (meaning Ten Thousand Springs) and created the **Early Ly Dynasty**. After his death his lineage proved weak and by 602 the Chinese were back in power.

The emergence of the **Tang Dynasty** in 619 heralded a period of prosperity for China and her colonies. The *Tangs*, ambitious to extend their empire, yet again renamed Giao Chau as the **Protectorate of 'Annam'** (the 'Pacified South') in 679 and used it as a base for penetration deeper into south-east Asia. As a result Annam became a frontier, and buffer, between the Chinese and their enemies beyond.

The Vietnamese finally rid themselves of the Chinese during the wane of the Tang dynasty. In 938 a Chinese fleet pursued the Vietnamese navy up the **Bach Dang River**. The tide was high, though quickly ebbing and the Vietnamese feigned retreat, luring the Chinese into their trap. As the water level fell the sharp iron-tipped wooden stakes the Vietnamese had implanted in the river bed and banks impaled the Chinese vessels and formed an effective barrage against the escape route back down river. The trapped Chinese had no chance in the ensuing onslaught. The victorious **General Ngo Quyen** went on to proclaim himself king of the independent state of **Vietnam** with his capital at the old city of Co Loa.

Power of the Tang

Victory through impalation

The Evolution of Vietnam
The untimely **death of Ngo Quyen** in 944 resulted in chaos. Twelve warlords emerged to take control of the country, but they were systematically challenged and defeated by **Dinh Bo Linh**, son of a senior mandarin, who in 968 reunited Annam under his control.

Dinh Bo Linh - later known as **Dinh Tien Hoang** - established this capital at **Hoa Lu** in Ha Nam Ninh province and re-named the country **Dai Co Viet** (the 'Great Viet State'). By reshaping the military and administrative hierarchies and promoting religion amongst his people he established a tribute to the powerful *Sung* rulers in China, and so he ensured their peace and their endorsement of his position. It was a delicate pact, but the independence was to last.

A lunatic assassin
Dinh Tien Hoang and his younger brother were murdered in 979 by a demented junior official. The next in line was barely six years old and so **La Hoan**, a mandarin-general and the lover of Dinh Tien Hoang's widow, took control. He warded off the Chinese in the north and repelled the *Chams* in the south, capturing their capital of **Indrapura** in the process.

A lauded hero, La Hoan was not popular either for his affair with the queen or the way he had gained his throne. Domestic political life was turbulent for him and also for his successors in the **Early La Dynasty** who killed each other off, finally leaving another child as the most senior royal candidate. It was the death of the dynasty and in 1009 the Court appointed **Ly Cong Uan** - who took the name **Ly Thai To** - as emperor.

Ly Thai To established **Thang Long** (Hanoi) as his capital and he and his successors built on the structure laid by Dinh Tien Hoang over half a century before. The **Ly Dynasty** provided, at last, relative stability and under them the country grew and prospered. The **Red River Delta** area remained the Vietnamese heartland, but with an increasing population they expanded southwards at the expense of the neighbouring **Champa kingdom**.

A hero to this day
The hero of this period was **General Ly Thuong Kiet**, who crossed into China in 1077 and defeated an enemy army. When the Chinese retaliated the following year, the general repelled them at the frontier passes. With victories over the *Cham* and *Khmer* armies in the south also to his name, Ly Thuong Kiet has become one of Vietnam's all time greats.

By the early 13th century the Ly Dynasty was in decline and the end of the line came when a 7-year-old princess inherited the empire. Waiting in the wings was the influential *Tran* family who seized the throne in 1225 and were to keep it for the next 175 years.

The **Tran period** is sometimes seen as the second phase of the golden era started by the Lys, with notable growth in cultural and, in particular, literary awareness.

Battles with the Mongols

The threat from the north now came from **Genghis Khan** and the **Mongols** who swept into northern China at the beginning of 13th century. The first of three Mongol-Vietnamese confrontations was not until 1267 when **Kublai Khan**, the grandson of Genghis, marched towards the *Sung* in southern China and captured **Thang Long** on the way.

The Mongol mission was unsuccessful and Kublai Khan was pushed back across the north-western border. He returned to conquer the **Sung Empire** in 1279 however, and then he reset his sights on the **Indochinese Peninsula**. Under the command of his son, **Toghan**, Kublai sent an army of 500,000 men into **Dia Viet** and overwhelmed a Vietnamese force of less than half the size. Thang Long was ransacked and **General Tran Binh Rong** imprisoned. Asked by his captors to switch sides, he responded with his famous fateful line. *'I'd rather be a ghost in the South (Dai Viet) than a king in the North (China)'*, before being decapitated.

Mongol occupation lasted until July 1285 when **Tran Hung Dao** launched a major attack on **Tay Ket**, southeast of **Thang Long**. The Mongol commander was killed and 50,000 men captured; the last of the enemy retreated across the border the following month. Tran Hung Dao had rid his country of half a million Mongols. He encouraged a fighting ethos whereby soldiers and **Everyman for** peasants alike rose against the enemy using both **his country** conventional and guerilla tactics - a method of warfare which has successfully defeated invaders ever since.

The **third Mongol incursion** was in 1299 when Kublai Khan's navy of 500 vessels sailed up the **Bach Dang** river, **Up the river** only to fall into the old river stakes trap (see page 58). **without a hope** On land a large Mongol force was slaughtered as it fled back to China through the **Noi Bang Pass**.

Peace survived Kublai Khan's death in 1294 and was strengthed under his son, **Timor**. Tran Hung Dao, veteran and hero of victories over the Mongols, died in 1300 aged over 70.

Viets versus Chams

While the peace with China was maintained by paying tribute **Emperor Tran Anh** turned his attention to the southern border, giving his daughter in marriage to the *Cham* King in return for the *Chams'* two northern territories. When the King died, **Tran Anh Tong** recalled his daughter rather than allow her to follow the local custom of burying herself alive next to her husband. Irate Chams invaded **Dai Viet**, but they were quickly quelled.

Cham success came during the reign of **Tran Du Tong**, in the mid-14th century, a low period for Dai Viet. At the same time the newly installed **Ming Dynasty** in China demanded an increase in tribute. In 1400 the **Tran**

dynasty ended when the 3 year old emperor was usurped by **Le Quy Ly** who then established his own *Ho* line.

Ho Quy Ly, as he became known, revitalised ailing Dai Viet, but the *Mings*, disenchanted with the new regime, invaded in 1406 and reinstalled the old family as the **Post Tran Dynasty**. The Chinese became increasingly influential and in 1414 they once again took direct control of Dai Viet.

The Lam-Son Uprising

The discontent of the Viets found embodiment as the **Lam-Son resistance movement**, originating in the village of Lam Son (Thanh Hoa province), under the charismatic leadership of **Le Loi**.

Le Loi's ten years of guerilla warfare against the *Ming* is a well loved episode in Vietnam's long history of resistance struggles. Guided by strategist **Nguyen Trai** and his principle *'Better conquer hearts than citadels'* the **Lam-Son Uprising** was a peoples' movement which culminated in 1427 after Le Loi cornered an enemy force of 100,000 men and took their generals hostage. Rather than slaughter them, he allowed the Chinese to sail home in peace.

Le Loi became emperor, calling himself **La Thuan Thien**, and consolidated the peace by offering triennal tribute to Peking. During his reign and that of the great **Le Thanh Tong** (1460-97), the fourth Le emperor, the Vietnamese enjoyed an unprecedented period of security and progress.

The **Le emperors** adopted the **Chinese Confucian** model for their society. The monarch was the father figure of the nation and commanded complete deference and respect from his subjects; he was the absolute ruler in the secular and spiritual worlds and had a quasi-divine status. The **mandarinate** - the bureaucracy administrating the country - was selected through tougher examinations and this led to greater efficiency in the running of the country.

Peace with China allowed the Vietnamese to pursue their ongoing war with the Chams. They pushed south, extending their authority beyond the **Hai Van Pass** by the end of the 15th century and over the next 200 years their colonisation virtually smothered the Champa culture.

The **Le Dynasty** began its decline under the ruthless **Le Uy Muc** (the 'Diabolical King') early in the 16th century and continued during the reign of his equally despotic successor, **Le Tuong Doc**.

Popular revolt

Adoption of Confucian principles

Internecine War

Mac Dang Dung, a tenuous descendant of the old **Tran Dynasty**, exploited the weakness and seized the opportunity to win the throne for himself in 1527.

The **Mac Dynasty** had its enemies and **General Nguyen Kim** restored the Le Dynasty 'in exile'. The Mac rulers continued to command the territory from **Son Nam** to the north, while the Le-Nguyen alliance held **Thanh Hoa** and the area to its south.

Fighting between the Les and Macs

Nguyen Kim, poisoned in 1554, was succeeded by **Trinh Kiem**. War between the Les and Macs continued until the Macs were defeated and their capital Thang Long was captured by Trinh Kiem's son in 1591. The Macs retired to Cao Bang Province where they ruled autonomously for the next 75 years.

A new contest now emerged between the Trinh and Nguyen families after a split in their allegiance. Both recognised the **Le Dynasty** as the legitimate, albeit 'puppet', rulers, but both established their own powerful dynasties with the Thrinh controlling the north for the Le emperors and the Nguyen in command of land south of the **River Gianh** with their capital at **Phu Xuan** (Hue).

The **Trinh-Nguyen Internecine war** broke out in 1627 and rumbled on until 1672 when the two dynasties agreed to respect the position of their common frontier. The pact withstood the next 100 years.

Nguyens push southwards

Meanwhile the **Nguyen faction** expanded southwards, absorbing the remnants of the *Chams'* territory as they laid claim to **Phan Rang** in 1653 and **Phan Thiet** in 1697. This date marks the end of Champa as a Kingdom. Beyond lay the fertile **Mekong Delta** inhabited by the *Khmer* people, a rich prize which the Vietnamese won easily. By the late 19th century the Nguyens had colonised present southern Vietnam.

Both the Trinh and Nguyen dynasties were becoming increasing corrupt and despotic however. Peasants revolted on numerous occasions in both the north and the south and the unrest finally climaxed with the popular **Tay Son Uprising**.

The Tay Son Brothers

Three brothers (also called Nguyen, though nothing to do with the ruling dynasty) had been amongst the wave of southbound settlers and in the 1770s they gathered grass roots support and rose up, first capturing areas around **Da Nang** and **Qui Nhon**, before finally winning **Saigon** and the rest of the south in 1783. **Nguyen Anh,** incumbent **Lord of the Nguyen clan**, fled to Siam where he collected an army of 20,000 Siamese soldiers and a large fleet. This force returned in January 1785 and sailed up the Mekong Delta, but fell into an ambush at the **Rach Gam-Xoai Mut** reach of the Mekong River. The army was annihilated and those who survived, including Nguyen Anh, fled westwards back to Siam.

The **Tay Son brothers** headed north, defeated the **Trinh Lords** and captured the capital **Thang Long**. They recognised the rather ineffectual Le Dynasty, but divided

**Tay Sons
control Vietnam**

command of the now united country between themselves: **Nguyen Hue** held the North, **Nguyen Nhat** the Centre and **Nguyen Lu** the South.

Emperor Le Man De tried to revive the glory of his dynasty with the help of the Chinese, who sent an army of 200,000 men across the border. Popular demand encouraged Nguyen Hue to counter the invasion and proclaiming himself as **Emperor Quang Trung** in 1789, he marched north with 100,000 men to meet the enemy.

It was just before **Tet** (the Lunar New Year), a time of huge celebrations and Quang Trung caught the Chinese unawares as they prepared for the event. His army routed the Chinese at the **Battle of Dong Da** (near Thang Long), killing 10,000 and putting the rest to flight.

After this promising start, the Tay Son era soon suffered internal problems, though more significant was the growing threat to Vietnamese independence, not from Chinese as in the past, but from the French.

The French Connection

**European
traders**

In 1535 the **Portuguese** reached **Cochin China**, as they called Dai Viet, and started trading at **Fai Fo** (present **Hoi An**, a port just south of Da Nang). They, like the Dutch, French and English who followed, dealt arms to the warring Trinhs and Nguyens but, with the conclusion of the civil war in 1672, business slumped and was virtually non-existent by the turn of the century.

The **presence of Christianity** was less ephemeral. Catholic missionaries had been in Dai Viet since the 16th century and the local mandarinate had generally treated them with suspicion, alternately tolerating and persecuting them. After all, the Christian dogma was at odds with the more worldly Confucian standard which demanded obedience to emperor, state and family. The missionaries did win converts amongst the poor however, and at the same time learned **Jesuits** made an impact on higher echelons of society. The Christian community

Minh Mang Mausoleum, Hue.

swelled to some 300,000 by the mid-19th century.

The French prelate **Pigneau de Behaine**, Bishop of Adran, had been in south Vietnam since 1767 and had

The Bishop who shaped Vietnam's destiny

formed a close friendship with **Nguyen Anh**, the Nguyen Lord who had been deposed by the Tay Son Uprising. He became obsessed with restoring Nguyen Anh to his throne.

Having failed to gain support from the French government, the bishop raised money from French merchants in the Mascarana Islands and gathered an army of mercenaries from the French settlement of Pondicherry in India.

With this army Nguyen Anh won back south and mid Dai Viet. In 1802 he was proclaimed emperor, adopting the name **Gia Long**, and he established his capital at Phu Xuan (Hue), where his family the Nguyen Lords, had previously held their court. He renamed the country **Vietnam.**

Pigneau de Behaine died of dysentery in 1799 and was buried by Nguyen Anh with great ceremony. The emperor had never accepted the bishop's faith, but he

The cyclo is a popular form of transportation in Vietnam.

The conical hat is a traditional style throughout Vietnam.

A colourful funeral in Hue.

A buddhist monk in saffron robe.

tolerated Christianity in Vietnam out of respect to this friend. His successors **Minh Mang**, **Thieu Tri** and **Tuc Duc** were less gracious to the religion.

Mission against Christianity

In 1833 **Minh Mang** publicly announced his campaign against Christianity; *'I, Minh Mang, the king speak thus. For many years men from the Occident have been preaching the religion of Dato* (Christianity) *and deceiving the public, teaching them that there is a mansion of supreme bliss and a dungeon of dreadful misery. They have no respect for the God Phat* (Buddha) *and no reverence for ancestors. That is great blasphemy indeed. Moreover, they build houses of worship where they receive a large number of people, without discriminating between the sexes, in order to seduce the women and young girls; they also extract the pupils from the eyes of sick people. Can anything more contrary to reason and custom be imagined?'* Minh Mang continued by outlining his purge on the religion. Churches were to be razed and Christians were to be persuaded to denounce their faith; if they did not, they would be *'punished with the last degree of severity, so that this depraved religion may be extirpated'*.

A clash of cultures

Minh Mang was more candid in a private note to his regional governors *'The religion of Jesus deserves all our hatred, but our foolish and stupid people throughout the kingdom embrace it en masse and without examination. We must not allow this abuse to spread. Therefore we have deigned to post a paternal edict, to teach them how to correct themselves.*

The people who follow this doctrine blindly are nonetheless our people; they cannot be turned away from error in a moment. If the law was followed strictly, it would require countless executions. The measure would cost our people dear, and many who would be willing to mend their ways would be caught up in the proscription of the guilty. Moreover, this matter should be handled with discretion, following the (Confucian) *maxim, which states: ' If you want to destroy a bad habit, do so with order and patience,' and continues: 'If you wish to root out an evil breed, take the hatchet and cut root.'*

Conquest to Colonisation

The French send in the navy

The French responded to the purge on missionaries by deploying their navy which, in September 1857, captured the port of **Da Nang** (Tourane).

From here the French turned southwards, capturing **Gia Dinh** (Saigon) and the provinces immediately to the west, before signing a treaty with **Emperor Tu Duc** in

1862 which acknowledged their conquest and excluded other foreign powers from the land. Five years later **Admiral de la Grandiere** annexed the remainder of the southern provinces claiming that they were a breeding ground for anti-French sentiment; in doing so he gained French sovereignty for all Cochin China (south Vietnam).

The French move in

Now, with their foot in the door, the French pursued their goal and by July 1884, they had won **Annam** (central Vietnam) and **Tonkin** (north Vietnam) as protectorates. The whole country was in their control; the Vietnamese had lost their independence.

The French divided Vietnam into its three regions: **Cochin China**, an official colony, directly administered by the French; **Tonkin** a protectorate and indirectly controlled by France; and **Annam**, also a protectorate, but with the Nguyen emperor at Hue still the head of state and the French domination a little less conspicuous. Further dealings in the region gave the French Laos and Cambodia as protectorates. Thus the federation of Laos, Cambodia, Tonkin, Annam and Cochin China became **French Indochina** under the supervision of a French Governor General who was appointed by the Ministry of Colonies in Paris.

Vietnam was swamped by French functionaries who were employed in even the most junior administrative posts. At home investors channelled large sums of money into projects via the newly established **Bank of Indochina**, first creating and then exploiting the rice fields and rubber plantations, mines and factories, with huge profits.

Nationalist Response

The French were disliked and in July 1886 **Emperor Ham Nghi's** soldiers attacked their troops at Hue. The nationalist struggle (known as the **Can Vuong** (Loyalty to the King) Movement), was thwarted and the emperor was eventually exiled to Algeria, where he died in 1947. Resistance continued under the now legendary heroes **Phan Dinh Phung, Cao Thang, Tran Van Du** and **De Tham.**

The Vietnamese react

The French continued to recognise the royal Nguyen dynasty and now placed **Dong Khanh** on the throne, but he died in 1888, to be followed by **Thanh Thai** who, on showing nationalist tendencies, was exiled to Reunion Island. Hopeful of nurturing a 'puppet', the French enthroned **Duy Tan**, the eight year old son of Thanh Thai but he too developed into a patriot, supporting a revolt which was discovered on the eve of its execution. Duy Tan was also banished to Reunion Island. He later joined the Allied Forces and was killed in a plane crash in 1945.

A cohesive anti-colonial movement began to take shape under the leadership of **Phan Boi Chau** and received a moral boost after Japan's victory over Russia in 1905. The peoples of the East suddenly realised they could topple Western powers.

In Japan, and then China, **Phan Boi Chau** united exiled Vietnamese into a group known as **Viet-Nam Quang-Phuc Hoi** (The Association for the Restoration of Vietnam) with **Prince Cuong De**, a direct descendant of **Emperor Gia Long**, as its figurehead and claimant to the throne of Annam. In 1925 Phan Boi Chau was captured and brought back to Vietnam to stand trial. He spent his final years under house arrest in Hue, while Cuong De travelled the world trying rather unsuccessfully to solicit support for his anti-colonial campaign. The prince died an exile in Tokyo in 1951.

The rise of nationalism

A Western-educated Vietnamese elite emerged and new anti-colonial movements mushroomed, most notably **Viet Nam Quoc Dan Dang** (VNQDD) or Vietnam Nationalist Party which styled itself on the **Chinese Nationalist Party** (Kuomintang). The VNQDD were committed to overthrowing the French and on the 9th/10th February 1930 they launched their insurrection at **Yen Bai**, in Hoang Lien Son province. The revolt failed, but it heralded the start of a new trend of anti-colonial reaction.

The repression of the VNQDD led to the rise of various communist groups, united as the **Indochina Communist Party** in 1930 under the leadership of **Nguyen Ai Quoc** (Nguyen the Patriot), later know as **Ho Chi Minh**.

The Emergence of Ho Chi Minh

Ho Chi Minh, a man of fifty names

Ho Chi Minh - the name is the best known of the man's fifty or so aliases - was born on 19th May 1890 in **Kim Lien**, a village near Vinh in **Nghe Tinh**, a province traditionally famed for its rebels. After studying at college in Hue, in 1911 he found employment in the kitchens of a merchant vessel travelling the oceans. In Paris he worked in a succession of odd jobs and at the same time became increasingly involved with the French Socialist Party and later its offshoot, the French Communist Party. He identified himself with Vietnam's fight for freedom and founded the **Association of Vietnamese Patriots**.

The Russian Revolution had a great impression on Ho. He was an admirer of Lenin, *'a great patriot who liberated his compatriots'* and he spent a year in Moscow before travelling to Canton where he met **Phan Boi Chau**; in 1925 he formed the **Vietnamese Revolutionary Youth Association**, a forerunner of the **Indochina Communist Party**.

Meanwhile, with an economy badly dented by the **First World War**, France demanded greater returns from her colonies. Nationalist feelings intensified and by 1932 the French had imprisoned 10,000 agitators and executed the ringleaders.

France's puppet kings

They maintained the ineffectual Nguyens on their throne in Hue. **Khai Dinh**, son of Emperor Dong Khanh, succeeded the exiled Duy Tan in 1916. But he was weak and is remembered more for his gambling excesses than his resistance to colonialism. He took his young son with him on a trip to France in 1922 and left him there to be educated. Three years later Khai Dinh died and his twelve year old son was pronounced **Emperor Bao Dai of Annam**.

Bao Dai remained in France, returning home in 1932 to take up the rather powerless position of emperor. As the **Second World War** drew to its conclusion the Japanese, in desperation, overwhelmed the weakened French forces in March 1945 and thus ended the era of French rule in Indochina. *'The French colonists either fled or surrendered, showing that not only were they incapable of 'protecting' us, but that in this span of five years, they had twice sold our country to the Japanese,'* commented Ho Chi Minh. French rule was supplanted by an 'independent' Japanese controlled government. Japanese capitulation to the Allies at the end of the Second World War immediately boosted Viet Minh chances. Their **August Revolution** of 1945 proved a resounding success.

Japanese Occupation

Back in Europe, France fell to Germany in June 1940. Her Eastern colonies were threatened by Japan, so the government in Vichy quickly signed a treaty with the Japanese allowing them to occupy Vietnam, though France's own colonial structure was to remain intact and operate as normally as possible. As Ho Chi Minh put it,

French-Japanese collusion

'the French imperialists went down on their bended knees and handed over our country to them'.

Ho Chi Minh was still abroad. Two years in a Hong Kong gaol were followed by trips to Moscow and China promoting the cause of his people. Finally he returned to Vietnam where he founded the **Viet-Nam Doc-Lap Dong-Minh Hoi** (later known as the League for Vietnamese Independence) which evolved into the **Viet Minh**. It was May 1941; Ho was back home after 30 years.

Under the command of **Vo Nguyen Giap**, Ho's military adviser, the Viet Minh organised a guerilla offensive against the French and the Japanese. Meanwhile Ho was now financed by his old adversary **Chaing Kai Shek** to provide intelligence about the Japanese and he even gained some sponsorship from the United States for the same purpose.

Ho's American sponsorship

The Declaration of Independence

Bao Dai, no more than a puppet emperor under the French and Japanese, chose to abdicate rather than cause division amongst the people. On 22nd August 1945 he publicly transferred power to the Democratic Republic government and became, at least temporarily, plain **Monsieur Nguyen Vinh Thuym**, taking an appointment as a counsellor of state in the new regime.

On 2nd September of the same year Ho Chi Minh proclaimed independence in Hanoi. He summarised France's exploitative colonial role in Indochina and praised the peoples' fight for liberty in a speech charged with passion, *'The French have fled, the Japanese have capitulated, Emperor Bao Dai has abdicated. Our people have broken the chains which for nearly a century have fastened them and have won Independence for the Fatherland. Our people at the same time have overthrown the monarchic regime that has reigned supreme for dozens of centuries. In its place has been established the present Democratic Republic.'*

And he finally declared, *'We, members of the Provisional Government of the Democratic Republic of Vietnam, solemnly declare to the world that Vietnam has the right to be a free and independent country - and in fact it is already. The entire Vietnamese people are determined to mobilise all their physical and mental strength, to sacrifice their lives and property in order to safeguard their independence and liberty'.*

Proud to be free

Colonial Conspiracy

'We are convinced that the Allied nations which at Tehran and San Francisco have acknowledged the principles of self-determination and equality of nations, will not refuse to acknowledge the independence of Vietnam'.
(Ho Chi Minh in his Declaration of Independence speech, 2nd September 1945).

The Allies decided at the **Potsdam Conferences** that Britain would officiate over the dismantling of the Japanese army in Vietnam south of the 16th parallel, while the Chinese (the **Nationalist Kuomintang**) would undertake the same task north of the line.

The Allies had their own reasons for restoring colonialism to Vietnam. Britain wanted nationalism in Asia suppressed while the Americans under Truman wanted to check the rise of communism.

On arriving in Saigon the British manipulated events in order to discredit the Viet Minh, who they claimed were now allying themselves to the Japanese. They imposed martial law, disarmed Viet Minh police and guards and at the same time armed many of the 5,000 French soldiers they had released from the surrendering Japanese army.

West fears nationalism and communism

A further attachment of French troops arrived and in the early hours of the 23rd September they staged a violent *coup d'état*, successfully overthrowing the Viet Minh government.

Viet Minh protests and agitation only led to greater reprisals. The French shipped in more reinforcements and they were further supported by British Indian troops and the Japanese, the old foe, whom the British - quite incredibly - re-equipped, embraced and set against the Vietnamese.

Britain's behaviour did receive widespread criticism. From **General MacArthur**, commander of the American forces in the Pacific: *'If there is anything that makes my blood boil, it is to see our allies in Indo-China deploying Japanese troops to reconquer these little people we promised to liberate. It is the most ignoble kind of betrayal'*. From **Pandit Nehru**, at the time supporting his own nationalist movement in India: *'We have watched British intervention . . . with growing anger, shame and helplessness, that Indian troops should be used for doing Britain's dirty work against our friends who are fighting the same fight as we are'*.

British duplicity

By the end of 1945 however the British were on their way home, while the French, with some 50,000 troops, were back in control of south Vietnam. In the north the Chinese had more justly fulfilled their obligation: the Japanese had been repatriated and Ho Chi Minh's government had been recognised; the Chinese, though, had indulged in much pillaging.

Prelude to the Indochina War

Early the following year, however, the Chinese returned the north to the French as part of a larger deal. Ho Chi

Minh tried to salvage what independence he could from the French, signing a treaty in March 1946 whereby *'The French Government recognises the Republic of Vietnam as a free state, having its Government, its Parliament, its army, and its finances and forming part of the Indochinese Federation and* **Revival of** *the French Union'.* It went on to state that a plebiscite **French interests** would decide whether Vietnam should be divided into Tonkin, Annam and Cochin China - as the French wanted - or should be one country as was Ho Chi Minh's wish. The Government of Vietnam agreed to *'receive the French army in friendly fashion when . . . it relieves the Chinese troops'.*

The last thing the French wanted was **referendum**. The people would vote for one country and that would mean the French would lose their monopoly on fertile Cochin China which was France's Eastern pot of gold, accounting for 60% of its Indochinese investments.

The unsettled peace was soon to break into war. In November 1946 the French shelled the port of **Haiphong** during a minor dispute over custom controls, killing hundreds of Vietnamese citizens. A few weeks later there was fighting in the streets of **Hanoi**. The time for war had come and on 19th December Ho Chi Minh rallied Viet Minh to take up arms against the French. It was the beginning of the **Indochina War** which was to drag on for 9 years.

Western Fears of Eastern Communism

Vietnam costs The war was disastrous for the French who were to **France dear** spend over half their military budget and deploy over a quarter of their armed forces (150,000 men) in Indochina; by the end of it they had over 90,000 casualties in Vietnam.

In mid 1949 the French attempted to woo the Vietnamese people away from the Viet Minh by resurrecting the old **Nguyen royal family**. Bao Dai, who had been living in Hong Kong, was brought home and made Chief of State of the **State of Vietnam**, a self-governing Vietnam within the French Union, but he was never seen as anything more than a colonial puppet.

October 1949 and the **Chinese Communists** overthrew the **Nationalist Party** in China and soon their forces were stationed on the border with north Vietnam. Early in 1950 Ho Chi Minh sent despatches to a number of governments requesting recognition of his **Democratic Republic of Vietnam**. The Chinese and Soviets were the first to respond favourably.

American fears that Ho Chi Minh was a front for

Chinese or Soviet communism led **President Truman** to give the French $10 million for their fight against (pro-communist) nationalism in Indochina. By the end of the Indochina War the Americans had channelled over $4 billion, often through the pro-French, Western recognised State of Vietnam governments, to this cause. At one stage they were paying 90% of the French war costs.

Meanwhile Ho Chi Minh gained military aid from **China** and the **Soviet Union**, happy to take support for his nationalist cause from wherever it was offered. The fact that it came from communists was of secondary importance.

The Viet Minh fought a patient guerilla war from the jungles, hills and paddies, places where the opponents' cumbersome military hardware had no access. For the French it was an increasingly frustrating, unsuccessful, expensive and unpopular war.

Dien Bien Phu and the Fear of Peace

The French generals in Indochina, under pressure for results, believed they could defeat the Viet Minh in a traditional pitch battle situation. They chose their battlefield - **Dien Bien Phu**, a village in a strategically important valley 275 km west of **Hanoi** - and in late November 1953 they airlifted in supplies and entrenched themselves within a massive fortified complex.

Dien Bien Phu was a disaster for the French, the 64 day siege sounding the **final death call of French Indochina** (see page 123).

Meanwhile, in late April, a conference was held in **Geneva** to try and resolve the Indochina crisis. Shortly before it convened **Vice President Nixon** gave his views: *'If the French withdraw, Indochina would become communist - dominated within a month . . . The United States as a leader of the free world cannot afford further retreat in Asia. It is hoped the United States will not have to send troops there, but if this government cannot avoid it, the Administration must face up to the situation and dispatch forces'.*

Bidault, the French Foreign Minister, asked for more direct American assistance. **Dulles**, the U.S. Secretary of State, supported the idea, but said he would have to get the backing of Congress and also of the British before acting. **Eden**, the British Foreign Secretary, responded that his government was against Allied intervention in Indochina.

A Peace Destined for War

On 7th April, the French called for peace. The Viet Minh's

success at Dien Bien Phu had played its part. It was decided, as a temporary measure, that Vietnam should be divided at the **17th parallel** and that the Viet Minh and their supporters should settle north of that line, while their former enemies - the anti-Ho Chi Minh nationalists who fought for Bao Dai's State of Vietnam government alongside the French - should re-group in the south. Furthermore, France should give Vietnam complete independence; national (North and South together) elections should be held by mid-1956; the people could move freely between North and South; no foreign military bases were allowed in Vietnam - nor could there be military alliances with outside powers or the import of new weapons or the increase of troop numbers. Though Vietnam was divided in two it was, for the time being at least, free from foreign domination.

A divided country, a divided people

The Americans, now led by **President Eisenhower**, feared the rise of communism in south-east Asia. It was anticipated that Ho Chi Minh would win 80% of votes in a nationwide election and such an outcome had to be prevented. Meanwhile Ho feared America would fill the void left by France and as early as July 1954 he told his party colleagues; '*At this moment American imperialism, the principle enemy of the peoples of the world, is becoming the direct principal enemy of the peoples of Indochina; that is why all our actions must be aimed at this one enemy*'.

Vietnam and America on a collision course

Also in July of that year Bao Dai chose **Ngo Dinh Diem**, a lawyer, a Catholic and staunch anti-communist to lead his government. Ngo went on to become **Chief of State** (taking over from Bao Dai who retired to France where he still lives) and then declared the country south of the 17th parallel as the **Republic of Vietnam** with himself as president. He consolidated a separate nation from the North by stopping trade, travel and even postal services across the demarcation line. Furthermore he refused to consent to the nationwide elections as stipulated in the Geneva Accords.

Despite his increasing despotism, ineffectiveness, unpopularity and nepotism Ngo Dinh Diem, leader of 'free' Vietnam, continued to receive American support. As **Johnson**, Vice President to Kennedy, re-affirmed on his journey to Vietnam in May 1961; '*The United States is . . . conscious of its responsibility and duty, in its own self-interest as well as in the interest of other free peoples, to assist a brave country in the defence of its liberties against unprovoked subversion and Communist terror*'.

America supports anti-communist Vietnam

Opposition to President Diem came in the shape of the

National Liberation Front (NLF or NFL) a political party created in December 1960 which was essentially Hanoi's representation in the South. Under the NLF umbrella there grew what became called the **Viet Cong** (VC), short for **Viet Nam Cong Son**, meaning Vietnamese Communist, the resistance fighters who succeeded the Viet Minh in the South. Meanwhile the regime in the North purged the landlords, including those of modest means. It was the darkest chapter of Ho's rule. Confiscated lands were redistributed as small plots to peasants, while an estimated 15,000 people were killed and many more were imprisoned.

America is dragged ever deeper into Vietnam

The Americans responded to the rise of the Viet Cong by intensifying their support for Ngo Nguyen Diem's war, a war which had in effect become theirs. By early 1963 the American presence in South Vietnam had increased to 12,000 'advisors', 25 times the number they had had three years before.

Diem attempted to prevent Viet Cong infiltration of the masses by creating **'Strategic Hamlets'** which were camps, fenced and guarded, into which villagers were forcibly re-located. One third of the South's rural population was interned in such places. This scheme failed not least because most of the people were already Viet Cong sympathisers and its unpopularity alienated them even further from Diem's regime.

In May 1963 Ngo Nguyen Diem, a Catholic, denounced the Buddhists' celebrations of Buddha's birthday. There were demonstrations and **Thich Quang Duc**, a senior Buddhist monk from Hue, publicly immolated himself in a Saigon street. The subsequent series of press pictures shocked the world.

Diem had become a liability to his sponsors. He had to go. On 1st November 1963 a military coup led by **General Duong Van Minh** assassinated Ngo Dinh Diem and his brother.

The Build Up to the Vietnam War

Kennedy was assassinated that November and Johnson, on entering the White House, pledged to prevent the **'Domino Effect'**, the chain reaction spread of communism in south-east Asia, with the promise, *'I am not going to lose Vietnam.'*

The 'Domino Effect' must be halted

Kennedy had brought America down the path which was to lead to the Vietnam War. Words from his inaugural speech were chiselled on his tomb: *'Let every nation know, whether it wishes us well or ill, that we shall pay any price, bear any burden, meet any hardship, support any friend, oppose any foe, in order to insure the survival and success of liberty.'* The cost for 'liberty' mounted. By the end of 1963 America had 15,000 MACV advisors helping the South Vietnam government and their annual aid budget to the country had topped $500 million.

Back in Vietnam, Viet Cong activities intensified and on 2nd May they blew up the *Card*, a US transport ship, while it lay anchored in Saigon harbour. The following day they hurled another bomb into a group of Americans who were surveying the ship's damage. The U.S. provided a further 12,000 advisors (MACVs) to **General Khanh**, the South Vietnamese leader; meanwhile Johnson assessed the consequence of direct U.S. intervention.

The Road to War

On 31st July South Vietnamese commandos attacked **Hon Me** and **Hon Nieu**, the North Vietnamese islands in the Gulf of Tonkin. Two days later the U.S. destroyers *Maddox* and *Turner Joy* were allegedly attacked by the North's torpedo boats while on a surveillance operation in the Gulf of Tonkin. On the 4th August there was another confrontation which led the Americans to bomb North Vietnamese torpedo boat harbours and an oil depot near Vinh, causing extensive damage.

Three days later Congress passed the **Gulf of Tonkin Resolution** which gave Johnson wide ranging powers to assist South Vietnam in their battle against the North. In effect it gave him freedom to wage his own war in South-East Asia.

On 1st November the Viet Cong shelled the **Bien Hoa airbase** near Saigon destroying B-52 bombers and killing five Americans. Johnson did not retaliate immediately, waiting for victory in the elections at home before he responded.

In early December Johnson bombed the **Ho Chi Minh Trail**, the Viet Cong's vital supply route and lifeline from the North, which cut through the jungles along the Vietnam-Laos border. The Trail was to become one of the Americans' hottest targets.

The Viet Cong attacked the U.S. base at **Pleiku** on 7th February 1965 - resulting in nine dead Americans, many wounded and heavy damage to planes. The same day Johnson ordered an air assault on North Vietnam and 49 US Navy jets dropped their bombs on the North Vietnamese base at **Dong Hoi**. The Viet Cong reacted by bombing U.S. army barracks at **Quinhon**, killing a further

The Gulf of Tonkin incident

Bombing the Ho Chi Minh Trail

23, which in turn led Johnson to send in another air attack. The **Vietnam War** was under way. On 24th February Johnson let loose **Operation Rolling Thunder**, a sustained airborne campaign bombing North Vietnam, which continued, with brief interruptions, until 31st October 1968. Only days later on 8th March 1965, the first of the U.S. combat troops, as opposed to 'advisors', landed at **Da Nang**.

American combat troops arrive

The Vietnam War

The Americans anticipated a quick, decisive 'limited' war. Their Vietnamese enemy were, however, prepared to wage a total war, sacrificing everything in the fight for their land. Ho had earlier warned the French: *'You can kill ten of my men for every one I kill of yours. But even at those odds, you will lose and I will win'*. It was as true now as it was then.

In response to the U.S. troops landing in Da Nang, the North despatched, for the first time, a contingent of their **North Vietnamese Army** (NVA) regulars to the South to support the 65,000 or so Viet Cong. In the summer of 1965 **General Westmoreland**, commander of U.S. forces in Vietnam, asked for and received more troops, a total of 184,000 by the end of the year, to help the **Army of the Republic of Vietnam** (ARVN).

The Americans secured their base at Da Nang and in October they were successful at **Ia Drang**, a valley near Pleiku and site of the **first major battle** of the war, where helicopters were effectively used to deploy soldiers into the fray. The Americans lost 300 men, against the Communists loss of approximately 2000 men. For the Americans the 'body count' equation was the means of calculating a victory. Statistics were virtually irrelevant to the Communists.

Strategies of War

Still the Americans believed they should intensify their campaign. They brought in more soldiers: 268,000 in 1966, 449,000 in 1967, 535,000 in 1968 and 542,000 at its peak in 1969. In addition, small contingents from elsewhere in the 'Free World', from Australia, New Zealand, Philippines, Thailand and South Korea also arrived to assist the Americans. And the men were supported by increasing amounts of weaponry - *'more bombs, more shells, more napalm . . . till the other side cracks and gives up,'* was the solution proposed by one general and endorsed by many others.

Vietnam suffering a growing arsenal

The pounding increased. the American airborne divisions of helicopters, fighter jets, bombers clouded the skies and let drop their arsenal like a relentless monsoonal downpour. The B-52 bombers, operating from U.S. airbases in **Guam** and **Thailand** and flying at high altitudes of 30 to 40,000 feet, were amongst the most potent, but least vulnerable of the U.S. weapons. Their bombs caused massive devastation mainly in the South which was 50% Viet Cong controlled by the end of 1966.

Initially **American ground troops** had been drafted to protect the airbases and defend the urban centres, but to track down the Viet Cong they had to go out into the field and get them.

Operating from a fire support base, teams of U.S. troops would venture out on **'search-and-destroy'** missions, to kill and capture Viet Cong suspects and destroy whole villages believed to be sympathetic to the Viet Cong cause. The massacre at the village of **My Lai,** where over 500 villagers were slaughtered on the 16th March 1968, is the most famous of many similar incidents (see page 170).

To the villages in search of Viet Cong

Khe Sanh

In early 1968 Khe Sanh, an isolated American stronghold just below the border with the North, became the **epicentre of the war**. In mid-January 40,000 Communist troops converged on the base intent on holding it under siege. Commentators saw Khe Sanh as America's **'Dien Bien Phu'**, but there are fundamental differences. For the Communists this was just a stage in the war and not a final showdown as Dien Bien Phu had been; furthermore, unlike the French 14 years before, the Americans had the support and air power to attack the enemy.

During the battle at Khe Sanh, which ended on the 14th April, the U.S. forces killed over 10,000 Communists, while their own casualties merely numbered hundreds of dead. The airborne attacks, code named **Operation Niagara Falls**, were once again their most potent weapon.

Communists suffer huge losses

For the Communists Khesanh was a component of a larger strategy, it served to divert attention in the prelude to the **Tet Offensive**. The North and South had agreed to a truce during Tet, the lunar New Year celebrated by all Vietnamese which, in 1968, fell on the last days of January. The North broke the agreement.

The Tet Offensive

On the night of 30th January 1968 the Communists

violated the Tet ceasefire and launched a wave of simultaneous attacks on centres throughout the South, catching both the Americans and the Saigon regime completely unawares. They anticipated, erroneously, that their force of 70,000 would be swelled by popular mass support and, in de-stabilising the country, they hoped to upset the relationship between the Amercans and the South Vietnamese.

American embassy targeted

While the Tet Offensive did not really succeed in these aims it did prove to be the **turning point** of the war. In the previous weeks 6,000 Viet Cong partisans had infiltrated **Saigon**. In the early hours of the 30th they attacked prominent targets around the capital including the American Embassy.

The most horrific image of the war

The American public had long been saturated by daily media coverage and, to an extent, the horror of the war had lost its impact. But their awareness was jolted on 31st January by the stark headline: WAR HITS SAIGON. TV stations broadcasted the assault on the Embassy, which resulted in the death of five Americans, the fighting in the streets of Saigon and the sight of recriminations as **General Nguyen Ngot Loan**, the South's chief of police, drew out his pistol and coolly shot in the head a young Viet Cong captive.

It took the Americans and ARVN three weeks to quell the insurrection in Saigon. The fiercest fighting, however, took place at **Hue**. Here, in the erstwhile royal capital on the banks of the beautiful Perfume River, the Communists managed to free 2500 political and military prisoners and are alleged to have killed 3,000 sympathisers' of the Americans and ARVN.

The Communists win and lose Hue

The Communists, having won Hue, established the old **Citadel** as their headquarters and held it for 25 days. The Americans and their ARVN allies were slow to react, partly because a significant quota of their forces were preoccupied in Khe Sanh and elsewhere. When they finally responded they destroyed much of the city. The **Communists' death toll** was 5,000 men in Hue; by contrast the Americans and ARVN suffered 119 and 363 dead respectively.

Eventually the remaining core of Communists, beaten into just a section of the Citadel, abandoned their defence and on the 25th February Hue was once again securely under American control. The Viet Cong and the North had lost the Tet Offensive, but **antiwar sentiment** in America, inflamed by the 'Tet episode', grew ever stronger.

Memorial to air clash over Hanoi.

The Turbulent 'Vietnamisation' of Vietnam

On 31st March Johnson announced the cessation of bombing north of the 20th parallel and proposed **peace talks** with Hanoi. To the surprise of the nation, he also declared he would not seek re-election as President, largely because of the growing unpopularity of the Vietnam war.

Nixon's promise 'to win the peace'

The war and the peace talks (held in Paris) rumbled on without any results. On becoming President in November, **Nixon** promised to 'end the war and win the peace', and proposed a process of 'Vietnamisation' (de-Americanising) - the gradual withdrawal of American troops, and simultaneous development and reinforcement of the ARVN so they could conduct the war by themselves.

However, the South would have been too weak without the Americans, and so Nixon intensified the battle, authorising the **Accelerated Pacification Campaign**, which, under the command of **General Creighton Abrams'**, Westmoreland's successor, set about clearing the Mekong Delta of Viet Cong as quickly and as destructively as possible. Also enforced was the **Phoenix Programme**, a purge on the South's alleged Communist sympathisers, of whom 40,000 were killed.

Withdrawal of American soldiers

The number of American troops in Vietnam peaked at 542,000 in March 1969, but in June Nixon announced the withdrawal of 25,000 soldiers and the limitations of economic and military aid. This became know as the 'Nixon Doctrine'. On 2nd September 1969 **Ho Chi Minh** died aged 79.

Though Nixon continued to withdraw troops, in early 1970 he also bombed Viet Cong and NVA sanctuaries across the border in Cambodia. Plans to intensify the **Cambodia campaigns** led to widespread demonstrations in America. In trying to contain a march in **Kent University, Ohio**, National Guardmen shot four students dead.

American public reacts to war

The continued bombing prompted **Prince Sihanouk**, the deposed Cambodian leader, to compare the Americans and the Nazis, ' . . . *what is the difference between burning and gassing people in ovens and doing it to a whole nation out in the open. That is just what the United States of President Nixon is doing today . . . Nixon is waging a war of extermination against the entire people of Indo-China.'*

As the number of American soldiers in Vietnam decreased, to 280,000 in 1971 and 140,000 in 1972, the **demoralisation** amongst the remaining soldiers increased. Amongst the ranks, crime, overt racism, drug addiction (in 1971 some 10-15% of GIs were addicted to hard drugs), desertion and 'fragging' - the killing of officers through the fragmentation of an exploding grenade - became more common.

Growing demoralization in the ranks

Countdown to Communism

On 30th March 1972 120,000 North Vietnamese soldiers supported by Viet Cong launched their major offensive. **Quang Tri**, just south of the 17th parallel, was won and the rest of the South's northern provinces also fell. Nixon renewed the bombing of the North and the mining of its ports. The North's anti-aircraft guns scored success, shooting down 15 B-52s amongst its toll of enemy planes.

The many rounds of **peace talks** between Washington and Hanoi over the years had been fairly fruitless, but in **Paris** on the 27th January 1973 a more hopeful treaty was signed. Nixon claimed to have 'achieved peace with honour'. By April the last of the American troops had quit Vietnam, leaving the 'Vietnamisationed' South pitched against the North and the Viet Cong for their ultimate test.

Last American troops leave Vietnam

The Southern army, equipped with their American weapons and training, regained territories lost during he North's 1972 offensive, but morale soon dwindled and the incapable **Thieu** - president since 1967 - faced mounting **civil problems**. Not least of them was the **millions of refugees** who had flocked to the relative safety of Saigon and who had provided numerous service jobs for the Americans. With the Americans' departure they were now redundant.

On 9th August 1974 Nixon resigned his Presidency over the **Watergate affair** and with him seemed to die some of the anti-Communist fire.

Meanwhile, in 1973 and 1974, the North consolidated its positions in the South, capturing the enemy's weaker bases and in **January 1975** the North Vietnamese machine rumbled southwards capturing all that lay in its path. The Southern army put up a token fight, before crumbling.

The Communists head southward

Thieu resigned on 21st April and was succeeded by **General Duong Van Minh**. The evacuation of American advisors and civilians and the Vietnamese who had been associated with them intensified as the Northerners neared Saigon. Thousands were airlifted by a fleet of helicopters to the American aircraft carriers waiting offshore, but many Vietnamese who had embraced the

---

CASUALTIES OF WAR

During a period of three decades - 1945-1975 - Vietnam's population was decimated. Some four million Vietnamese - fighters and civilians, including the aged and children - were killed during the **civil war**. The exact death toll is unknown. The number is significantly enlarged if the casualties of the earlier **Indochinese War** are added. Furthermore in 1978 Vietnam invaded **Cambodia** after the Khmer Rouge had killed thousands of its villagers along Vietnam's southern border. According to Hanoi 50,000 of it soldiers died during Vietnam's subsequent nine years of military occupation of Cambodia.

Foreign invaders also lost much blood in this corner of South East Asia. In purely financial terms, the Vietnam Var cost the **Americans** around $150 billion. Some 90,000 **French** were casualties of the Indochinese War between 1945 and 1954. Nearly 58,000 Americans were killed and 200,000 permanently disabled. Over 60,000 American **'Vietnam Vets'** have since committed suicide as result of traumas caused by the conflict. Furthermore, the divorce and mental breakdown rates amongst these former military personnel is extremely high and 2646 U.S. servicemen, 1820 believed to have been lost on Vietnamese soil, still remain unaccounted for. Stories of these MIAs - **soldiers Missing in Action** - being interned as slaves by fiendish Orientals have been the inspiration for blockbusting films and bestselling novels. Such tales are fantastic fiction according to Hanoi; Washington seems less willing to dismiss them as mere myths.

In addition to the many direct casualties of war there are other 'losers'. Noticeably the **half-castes** - the offspring of French or American fathers and Vietnamese mothers - who traditionally fall between two cultures and are customarily discarded by both. The French took 25,000 children of mixed heritage with them on leaving Vietnam in 1954. Many **Amerasians** - the result of American paternity a generation later - have now, fifteen years on, found homes in America with adoptive families if not with their real fathers. Others remain in Vietnam, often having spent their childhood in an orphanage. Another conspicuous legacy of the Vietnam War is the **deformed children** who are still being born. The effects of America's **chemical warfare** manifests in the foetus and deformities amongst Vietnamese babies are, for example, ten times more common than in Britain.

American movement were left behind to face an uncertain fate at the hands of the Communists.

Vietnam re-united The Communist tanks rolled into Saigon on 30th April. They headed for the Presidential Palace, where President Minh calmly accepted defeat. The North Vietnamese flag was hoisted, the war for liberation had been won and Vietnam was re-united.

Post War Vietnam

There was no calm with the peace. North and South were officially reunified in July 1976 and in December that year the **Fourth Party Congress** implemented a dramatic specialisation programme of the old South. The hasty **collectivisation of agriculture and industry** proved economically and socially disastrous; people were forcibly relocated to the countryside from the overcrowded cities and there was **malnutrition** in the Mekong, traditionally one of the rice bowls of the world.

Loyal cadres from the North were given positions of authority in the South in preference to locals. Thousands of supporters of the South's old non-communist regime ended up in **'re-educational' camps**, as did drug addicts, prostitutes (an estimated 500,000 had served the Americans), criminals and Buddhist monks, Christian clergy and intellectuals, many of whom had in fact supported the Northern regime. The purge led to mass flight from the country.

Attempts to normalise American-Vietnam relations in 1977 came to nothing. Now, in the early 1990s, when most nations of the world, as well as the UN, recognise Vietnam, the Americans still boycott the old enemy by enforcing the **Trading with the Enemy Act** on the country. Two main obstacles have prevented normalisation, first, the whereabouts of around 2000 MIAs (soldiers missing in action) lost in Vietnam, and, second Vietnam's presence in Cambodia.

In 1978 the **Khmer Rouge** attacked villages on the Cambodian-Vietnamese border, areas which were once part of the ancient Khmer kingdom. The Vietnamese responded by invading Cambodia and overthrowing **Pol Pot** and the Khmer Rouge. They placed an allied government in Phnom Penh and left a force of 200,000 men in the country.

The **Chinese**, who were staunchly pro-Khmer Rouge, retaliated by attacking Vietnam's northern frontier town of **Lang Son** in February 1979. Hundreds of thousands of Vietnam's ethnic Chinese fled the country for fear of reprisals against them.

In 1982 Cambodia's **Prince Sihanouk** formed the **Coalition Government of Democratic Kampuchea** as the opposition in exile. Despite its despicable members, notably the Khmer Rouge, the Chinese backed coalition won the approval of most of the West and even gained Cambodia's seat at the UN in preference to the incumbent government in Phnom Penh.

In 1989 Vietnam withdrew its army from Cambodia and early in 1993 the UN organised **democratic elections**. Vietnam has now met the American conditions. Teams

Margin notes:
- Unsavory aftermath to the war
- American boycott of Vietnam
- New conflicts with old enemies

In search of lost loved ones from the US are allowed to search for MIAs, and the remains of over 100 have been discovered and returned home during the past few years. Vietnamese forces have also finally quit Cambodia. Still America continues to blacklist Vietnam, but it is hoped that **'normalisation'** will soon be sanctioned.

On the domestic front there have also been marked changes of policy in recent years. The **Sixth Party Congress** held in 1986 decided to follow the Soviet trend towards *perestroika* (the local version is known as *doi moi*) and *glasnost*; collectivisation and re-education are no longer the trend. The most recent crumbling of the Soviet block initially alarmed the regime in Hanoi and in late 1989 **Nguyen Van Linh**, General Secretary of the Communist Party, wholeheartedly confirmed his rejection of a multi-party system. The notion of a one party state remains rigid; however without a Soviet sponsor, which at one stage provided $1 million a day, Vietnam must compete on the world market. The country has tremendous natural resources and a vast untapped population. It requires aid and investment, but the **American embargo** continues to keep Vietnam isolated and underdeveloped.

Vietnamese enterprise stifled

For a quick rundown of key dates and dynasties see Appendix I.

SECTION 2:
AROUND VIETNAM

Bac Phan (including Hanoi)

Trung Phan (including Hue)

Nam Phan and the Mekong Delta
(including Ho Chi Minh City)

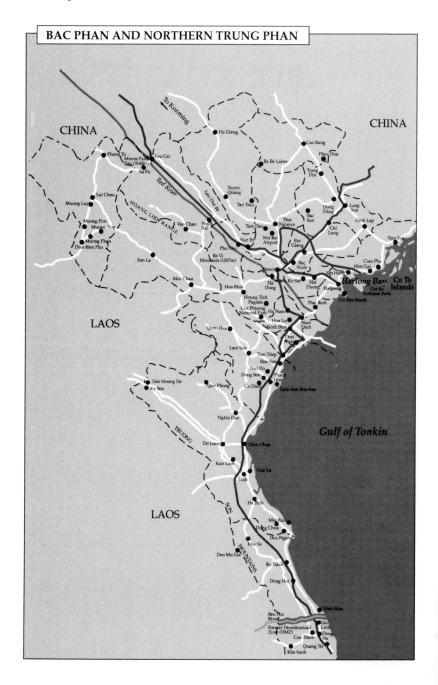

BAC PHAN AND NORTHERN TRUNG PHAN

BAC PHAN

Bac Phan - Bac Bo, Bac Ky or Mien Bac - is the area of Vietnam north of **Thanh Hao** province. It can be divided into three zones:

Vietnam's cradle

• **Trung Chau** - the flat lowlands which encompass the Red River Delta. This the cradle of Vietnamese culture and is densely inhabited, by almost entirely ethnic Viets and intensely farmed - predominantly with rice. **Hanoi** and **Haiphong** are the largest of several cities.

• Pushing out from this region is an intermediary zone known as **Trung Du**, a higher plains area where the population is less dense and more diverse, with a mixture of Viets and ethnic minority peoples. Rice cultivation gives way to tea and coffee farming.

• Beyond this, to the north and west, the land becomes the mountainous region called **Thuong Du**, a natural barrier serving as the border to and shield against China and Laos. Up here, the sparse population is almost entirely comprised of the ethnic minorities whose lives traditionally revolve around slash and burn farming and hunting and gathering.

Emergence of the Vietnamese culture

The history of *Viets*, the peoples who went on to colonise all of present Vietnam, starts to take shape in the **Red River Delta** region. The legendary **Hong Bang Dynasty** (2879 to 258 BC) had its capital at Phong Chau in Ha Son Binh province, to the south of Hanoi. This was succeeded by the **Thuc Dynasty**, the first accountable dynasty, which built its capital at Co Loa just to the north of Hanoi.

Bac Phan, in the shadows of China, was always threatened by its larger, superior neighbours to the north, and, with the fall of the Thuc Dynasty, the Viets did come under the tentative control of the Chinese who governed them from Phien Ngung (Canton). What is known as the **1000 years of Chinese domination** began only after the **Han Dynasty** sent forces southwards, overwhelming the Viets in 111 BC and annexing Bac Phan - and beyond - as their province of **Giao Chi**. It came to an end in 938 AD with the famous defeat of the Chinese at the **Battle of Bach Dang**.

Over shadowed by China

Such was the history of the ethnic Viets who had evolved in the Red River Delta. Life up in the hills of the Thuong Du region was comparatively uneventful. Tribes from, in particular, the *Tay-Thai* and *Sino Tibetan* language groups had migrated here for varying reasons at different periods over the past thousands of years (see page 43). For the most part their remote habitats were not really affected by the activities down on the lower lands, though certain places were in the path of invading Chinese and some of the tribal groups did fight alongside the Viets.

TRAVELLING IN BAC PHAN

Roads head out of **Hanoi** in all direction. **Northwards and westwards** they gradually ascend, following the river valleys deep into the mountainous regions - to Lang Son, That Ke, Cao Bang, Be Be, Ha Giang, Lao Cai, Son La, Lai Chau, Dien Bien Phu - and onto the borders with China and Laos. The old railway lines lead from Hanoi to Lang Son and up the Red's valley to Lao Cai.

From the Red River Delta into the mountains

Eastwards, the main road from Hanoi leads to **Haiphong**, the major port in the north, and then - after the river crossings - it continues north, parallel to the coast, up to Ha Long Bay, Tra Co and China. There is also a train, between Hanoi and Haiphong.

Highway One is the main road to the **south**, and alongside it runs the Hanoi-Ho Chi Minh City rail track.

The **waterways** of the Red River Delta are not as extensive as those down in the Mekong. Nonetheless the rivers and linking canals offer an **important means of transport** for freight and passengers and often lead to places where there are no roads. Up in the hills the rivers also serve as paths deep into the interior and provide the locals with a way of getting around. The peoples living down on the coast travel the shores and islands of the **Gulf of Tonkin** in small fishing boats and ferries.

HANOI

Hanoi lies on the west bank of the **Red River** - the Song Hong - 130kms upstream from the Gulf of Tonkin and the South China Sea.

The Viet culture evolved in the Red River Delta and Hanoi has long been the focal point of the civilisation. A **citadel** was built on the site of present Hanoi in the 3rd century AD, during the long period when northern Vietnam was **Gia Chau**, a province of China.

Choice capital

The citadel was developed in the ninth century and in the 11th century, the **Ly Dynasty** - the first of Vietnam's great dynasties after the ousting of the Chinese - established it as their capital.

Emperor Ly Thai To, founder of Ly Dynasty, visited the citadel on coming to power in 1010. As he stepped from his boat onto the jetty a golden dragon soared from

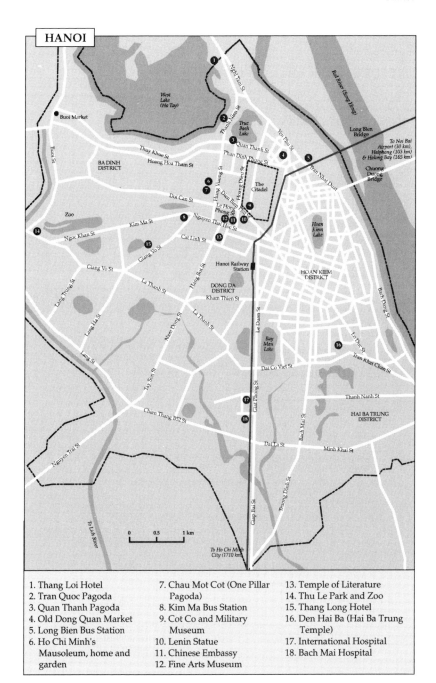

HANOI

West Lake (Ho Tay)

Nghi Tan St

Red River (Song Hong)

Buoi Market

Thanh Nien St

Truc Bach Lake

Long Bien Bridge

Bưởi St

Thuy Khue St

Quan Thanh St

Yen Thu St

To Noi Bai
Airport (30 km),
Haiphong (103 km)
& Halong Bay (165 km)

BA DINH DISTRICT

Hoang Hoa Tham St

Phan Dinh Phung St

Tran Nhat Duat

Chuong Duong Bridge

Doi Can St

Hung Vuong St

Hoang Dieu St

The Citadel

Le Hong Phong St

Zoo

Ngoc Khan St

Kim Ma St

Nguyen Thai Hoc St

Hoan Kiem Lake

Giang Vo St

Cat Linh St

HOAN KIEM DISTRICT

Giang Vo St

Hang Bot St

Hanoi Railway Station

Bach Dong St

Giang Vo St

La Thanh St

DONG DA DISTRICT

Kham Thien St

Lang Trung St

Lang Ha St

Nam Dong St

La Thanh St

Le Duan St

Bay Mau Lake

Lo Duc St

Tran Khat Chan St

Lang St

Tay Son St

Dai Co Viet St

Thanh Nanh St

Chien Thang B52 St

Giai Phong St

Bach Mai St

HAI BA TRUNG DISTRICT

Nguyen Trai St

Dai La St

Minh Khai St

To Lich River

0   0.5   1 km

Cau Bai St

Truong Dinh St

To Ho Chi Minh
City (1710 km)

1. Thang Loi Hotel	7. Chau Mot Cot (One Pillar Pagoda)	13. Temple of Literature
2. Tran Quoc Pagoda	8. Kim Ma Bus Station	14. Thu Le Park and Zoo
3. Quan Thanh Pagoda	9. Cot Co and Military Museum	15. Thang Long Hotel
4. Old Dong Quan Market	10. Lenin Statue	16. Den Hai Ba (Hai Ba Trung Temple)
5. Long Bien Bus Station	11. Chinese Embassy	17. International Hospital
6. Ho Chi Minh's Mausoleum, home and garden	12. Fine Arts Museum	18. Bach Mai Hospital

HANOI FACTS

TOURIST OFFICES:

Vietnam Tourism, 54 Nguyen Du, Tel: 57080, 52986.

Hanoi Tourism, 18 Ly Thuong Kiet, Tel: 54209, 57886

Hanoi Tourism and Service Company (often referred to TOSERCO), 9 To Hien Thanh, Tel: 52937

Immigration Police, 83 Tran Hung Dao
Opening times: 8-11 and 13-17 Monday to Saturday

Chamber of Commerce (Vietcochamber), 33 Ba Trieu, Tel: 25961

Post Office, 75 Dinh Tien Hoang, Tel: 54413
Opening times 6.30-20

Bank of Foreign Trade, 47-49 Le Thai To, Tel: 52831
Opening Times 8-11.30 and 13.30-15.30 Monday to Saturday (closed Saturday afternoon)

TRANSPORT

Vietnam Airlines (Domestic), 16 Thai To

Vietnam Airlines (International), Quang Trung, Tel: 55284
Bookings on other airlines can be made here.

Railway, Duong Le Duan (on the west side of town), Tel: 52528
Opening times for tickets: 7.30-11.30 and 13.30-15.30

Bus Terminals
Kim Lien terminal, on Duong Le Duan to the south of the railway station, is the station for southbound services. *Kim Ma* and *Long Bien* terminals are stations for services to the north-west and north-east respectively.

ACCOMMODATION
Faded colonialism and communism have finally been restored for the new capitalist. The old French Hotel *Metropole* and the Cuban built, Soviet style *Thang Loi,* relics of past eras, are undergoing much needed renovations. For a large capital city Hanoi has a very low standard of accommodation. Doubtless this will change, but for the moment it is a matter of puffing life into the dinosaurs.

Thong Nhat, *15 Ngo Guyen, Tel: 58221, 52785.* The white, old Metropole, well located in a pleasant central boulevard, is the best of the downtown hotels. Its decline into complete decay has been arrested; its shabby charm will probably be sacrificed in the renovation, but hopefully its character will remain.

Thang Loi, *West Lake, Tel: 58211, 52004.* Built in 1970s with Cuban-Soviet assistance, the Thang Loi is Hanoi's flagship hotel. The cracks are showing, but are patched up. It has a pleasant setting overlooking West Lake, however it is about 5km from the city centre.

Dan Chu, *29 Trang Tien, Tel: 53323.* Another old colonial hotel, the former Hanoi Hotel, the Dan Chu is around the corner from the Thong Nhat; it was renovated fairly recently, but needs a further facelift.

To the south of the Thong Nhat-Dan Chu area are:

Hoe Binh, *27 Ly Thuong Kiet, Tel: 53315.*

Hoan Kiem, *25 Tran Hung Dao, Tel: 54204.* A not so central or desirable alternative is the high rise, many-roomed Soviet-type **Thang Long** by *Lake Giang Vo (tel: 57796)* to the west of the Temple of Literature.

NIGHTLIFE

The **weekly dances** at the main hotels are the highlight of the night scene. The music and dance, a hotch-potch of styles and standards, is only of part of the attraction. More significantly, the dances are one of the few outlets for 'having a good time'; they are a relaxed meeting place for both Vietnamese and Westerners. A hotel's **Dance Night** is usually one night over the weekend and tends to end punctually at 11pm or midnight. Receptionists have details. Other dance venues will probably open in response to demand.

A celebrated nightspot amongst expatriate Westerners in this quarter of the Orient is the Australian Embassy's **Billabong Club.** It is held on Friday evenings at the embassy *(66 Ly Thuong Kiet, Tel: 52763)* and Australians are welcome, as are other nationals with invitations. Guests are obliged to buy a book of tickets ($10) which serve as credits for famous Australian party drinks.

The **Municipal Theatre** at the end of *Tran Tien (Tel: 54312)* provides alternative entertainment. Or, like thousands of locals, take an evening promenade around Lake of the Restored Sword.

RESTAURANTS

Besides the main hotels there are several well known restaurants such as the **Cha Ca** (fish), *14 Cha Ca,* the **Thuy Ta,** overlooking *Lake Hoan Kiem at Le Thai To;* and **Restaurant 202,** *202 Pho Hue.* Alternatively there is a growing number of excellent small, unpretentious places. Sometimes they are no more than a room in a flat with half a dozen tables and they may be down a back alley and without any indication of existence. More conspicuous are the many **street kitchens.** Locals and expatriates can provide current restaurant recommendations.

the river into the sky. He interpreted this incident as a
good portent and shifted his capital here from Hoa Lu, in
Ha Nam Ninh province, naming it Thang Long (Soaring
Dragon).

Thang Long - on the western side of present Hanoi -
remained as capital until the 19th century, though it
underwent several name changes. At one stage, in the
15th century, it was called **Dong Kinh**, (Eastern Capital),
from which the name **Ton Kin** (Tonkin) is derived.

Early in the 19th century the **Nguyen Emperors** - rulers
of a united Vietnam - moved their royal seat to **Hue**, and
Thang Long, reduced to a provincial capital, was, in 1831,
renamed Hanoi, meaning the **City Inside the Bend of the
River** (*Ha* means 'River' and *Noi* means 'In'). The **French**
on procuring all of Vietnam in 1884, established the
northern part of the country - approximately the region of
Bac Phan - as their **Protectorate of Tonkin** with the city of
Hanoi being its capital and a major administrative centre
for Indochina.

After the departure of the French in 1954 and the
subsequent dividing of Vietnam into two, Hanoi became
capital of the **Democratic Republic of Vietnam** - the
North. Twenty one years later the Northern Vietnamese
won Saigon and the **Republic of Vietnam** - the South -
thus re-uniting the country as one, with Hanoi as its
capital.

Life in Hanoi

With the North's victory the South's door to the West was
closed. **Ho Chi Minh City** (Saigon) may be stuck in a
time warp, but it had contact with the West as recently as
1975. Now, with *doi moi*, its people are quick to re-
immerse themselves in the spirit of free enterprise and
refresh their taste for the Western culture. While Ho Chi
Minh City is starting to buzz, Hanoi, which has had little
contact with the West since the mid-1950s, is languishing
in an even more ancient era. For over 35 years its peoples'
vision of the outside world has been the Soviet Block and
it will take longer for them to adjust to new influences
when they eventually arrive. And during all the excited
talk of Ho Chi Minh City becoming the new 'Bangkok'
there is no mention - yet - of a flashy future for Hanoi.

In Hanoi and the old North, you are struck by the
insipid, grey poorness of life. It is different, say, to India
where there is grotesque poverty, but also fabulous
wealth. Here, it seems, the struggle to make ends meet is
shared by all. There are exceptions, including those

Hanoi, hub of Indochina

Hanoi remains in a time warp

making good, quick money in the growing **black market**, but none go starving. *'We have had to tighten our belts, but at least we have belts'*, pronounced one Hanoi shopkeeper. *'All small size'*.

Sightseeing

Hanoi is by no means unattractive, despite its overall state of disrepair. There are many lakes, wide tree-lined boulevards, which are particularly pretty when the bright red flowered **Student Trees** are in blossom, and many of the handsome cream and ochre, green-shuttered **colonial buildings** still stand, though most look as if they have received little attention since the departure of the French.

Handsome colonial architecture

The Lake of the Restored Sword

Hanoi's **historical sights** cover a greater time span than those in Ho Chi Minh City by virtue of the comparative ages of the cities. The heart of Hanoi is **Ho Hoan Kiem** - the Lake of the Restored Sword. **Le Loi**, the great 15th century warrior king, had been given a magical sword by the gods to fight off the Chinese invaders. Ten years on and his mission successfully completed, Le Loi was boating in **Luc Thuy** (the Small Lake) when a golden tortoise rose from the waters, snatched the sword from the king's hand and disappeared back to the depths. Le Loi believed the gods wanted to retrieve the sword - possibly to bestow it to another soldier in the future - and he renamed the small lake the Lake of the Restored Sword. In the centre of the lake is a small pagoda, the **Tortoise Tower**, in memory of the golden tortoise.

At the northern end of the lake is the 19th century **Ngoc Son** (Jade Hill) **Temple** on a small island linked to the shore by the **The Huc** (Sunbeams) **Bridge**. The temple dedicated to **Tran Hung Dao**, conqueror of the Mongols, has a pretty setting and **concerts** are sometimes held here. There is a **craft shop** by the entrance gate. The temple is *open from 0800 to 1700 hours.*

A walk around the lake

A circumnavigation of the lake is a pleasant and gentle introduction to Hanoi. Join the dawn crowd of earnest walkers and joggers, or the thousands of rush hour cyclists a few hours later, or the more relaxed promenaders in the evening. The streets beyond the south and south eastern sides of the lake constitute the downtown.

East of the lake in **Pho Ngo Quyen**, a block behind the large Post Office, is the white **Hotel Thong Nhat**, still the best of the central hotels. Opposite, behind wrought iron

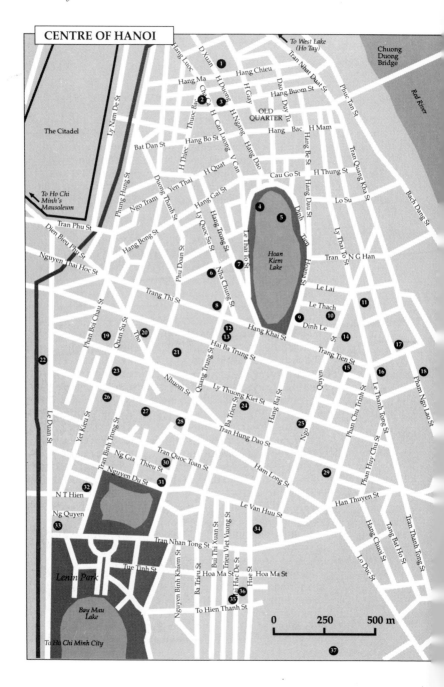

CENTRE OF HANOI

KEY TO HANOI MAP

1. Cho Dong Xuan Market Hall
2. Cha Ca Restaurant
3. Ho Chi Minh's Lodgings
4. Thuy Ta Restaurant
5. Ngoc Son Temple
6. Nha Tholon (St. Joseph's)
7. Vietnam Airlines (Domestic)
8. Aeroflot
9. Post Office
10. French Palace of the Royal Governor of Tonkin
11. Bank of Foreign Trade
12. Vietnam Airlines (International)
13. Air France
14. Thong Nhat Hotel
15. Dan Chu Hotel
16. Municipal Theatre
17. Revolutionary Museum
18. History Museum
19. Australian Embassy
20. 'Hanoi Hilton' P.O.W. Prison
21. 19th December Market
22. Railway Station
23. Quan Su (Ambassador) Pagoda
24. Vietcochamber
25. Hoa Binh Hotel
26. Palace of Labour
27. Immigration Police
28. Cambodian Embassy
29. Hoan Kiem Hotel
30. Laos Consular Office
31. Vietnam Tourism
32. Laos Embassy
33. Kim Line Bus Station
34. Hom Market
35. TOSERCO
36. Restaurant 202
37. Den Hai Ba (Hai Ba Trung Temple)

A market scene in Hanoi.

Steam engines in the train yard at Hanoi.

gates, is the old **French Palace of the Royal Governor of Tonkin**, which was stormed by the Vietnamese during the **August Revolution of 1945**. It is now a government guest house. In the other direction, left around the corner and into Trang Tien, is the **Hotel Dan Chu**.

Trang Tien
Trang Tien and the neighbouring streets form the **main shopping area**. There are a couple of old department stores which attract many 'window shoppers' who cluster around display cabinets exhibiting dusty drab and mundane merchandise. Some shops smartened and sharpened themselves for the market economy, others remain bogged down in their time warp and will be successful only if they adjust to the changing times.

Window displays devoid of luxury

There are **book shops** but the titles - mainly in Vietnamese and Russian, with a few in French and English - are not of interest. Occasionally you stumble across a fine volume dating from the colonial era and there is a good series of books on Vietnam published in English by Hanoi's **Foreign Languages Publishing House** whose HQ is at **61 Trang Tien Street**. Girls on the street corners sell post cards, city maps, 'tourist books', though their 'cut prices' are often inflated.

The colonial **Municipal Theatre**, in a clearing at the top end of Trang Tien, looks splendid and pompous compared to the grimy facades along the street, especially towards sunset when it glows a rich honey colour. Behind the theatre is the excellent, large, pagoda-shaped **Museum of History** which was built by the French in 1895 and was home for their *Ecole Française d'Extreme Orient* before becoming a museum in 1958. Opposite is the **Revolutionary Museum** and beyond are the murky brown waters of the Red River. As yet there is no congenial walk along the river bank.

Hanoi's sights are well scattered and if you want to explore beyond this central area, it will be more convenient to hire a bike or the services of a cyclo rather than walk. Most places of interest lie to the north and to the west of the Trang Tien-Theatre neighbourhood. However there are some sights to the south.

Districts of interest

Quan Hai Ba Trung

Heading southwards from the theatre down *Pho Chu Trinh* you pass the *Hotel Hoan Kiem* on the right after a few blocks. Behind, on the parallel *Pho Ngo Quyen*, is the *Hotel Hoa Binh* and, continuing down *Pho Lo Duc*, you enter the Quan (District) Hai Ba Trung. On the right is the **Den Hai Ba**, the temple honouring the **Hai Ba Trung** - the Trung sisters who routed the Chinese in 40 AD and were, for three years, proclaimed queens of independent Vietnam. The Chinese returned with a powerful army and with defeat inevitable, the sisters chose suicide rather than face capture. Their **statues** depict them kneeling, arms raised, addressing the people.

Side streets to Lenin Park

Turn westwards through the side streets to **Lenin Park**, or Thong Nhat (Reunification) Park as it is sometime called, a large pleasant park built on reclaimed land and popular as a picnic spot. There is also boating on the **Bay Mau Lake**. On the far side is the main *Duong Giai Phong*, the start of **Highway One**, the road to the south. To the north of Lenin Park, you pass the modern, spectacular

Palace of Labour - a gift to the Vietnamese from the All Union Central Trade Union Council of the USSR. Across *Trang Hung Dao* from here is the **Quan Su (Ambassador) Pagoda**, one of the main Buddhist centres in the city. In the 15th century this was the site of a lodge for visiting Buddhist ambassadors - *quan su*. The present pagoda was restored in the 1930s. **Important ceremonies** are held on the 1st and middle days of the lunar month; times: *7:30 to 11:30 and 13:30 to 17:30.*

Lodgings for Buddhist ambassadors

Quan Dong Da
Nearby, at the end of *Tran Hung Dai*, is the **Central Railway Station**. Just metres down the line is the most central of the several steam engine yards. It is probably wisest to seek permission from the station master before attempting a visit. West of the track is **Quan Dong Da** - once a separate village, now part of Hanoi proper - where the legendary **Emperor Quang Trung** (Nguyen Hue, the leader of the Tay Son brothers) routed the 200,000 strong Chinese army during Tet in 1789. A **festival** to commemorate the battle is held here on the 15th of the first lunar month, with a **wrestling competition** as the highlight of the event.

While central Hanoi was relatively unscathed by the American bombs, **Dong Da** was severely damaged. America's bombing of Hanoi and other strategic centres started on 17th April 1966 and persisted until the last days of 1972, with few respites. On Boxing Day 1972, the residential quarter of **Kham Thien**, just to the south of the railway station, was badly bombed by the US's B-52's. Hundreds were killed and much of the district was razed to the ground. A memorial in **Pho Kham Thien** marks the occasion. For their part the Vietnamese shot down 358 U.S. planes over Hanoi during the war. Many of the pilots who survived were detained in the **Hoa Lo**, the infamous French built prison dubbed the **'Hanoi Hilton'** by its American inmates. The POW prison, which still stands on the Hai Ba Trung half a kilometre east of the station, is now the **city gaol**.

Hanoi's unsalubrious Hilton

Continue northwards from the station for a few blocks and you reach **Trang Thi-Pho Nguyen Thai Hoc**, the westward extension of Trang Tien. Down here is **Van Mieu**, the **Temple of Literature**, and, opposite the **Museum of Art** (see page 105). There is also a cluster of former Soviet satellite embassies round here. Roads north of the museum lead into **Duong Dien Bien Phu**.

Duong Dien Bien Phu

Lenin still
honoured

On the south side of Duong Dien Bien Phu stands a large pensive **statue of Lenin** in one of his typical stances. Once a common sight in thousands of cities and towns across half the world, it is now a rare icon from a dying philosophy. Opposite is the site of the **old citadel**, now an army headquarters, made conspicuous by the **Cot Co**, the 60m, hexagonal tall Flag Tower, which survived the fort's destruction in the 19th century. It has become a national symbol, surmounted by a nation's flag, a golden star on a red background. Here, too is the **Military Museum** (see page 105).

Continue north-west along Duong Dien Bien Phu. This is an area of **government ministries** and **embassies**, some housed in the old colonial buildings. The road leads into *Duong Hung Vuong* and the *Ba Dinh*, a wide space dominated by the solemn looking **Mausoleum of Ho Chi Minh**, an exact replica of the Lenin's tomb in Moscow. In this square, on 2nd September 1945, President Ho Chi Minh read the Declaration of Independence, giving birth to the Democratic Republic of Vietnam. On **2nd September (National Day)**, a rally is held in front of the mausoleum and there are festivities at the Lake of the Restored Sword and elsewhere in Hanoi.

You may - and should - visit the mausoleum, which

Ho Chi Minh mausoleum.

tops Hanoi's list of attractions. However its opening hours are rather limited: *open daily between 07:30 and 11:00 except Mondays and Fridays and closed annually from the 3rd September until 6th November.*

Check in at the nearby bureau prior to your visit; you will need your **passport** for registration and **cameras** must be left here. A white-gloved, uniformed guard will then accompany you around the mausoleum.

This is a solemn pilgrimage made by thousands every day. Vietnamese - whether they come from the old South or North and of every political persuasion - revere Uncle Ho as the country's father figure of freedom.

Uncle Ho embalmed

Embalmed, Ho lies in state in the central chamber of the mausoleum. You file past his glass coffin. Young cadets, with fixed expressions and dressed all in white, stand smartly to attention, only responding when a pilgrim, emotionally overwhelmed by the occasion, breaks down and needs assistance.

From the mausoleum you are led into a pretty garden, and around a large pond to the simple,traditionally styled house which Ho chose as his home for his last years, in preference to the grand old colonial presidential palace. There are no walls. Instead, thin bamboo blinds serve as breeze breakers between the modest conference area, Ho's bedroom and study. Everything is as it was on his death in 1969. The house overlooks the pond and steps lead down to the water, where you, like Ho, can feed and stroke the plump orange carp.

Modesty preserved

Behind the mausoleum is the **Ho Chi Minh Museum**, soon to be opened, which will recount Ho's life through pictures, commentaries and displays of his paraphernalia.

A symbol of Vietnam

Opposite is the **Chau Mot Cot**, the One Pillar Pagoda. Of traditional design and measuring 3 metres square, the pagoda, perched on a single cement column rising from a small pond, represents a lotus. Promoted as a great national monument and major sight it's appearance is rather an anti-climax. It was originally build in the 11th century by **Emperor Ly Thai To** who had a vision of the **Goddess Quan Am** sitting cross-legged on a lotus, with arms outstretched offering him a baby boy. The emperor, desperate to have an heir, married a village girl who bore him a son. The pagoda is dedicated to Quan Am. Badly damaged over hundreds of years by nature and invading armies - including the departing French on 10th September 1954 - this simple structure is seen to symbolise Vietnam.

Continue northwards up Duong Hung Vuong and you

reach the **Quan Thanh Temple** on the far side of the junction of roads. In its pleasantly untended garden this large temple does not initially appear to be of much consequence. It is, however, one of the most important of Hanoi's 600 or so temples and pagodas. Built by the Ly emperors, probably in the 11th century (though later restored), it is dedicated to **Tran Vo**, who helped **An Duong**, founder of the legendary 3rd century BC **Thuc Dynasty**, destroy the evil spirits which tried to prevent him building his capital of Co Loa. Inside are a 4 metre tall bronze statue of Tran Vo, which was cast in the 17th century, and a 1.5 metre high bronze bell.

Important Buddhist temple

Duong Thanh Nien

Duong Thanh Nien, also known as the Youth Promenade because it is lined by the red blossomed Student Tree, continues northwards. On the right is the small **Lake Truc Bach** where the 18th century Trinh Lords built their Summer Palace. The residence was later converted into a rehabilitation centre for disgraced royal concubines. Here the women were employed in weaving fine silk known as *Truc Bach*, hence the name of the lake. The palace was destroyed and today the lake shore is a popular promenade with young couples. A **stone plaque** on the roadside commemorates American airmen shot down over Hanoi; it is one of several such memorials in the city.

In memory of American pilots

Ho Tay (West Lake, or Grand Lac as the French called it) is on the left. In the 11th century the Chinese Emperor gave **Khong Lo**, a local Vietnamese monk, a large quantity of bronze. The monk cast this into a huge bell and when he rang it the Golden Calf came stampeding from the north and trampled the ground around here so hard that he created the lake. Today Ho Tay covers 5 sq km and is the city's main boating lake.

Overlooking Ho Tay is the pretty **Tran Quoc Pagoda**, unusual because its layout is different to most pagodas. **Monks can give you a tour** and explain the complex's design as well as the significance of the many statues of Buddha on the altar. This small pagoda is one of the oldest in Vietnam, dating from the 6th century AD and the time of **Emperor Ly Nam De**. The 17th century *stele* gives an account of the pagoda's history. There have been several renovations, the most recent in the mid 19th century.

At the end of the causeway the road joins the main *Duong Yen Phu* which follows the shores of West Lake to the *Thang Loi Hotel*, on the northern perimeter of the city.

Northern end of the city

The Red River

On returning, follow Duong Yen Phu back into town. It leads to **Cau Long Bien** (Bridge of the Quiet Dragon) which spans the Red River. Built at the end of the last century by the French, the **Long Bien** (Doumer Bridge) is the old link between Hanoi and the north and the port of Haiphong and the coast. It is across this bridge that the French marched when they finally quit Vietnam in 1954/55. During the Vietnam War the **Long Bien** was badly bombed by the Americans who saw it as a strategic supply line for the Communists. Beyond the Long Bien is the decrepit looking **Chuong Duong Bridge**, which has also suffered attacks in the past.

Bridges over murky waters

The recently constructed **Cau Thang Long** (Bridge of the Soaring Dragon) is further upstream, around the bend in the Red.

Dang Xuan

Dang Xuan - to the right, off *Tran Nhat Duat*, the continuation of *Duong Yen Phu* - is the most fascinating of Hanoi's districts. This is the northern part of the **'old quarter'** where the architecture is colonial French and no older than a hundred years or so. The names of the streets however - *Tin Street, Broiled Fish Street, Vermicelli Street, Medicine Street, Silk Street, Paper Street, Jeweller Street* - date back to the 15th century when the city was divided into 36 guilds and the streets bore the names of the merchandise their occupants manufactured and sold.

Evocative names in Hanoi's old quarter

Walk down a lane off *Tran Nhat Duat* and then down an alley and penetrate beyond the colonial facades. You will come to a **maze of paths** which thread their way around numerous stalls selling huge arrays of dried fish, poultry, goats, vegetables, fruits, rice, spices, herbs, cloth, cheap Western-style clothes, domestic utensils . . . Men stagger to and fro under heavy loads and women, squatting behind mounds of goods, haggle and deal, hauling large grubby bundles of banknotes in and out of the folds of their aprons. It is a medieval market and, though abundant, it is not opulent.

The **main market**, the enclosed **Cho Dong Xuan Market Hall** and its surrounding area, is not far away in *Hang Giay-Dong Xuan*. *Hang Luoc*, the parallel road beyond, where they hold the flower market, is fabulously colourful and active just before and during the Tet celebrations.

Continue down Hang Diay-Dong Xuan and you enter *Hang Ngang*. Ho Chi Minh stayed at *No. 48* and here, in

August 1945, he wrote his **Declaration of Independence**. This is now a **museum**. The road leads into *Hang Dao*, the old Silk Street, where there are **souvenir/curio shops** and stalls selling inexpensive, gaudy Western-styled clothes.

The French returned to Vietnam soon after Ho's proclamation of Independence. Resistance against the old colonials was fierce and on 17th December 1946 the French fired upon the Dong Xuan district. In the following days skirmishing broke out in the streets. The poorly armed Vietnamese regiment was forced to retreat, but they vowed to continue the fight. This was the **start of the French Indochina War** which would culminate with the Battle of Dien Bien Phu in 1954.

Fighting in the streets

At the end of *Hang Dao*, you reach the **bus-tram terminus** and the Lake of the Restored Sword. If you walk along the west shore, past the lakeside restaurant and cut down a side street into *Hang Trong*, you will come to the **Ba Da** (Stone Lady) **Pagoda**. When, in the 11th century, the labourers were digging the foundations for Thang Long, they unearthed a stone statue of a woman. A temple, later proclaimed a pagoda, was built on the site. Around the corner is the typical colonial stained-glassed, medieval-styled white cathedral of **Nha Tholon**. Consecrated St Joseph's on Christmas Day, 1886, it is a quiet island of Christianity amongst all the Confucianism.

Shrines to different religions

Back by the lake, continue around its southern end to return to **Trang Tien** and the city centre.

Museums

Museum of History (Bao Tang Lich Zu)

The pagoda-shaped Museum of History built by the French at the end of the last century is well worth visiting as it documents the evolution of the Vietnamese culture, the peoples' age old fight against the Chinese, their contest with the French and their own colonisation of the Cham and the Khmer kingdoms to the south. While there are no captions in English there is a **short guide book** *'The Historical Museum of Vietnam'* - published by the Foreign Languages Publishing House and written in Russian and English, available at the entrance. Erudite locals hanging around the entrance are usually willing to act as a guide.

The museum is divided into **eight sections**, each one concentrating on a period in Vietnam's history. Palaeontological and archeological finds, numerous artifacts and historic relics, royal paraphernalia, costumes, weapons, statues, diagrams, models, maps, paintings, photographs and commentaries gathered from around the country illustrate the different eras.

But, first, to put everything into perspective, there is a huge map of Vietnam and its different cultural areas and, in red and gold lacquer, Ho Chi Minh's immortal words - the country's 'motto': *'Nothing is more precious than independence and freedom'*.

The eight sections:

A history outlined *First:* The evolution of *Homo sapiens* in Vietnam and the Palaeolithic and Neolithic Ages.

Second: Bronze and Iron Ages and the Dong Son, Sa Huynh and Cau Set Cultures; the legendary Hong Bang Dynasty.

Third: The Dong Son Culture; the Thuc and Trieu Dynasties and the subsequent '1000 years of Chinese domination'; the struggle against the Chinese; the independent civilisations of Champa and Oc Eo (Funan) in central and southern Vietnam.

Fourth: Independent Vietnam, the golden era of Dai Viet (Great Viet) including the Ly and Tran Dynasties.

Fifth: Return of the Chinese and the Ming Period; the great Le Dynasty.

Sixth: The decline of the Le Dynasty; the Trinh Lords of the North and the Nguyen Lords of the South; the popular Tay Son Uprising.

Seventh: The Nguyen Dynasty; the rise and role of the French missionaries; the arrival of the French and the Viet fight against colonialism.

Eight: The rise of Ho Chi Minh and the Communist Party; Ho's Declaration of Independence, 2nd September 1945.

Address: *Phan Ngo Lao (Behind the Municipal Theatre).*

Opening times: *07.30-11.30 and 13.00-15.30. Open daily, except Mondays and some holidays.*

Museum of the Revolution (Bao Tang Cach Mang)

On display is material depicting Vietnam's long history of struggle against outside oppressors: The Chinese, French, Japanese and Americans.

One room is devoted to **Ho Chi Minh** and includes interesting photographs and memorabilia taken from different periods in his life.

The rest of the museum depicts with gruesome clarity the **horrors of the wars**. There are the weapons, the

War momentoes booby traps, the instruments of torture, the propaganda and a wealth of archival photos, mainly from the Vietnam

War era, featuring the US politicians and military officers and the carnage - death, grotesque mutilation, terror and flagrant destruction - for which they were responsible.

The tale of Communist victory
Finally, the fall of Saigon on 30th April 1975 and the North's victory is recounted.
Address: *25 Tong Dan (opposite the Museum of History)*
Opening times: *07.30-11.30 and 13.00-1530 daily, except Mondays and some holidays.*

Military Museum (Bang Tang Quan Doi)
Weapons of friends and foes: Soviet and Chinese armaments are shown with items captured from the French and American arsenals; amongst the displays are a MIG-21 and US F-111. Proudly presented are models of victorious battle scenes.
Address: *Duong Dien Bien Phu (next to the Army Headquarters)*
Opening times: *07.30-11.30 daily except Monday.*

Museum of Fine Arts (Bao Tang My Thuat)
The art on display in this former colonial Ministry of Information includes magnificent bronze drums which were cast in the 1st millenium BC (Dong Son Age), temple and pagoda art, bronze statues, ceramics, stone carvings, lacquerware, paintings, costumes. More recent art honours the joys and victories achieved through communist solidarity as well as non flag-waving work by contemporary artists.

Also exhibited are **ethnographic displays** relating to Vietnam's ethnic minorities.
Address: *66 Pho Nguyen Thai Hoc*
Opening times: *8-12 and 13.30-15.00 daily.*

The Temple of Literature (Chua Van Mieu)
Built in 1070 by **Emperor Ly Thanh Tong**, the temple is dedicated to Confucius and honours scholars.

Vietnam's ancient seat of learning
Five years later Emperor Ly Nhan Tong founded the National Royal College *(Quoc Tu Giam)* which was an elitist institution reserved for young royalty and sons of the senior mandarins. Later when it opened its doors to commoners, who could achieve their place by passing regional exams, it was renamed and the 'Royal' was dropped.

In 1484 the great Emperor La Thanh Tong, who had expanded the educational system, had stelae placed in the temple courtyard. Each one recorded the results of the triennial exams, giving a brief background on each of

Stelae in the courtyard of the Temple of Literature.

the successful candidates. These exams were tough and there was a huge failure rate; only a dozen or so out of several thousand candidates passed.

This registering of student names ceased in 1779, however, 82 out of the 116 stelae remain in the temple compound. The centre for the *Quoc Tu Giam* was shifted to Hue by the Nguyen Emperors early in the 19th century, where it became known as the *Quoc Hoc.* Amongst its many illustrious old boys are Ho Chi Minh and his younger adversary, President Diem.

Beyond the main gate are a couple of neat, grassed courtyards before the **Heavenly Glory Pond** which is flanked by the stelae mounted on the backs of stone tortoises. Beyond, through the aptly named **Great Success Gate**, are the rooms and shrines where devotees

Confucius revered

would, and still do, revere Confucius. Students are usually willing to take a break from their books and act as guide.

Address: *Pho Nguyen Thai Hoc*
Opening times: *08.30-11.30 and 13.30-16.30*

Zoo
The zoo, by a lake in **Thu Le Park** to the west of the city, is home for elephants and other local fauna. The **Temple of the Kneeling Elephant** *(Den Voi Phuc)* was built in the 11th century and commemorates **Prince Linh Lang** and his soldiers, who, mounted on elephants, defeated a Chinese army.

The Environs of Hanoi
Co Loa
The ancient **citadel** of Co Loa is 16 kms north of the city
centre, over the new **Thang Long Bridge**, on the way to
Noi Bai International Airport which is 48 kms from
town. Co Loa, Vietnam's first citadel, was founded in 255
BC by **An Duong Vuong**, who established it as the
capital of his **Kingdom of Au Lac**. The capital was
shifted, initially to Phien Ngu (Canton), during the '1000
Years of Chinese domination', but was susequently
returned to Co Loa during the brief **Ngo Dynasty**
between 939 and 965 AD.

The remains of the citadel's ramparts enclosing an area
of about 5 sq km, can be visited along with its **temples**.
These include memorials to **An Duong Vuong** and his
daughter **My Chau**, whose husband, **Zhong Shui**, stole
the king's magic bow and took it to his own father, a
Chinese general, who used it against the Viets causing
the downfall of the Kingdom of Au Lac (see page 56).
My Chau, the unsuspecting catalyst in this dupe, was
beheaded by her outraged father and the statue of her in
the temple is without a head. Zhong Shui, overwhelmed
by his disloyalty to his wife and father-in-law, eventually
drowned himself in the well beside An Duong Vuong's
temple.

A tragic
domestic drama

Me Linh
Me Linh, to the **north-west of Co Loa** and 65 kms from
Hanoi, was also an **ancient capital**, though only from 40-
43 AD - the period when the Trung girls regained
independence from the Chinese. To the south, the **Hai Ba
Trung Temple** stands in the sisters' home village of **Ha
Loi**. A **festival**, held here on the fifteenth of the first lunar
month, includes a procession of 150 boys and 150 girls.

Pagodas
There are many temples and pagodas honouring Buddha
and past heroes in this ancient heartland of the Viet
culture. Two of the most famous within reach of Hanoi
are: The **Thay Phuong (or Thien Phuc) Pagoda**, about 40
km to the west of Hanoi in the village of **Sai Son** which
was built during the reign of Ly Than Tong in the early
12th century. The much decorated pagoda honours **Tu
Dao Hanh**, a celebrated monk from the Ly Dynasty,
Emperor Ly Than Tong and the **sect of Sakyamuni
Buddah**. The pagoda, beautifully set on the hillside, is
also a centre for **water puppetry**. Also in this area is the

Temples and
pagodas around
Hanoi

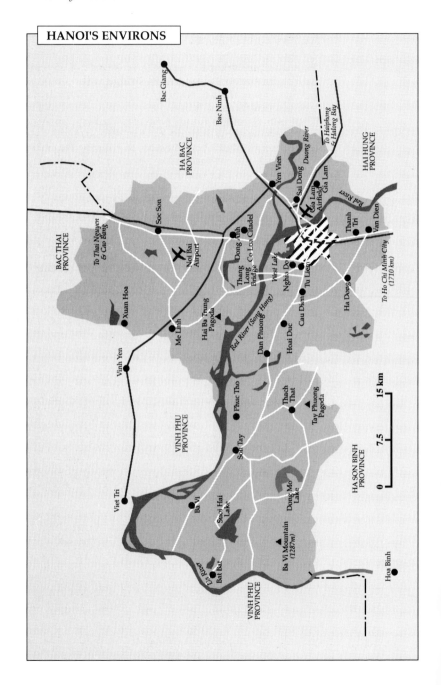

HANOI'S ENVIRONS

Bac Giang

Bac Ninh

To Haiphong & Halong Bay

HA BAC PROVINCE

Yen Vien

Sai Dong

Duong River

HAI HUNG PROVINCE

Gia Lam

Gia Lam Airfield

Red River

BAC THAI PROVINCE

To Thai Nguyen & Cao Bang

Soc Son

Thanh Tri

Van Dien

Noi Bai Airport

Dong Anh

Co Loa Citadel

Thang Long Bridge

West Lake

Nghia Do

Fu Liem

To Ho Chi Minh City (1710 km)

Xuan Hoa

Me Linh

Hai Ba Trung Pagoda

Red River (Song Hong)

Dan Phuong

Cau Dien

Hoai Duc

Ha Dong

Vinh Yen

Phuc Tho

Thach That

Tay Phuong Pagoda

15 km

Son Tay

VINH PHU PROVINCE

7.5

Dong Mo Lake

HA SON BINH PROVINCE

0

Viet Tri

Ba Vi

Suoi Hai Lake

Da River

Bat Bat

Ba Vi Mountain (1287m)

Hoa Binh

VINH PHU PROVINCE

Tay Phuong (or Bung Phuc) Pagoda, the West Pagoda, high on a hill at the village of **That Xa**. Originally built in the 8th century, the pagoda is highly ornate and is well known for its many **lacquered wooden statues**.

Factories, Crafts and Old Soldiers
There was a time, not too long ago, when the local authorities proudly promoted visits to **Workers' Co-operatives** as some of Hanoi's main attractions. Recently, though, such excursions have slipped from prominence. Those interested can liaise with the *Tourist Office* who will gladly arrange a visit to a **carpet or ceramic workshop** in the environs of Hanoi, where you can buy **handicrafts**.

Rehabilitation of old soldiers

Outings are also organised to the **rehabilitation centres** where the war wounded are employed in suitable jobs. So many of the U.S. Vietnam veterans have been psychologically damaged by the war, it is hard to appreciate how much mental anguish their Vietnamese counterparts suffer. It would seem that ex-soldiers and civilians alike just want to blank out the war, look forward and just get on with life.

EAST OF HANOI

Hai Hung Province
The road and railway from Hanoi eastwards through Hai Hung province to Haiphong have long been vitally important avenues of communication between the capital and its outlet to the world. During the French rule they were the targets of Viet Minh terrorism and at the time of the Vietnam War they were bombed by the Americans.

The flatlands of Hai Hung province - criss-crossed by canals and dikes - are intensively cultivated, with rice as the main crop. Here, in the heartlands of the ancient Viet culture about 35 km out of Hanoi is **Ke Sat**, a centre of Catholicism as early as the 17th century.

Hai Duong, the provincial capital, is 53 km from Hanoi and 42 km from Haiphong and, though rather drab, a convenient half-way halt along this route. In the north the plains give way to foothills where coffee and tea are grown. The **Keip Bac Temple**, at Van Yen, was built in 1300 in memory of the great **Tran Hung Dao** who rebuffed the Chinese armies on three occasions in the 13th century. **Kiep Bac** was a refuge for the old warrior, who died up here in 1300. He created the gardens, and

Treatment for war wounds

from the various plants he concocted medicines used to treat his wounded soldiers. **Other temples** in the surrounding hills are dedicated to his generals.

Haiphong Province

Haiphong, on the south bank of the **River Cua Cam** and
16km inland from the **Gulf of Tonkin**, is northern
Vietnam's main port, second city and capital of its own
small province of Haiphong.

The north's premier port

The place was no more than a local market town until
the French arrived in the late 19th century and took
possession of the area. They dredged channels and
drained marshes and developed Haiphong into an
industrial centre and port. Produce gathered from the
Tonkin hinterland was brought to Haiphong to be
exported and imports, too, would pass through its docks.

Battered and Beaten

The most significant event in its history occurred when
the French returned to Vietnam in 1946. **Ho Chi Minh**
signed a controversial agreement with the **French**
allowing French troops to post garrisons at various
centres around the north in exchange for Vietnamese
autonomy. He was not in a strong bargaining position,
for the Chinese, in North Vietnam to monitor the
surrender of the Japanese army after World War II, had
already allowed the French back to their old protectorate
of Tonkin. The French, physically more powerful, held
the upper hand over Ho and his Viet Minh.

The French came ashore at **Haiphong** on 6th March
1946. There was an uneasy relationship between their
contingent and the Viet Minh, who were each in charge
of different quarters of the city. On the 20th November a
French patrol arrested a group of Chinese smugglers,
only then to be seized themselves by the Viet Minh who
believed such customs duties were their prerogative.

Altercation over customs duties leads to war

The event sparked off strong French retaliation and, on
23rd November, the French mobilised their forces. Their
cruiser *Suffren* shelled Haiphong from the harbour, the
airforce fired the city and tanks rolled through the streets.
The battle continued for days and concluded with a
French victory. The death toll was estimated at between
six and twenty thousand, comprising mainly Vietnamese
civilians, though today even the lower figure is seen as an
exaggeration.

Less than a month later a similar conflict between the
French and Viet Minh occurred in the streets of **Hanoi**,
after which Ho declared open war against the French.

As an industrial and strategic centre, Haiphong was a
natural target during times of war and on occasions its
port was heavily mined by the enemy to prevent the

traffic of supply ships. The most intensive assault on the city was launched by the **Americans** on 18th December 1972 and lasted for eleven days. During that period American planes dropped 40,000 tons of bombs on Hanoi, Haiphong and the land between the two cities. The targets were factories and depots, but inevitably some bombs strayed and there were civilian casualties, though the numbers were relatively low because many people had been evacuated to the country side.

Haiphong Today

Haiphong appears a hard place pinched by poverty. In some districts you see the tumbledown houses and wonder whether they are relics of past bombings or just neglected buildings fallen into disrepair. The wide treelined boulevards and old municipal buildings in the centre of town are typically French, though they are in need of maintenance. The grandiose **theatre/opera house** - a normal colonial feature in the larger towns - seems particularly incongruous in this grey depressed city.

A drab city

Tourists pass through Haiphong on their way to **Ha Long Bay**; the city itself has little to offer them. The main attractions are: the central early 20th century **Nghe Temple** dedicated to Le Chan, who fought alongside the

Haiphong ferry.

111

Trung Sisters in 40 AD; and on the far side of the railway line the 17th century **Du Hang Pagoda** and the **Hang Kenh Temple and Communal House** with its 500 wooden sculptures. Nearby is the **Hang Kenh tapestry factory**. Out of town on **Elephant Mountain**, is the site of a 16th century temple.

Despite the city's overall drabness, it is interesting to wander around the downtown, *Dien Bien Phu Street* and its neighbourhood, and visit the **market** where they sell a large variety of **seafoods**.

The wide, brown, murky **Cua Cam** and its ferry point are down the road from the *Duyen Hai Hotel*. The **main port** is visible just downstream. These waters, having been dredged, can take ocean-going vessels of up to 10,000 tons. Dwarfed by these ships, the locals' Tonkinese junks and their smaller craft nip across the waters at a fair rate of knots, the wind billowing in their tatty hessian-like sails.

Junks and ocean vessels

HAIPHONG FACTS

Haiphong Food and Accommodation
There are three hotels regarded as suitable for tourists. The **Huu Nghi** *(Tel: 47206)* and the smaller **Back Dang** *(Tel: 47244)*, both on *Dien Bien Phu Street*, and the **Duyen Hai** *(Tel: 47657)*, behind them on *Nguyen Tri Phuong*. All three have restaurants and bars and there is dancing a couple of times a week at the Duyen Hai. There are **other restaurants** within the vicinity, where they serve such local specialities as **seafood** and **roast dog**.

Quang Ninh Province
To Ha Long Bay by Boat

Passenger ferries travel up and down the river. Heading downstream the **Cua Cam** widens beofre flowing into the Gulf of Tonkin. At its mouth it merges with the **Bach Dang**, at the site of two famous **river battles, one** in 939 and the other in 1288, at which the Vietnamese overcame the Chinese fleets.

On the southern lip of the Cua Cam is a **temple** dedicated to the great **Ngo Quyen** who routed the Chinese in the first of the battles of Bach Dang. Beyond, further to the south, nine hills form a peninsula protruding into the sea providing shelter for the sandy beaches of **Do Son**, Haiphong's main coastal resort, only 22kms away by road from Haiphong. The **Do Son Hotel** provides modest accommodation.

Nine hills shelter Do Son

Turning northwards you pass through a narrow channel which divides the mainland on the left from the island of **Cat Ba** on the right. Part of the scenic, hilly forested 188 sq km island has been declared a **national park**. Cat Ba is rich in flora and fauna - the **local warden** can provide you with a list of the hundreds of species - and a guide can show you around the island's **grottos** and take you to the best **swimming spots**. The island has been earmarked for tourist development, but due to its remoteness, it is unlikely to attract large numbers for a while at least.

Island reserved for nature

Cat Ba is by far the largest of a cluster of over 350 bizarrely shaped islands, many of which are easily visited by boat. However, continuing northwards, the ferry enters **Ha Long Bay** with its archipelago of thousands of extraordinary Karst limestone islands.

To Ha Long Bay by Road
Ferries, capable of taking vehicles, cross the **Cua Cam** and from the far side, there is a short drive before another ferry ride, this time across the historic **Bach Dang** (see page 87) to **Quang Ninh** province. The road veers inland, through **Yen Hung - Quang Yen** - to the shadows of the foothills. This area has some of the largest **coal deposits** in South East Asia, being rich in high quality anthracite. On the scenic **Mount Yen Tu**, to the north of here, there are many pagodas, including the **Dong Pagoda** where Emperor Tran Nhan Tong - during whose reign Tran Hung Dao defeated the Mongols at the second **Battle of Bach Dang** in 1288 - retired to a monastery. Unwilling to allow him his life of restraint, his harem of 300 women followed him to his refuge. He ordered them away, but they refused to go. Locals think that faced with these two extreme options,the emperor chose the chastened life. From the foot of the hills the road turns coastwards to **Ha Long Bay** and the town of **Hong Gai**.

Great coal reserves

Ha Long Bay
Ha Long Bay, an *'internationally classified Top Natural Wonder of the world'* according to the Vietnamese, is indeed a most unusual place.

In a country of poets, many have waxed lyrically about Ha Long Bay, but no verse has yet satisfied the locals, as their tourist handbook points out: *'So far no poet or writer has been able to fully describe the beauty of the bay'*. Long may it stay that way.

Ha Long means **'Descending Dragon'**, according to

local folklore a dragon swooped down on the bay and
dropped 1000 pearls into the glistening turquoise sea. The
pearls sprouted into small islands and these soft
limestone islets were carved by sea, salt spray, wind and
other natural forces into their strange shapes. Most rise
sheer from the water, curving gradually to form a profile
of a half oval. The locals with a more vivid imagination
have given them appropriate names - Sailing Boat Island,
Elephant Island, Virgin Island, Horse Island, Dog Island,
which guards the Gates to Heaven, and there are Monkey
Islands, one looking like a monkey, the other inhabited
by them. Contained within these islands are countless
grottos and they too have been given names - Surprising
Grotto is so called because its **stalactites**, to everyone's
surprise, look like fishermen. And there are islands with
tunnels you can sail through, some of them reaching one
or two kilometres in length.

Ha Long's curious sea mountains

Most of the islands reveal their stark grey rock face,
some are covered with vegetation and some are skirted
with beaches. There are about 1000 islands in Ha Long
Bay itself - an area of 1500 sq km - and a further 2000,
many of them quite large, elsewhere off Quang Ninh's
shores. The range, of which these islands are the peaks,
continues above ground in southern China.

The vast majority of the islands are rarely touched and
remain unexploited, though the **Japanese**, while
occupants of Vietnam during World War II, took sand
from some of the beaches to use in their **glass industry**.
Today, on one of the islands, Vietnamese biologists breed
monkeys for use in **medical research**.

The road turns down to Ha Long Bay and runs
alongside **Bai Chai beach** for several kilometres. The
islands are quite a distance out in the bay, but perfectly
visible. To the left are the hills and, on their slopes, the
hotels. There is no town, but, at the end of the corniche,
there is a small harbour and car ferry across the narrow
mouth of an inner bay. On the far side local transport
provides a service up the road to **Hon Gai**, capital of
Quang Ninh province.

The Ha Long Bay corniche

Hon Gai
Bombed by the Americans during the Vietnam War, Hon
Gai is an **administrative centre** and a **coal town** servicing
nearby mines and has no beauty in itself. However,
beside the squalid market there is a bay where local
sampans moor and take shelter. Most of them also serve
as houseboats for the fishing families. Here in this bay

THE BOAT PEOPLE AND THE ODP

The **1954 Geneva Accords** divided Vietnam at the 17th parallel and stipulated that the French and their allied soldiers should leave the North, while the **Viet Minh** in the South should return to the North. 100,000 Viet Minh made this journey, leaving 5000 behind who later formed the core of the **Viet Cong**.

Over a short period, citizens were allowed to choose on which side of the demarcation line they wanted to live. 700,000 Northerners fled to the South, many of them being Catholics who feared persecution under Ho's regime. A third of these travelled on U.S. naval vessels which provided a ferry service from Haiphong to Saigon. The South to North migration was less significant, though 40 people, as one source suggested, seems an underestimate.

200,000 Vietnamese fled the country in the wake of the **North's victory in 1976**. Many escaped overland into neighbouring countries, while others took to boats for overseas destinations. These, the first of the **'Boat People'**, often gave their life savings for passage on crowded, barely seaworthy vessels. Their clandestine voyages risked the storms, piracy and other perils of the South China Sea.

The flow of Boat People continued through the 1970s, 1980s and into the 1990s. **China's invasion of Vietnam** in 1979 inspired many of the country's **ethnic Chinese** to take to the seas for fear of persecution if they stayed behind; and in a desperately poor country, the further poverty caused by each bad harvest would encourage a new wave of refugees.

Those who survived their plight were detained in camps in the reception countries (Hong Kong had 43,000 refugees in 1989) from where they hoped they would be despatched to a new life in America or Europe. However the dream turned into a nightmare as a ticket to a third country grew increasingly difficult to obtain. The procedure of screening and dividing the Boat People into 'genuine political refugees' and 'economic migrants' became more rigid. In 1989 the Western countries committed themselves to resettling 55,000 of the former group, while those of the latter group would be sent back to Vietnam. By July 1990 3,160 Vietnamese had been voluntarily repatriated under a **UN scheme** which ensured no punitive action from the Vietnamese government against the returnees. In 1990 a more drastic scheme of involuntary repatriation was sanctioned.

A further legacy of the war is the **Amerasian children**, the offspring of American servicemen and Vietnamese mothers. Often abandoned as a product of a shameful past, these children ended up as orphans and street kids. (The French had taken 25,000 children of mixed parentage with them on leaving Vietnam in 1954). The **Orderly Departure Programme** was initiated in the 1980s with a view to finding homes for these children (and other legitimate refugees) in the West. Under this scheme 22,000 Vietnamese emigrated to the USA in 1988. Furthermore, Vietnam is now allowing supporters of the Southern regime, many of whom ended up in 're-education' camps after re-unification, to emigrate to America on condition they do not involve themselves in 'anti-Vietnamese activities'.

within a bay, the spectacular **Karst islets** are as close to the shore as anywhere.

Hon Gai's fame in recent years has been as a main starting point for **'Boat People'** fleeing Vietnam's shores. The sea route from Ha Long Bay across the Gulf of Tonkin, through the Hainan Strait to Hong Kong is only 1300 km and, never far from the Chinese coast on the port side, it is considered safer than the open waters of the more southerly South China Sea where the storms are wild and the pirates merciless. The boatmen from these shores charged desperate emigrants huge sums to provide transport in their junks.

Starting point for the 'Boat People'

Beyond Hon Gai the road continues parallel to the coast to **Cam Pha** and on, finally reaching the beach resort of **Tra Co**. This border area, which was invaded by the Chinese in 1979, remains militarily sensitive and possibly out of bounds.

Tourism in Ha Long Bay

There is not much to do in Ha Long Bay except visit the islands and relax. Ideally, you should travel **by boat from Haiphong via Cat Ba** and then sail amongst the islands en route to Ha Long Bay. Alternatively **join an excursion** from the harbour. It takes an hour or so to get in amongst the islands and, on a half day trip, you can chug around a while, disembark and visit a grotto and then return back to the mainland. Having come all the way to Ha Long Bay it is worth going on a full day tour which allows you more time for exploration and maybe a swim and a picnic on one of the islands. At **Hon Gai** the islands are closer to the shore and a tour from here would give you a quicker introduction.

A trip out to sea

The inverted U-shaped sails on the **fishing craft** parody the silhouette of many an island. The fishermen may offer you a trip out in the bay, but at present such expeditions are officially discouraged.

There is a **ferry**, though its timetable is irregular, covering the 100 km **from Ha Long Bay and Cam Pha**, up the coast, to **Co To**, an island inhabited mainly by ethnic Chinese who grow **rice** and **oranges**. The beach here is supposedly very lovely.

Ha Long Bay's hotels are on the left side of the **Bai Chai corniche**. The best is the **Ha Long** *(tel: 238)*, a colonial styled building with wide verandahs and large rooms, on the hillside amongst the pines and overlooking the bay and its islands. Nearby is a holiday complex previously used by Soviet holidaymakers, which may well be redeveloped as a hotel. At the far end of the beach, near the harbour and ferry crossing, are the **Vuon Dao** and **Bach Dang** hotels.

The cluster of buildings down here constitutes the centre of **Bai Chai** and there are a **post office, Tourist Office** and a **souvenir kiosk. Restaurants** are at the hotels and the speciality is, naturally, the **excellent seafood**.

In this potentially prime tourist spot, there is currently nothing in the way of nightlife. Nevertheless a marvellous evening can be had on the beach or in the bar, chatting to local fishermen who spin yarns about the sea and rattle off fantastically imaginative descriptions of the islands.

Down on the waterfront

Heading North

A road at **Tien Yen** - about half way between **Hong Gai** and **Tra Co** - cuts across Quang Ninh's remote hills into **Lang Son** province and onto Lang Son town. At **Dinh Lap** there is a turning to the south-west, leading into **Ha Bac** - a province famed for the sweet **Bo Ha orange** and the evocative **Quan Ho folk songs**. The route descends to the flatter lands and **Bac Giang**, the provincial capital, and **Bac Ninh** before reaching Hanoi.

THE NORTH

Through Ha Bac to Lang Son Province

The road and railway heading north-east out of Hanoi crosses the Red and, soon after, enters Ha Bac province passing through the town of **Bac Ninh**, and **Bac Giang**, the provincial capital. Bac Giang has a **local tourist office** and **accommodation**. North of here, upstream along the **River Thuong**, is the **Bo Ha orange** growing region.

North to the Chinese border

The routes continue into **Lang Son** province, along the valley, gradually ascending into a **scenic Alpine zone**. It was at **Chi Lang** that Le Loi defeated the Chinese in 1427. The mountains become more rugged and spectacular, finally reaching **Lang Son**, the provincial capital, 147 kms after Hanoi.

Lang Son

Lang Son, a busy market town, owes its importance to being only 18km from the border with China. The way between the two countries is through the **Nam Quan Pass** (the Gateway to the South), a path into Vietnam for many Chinese armies over the centuries.

The most significant of recent invasions was in 1979, when the Chinese briefly captured Lang Son. This area became politically sensitive and was put out of bounds to foreigners, only being re-opened in 1989. Today, locals cross the border into China and return with goods which they sell down in the town's **Ky Lua market**.

The skirmish at Long San

The **Tam Thanh Grottos**, just to the north-west of town, were badly damaged during World War II when the Japanese attacked Lang Son , and the settlement of **Dong Dang**, which lies beyond and almost on the border, was destroyed by the Chinese. Also on this border, **Nguyen Trai**, strategist and close associate of the 15th century emperor Le Loi, bid farewell to his father who had been captured by the Chinese. The emotional parting is evocatively recounted in Nguyen Trai's famous poem *Uc Trai Tag*.

Here, too, is **Nang To Thi**, a stone statue of a woman with her baby awaiting the return of her husband from war. She draws pilgrims especially on 2nd July, her special festival day.

Lang Son's basic accommodation is currently being improved to cater for tourists.

Site of an ancient culture

Stone axes, pottery and **fragments of other artifacts** found in caves in the **Bac Son mountains**, directly to the west of Lang Son, date back to the mesolithic-neolithic stone age culture now known as the **Bac Son Civilisation**. Judging from the skulls discovered, anthropologists believe these early people to be *Austronesian* - a human type that now lives further to the south, in the **Central Highlands** (see page 42). Over more recent centuries the region has been inhabited predominantly by the *Tay* peoples, and Bac Son is famous for the **1940 Tay Uprising** against the French.

The road continues north west from Lang Son, through **Dong Dang** and on, parallel to the border, through the mountains via **That Khe** (Trang Dinh) to **Cao Bang**, capital of Cao Bang province.

Cao Bang Province

The garrisons posted by the French in the outlying hill towns of the far north were isolated and vulnerable to Viet Minh attacks. This became all too evident in 1950 when the Viet Minh won Lang Son, That Khe and Cao Bang - and the vitally important road the *Rue Sans Joie*, (Street without Joy), as the French troops called it, between the towns.

The French not only lost many thousands of soldiers

trying to defend this route, but also a significant strategic advantage. **Mao Tse Tung** and the Communists were now in power in mainland China and were willing to support the **resistance movement** in Vietnam. Once in control of the northern border region, the Viet Minh were able to ferry arms from China and also use China as a sanctuary from the French. This was one of the rare occasions in history when the Chinese and Vietnamese were allies in war and it was due to Chinese assistance that the Viet Minh developed sufficient military strength finally to overthrow the French in 1954.

Cao Bang, located 295 km by road from Hanoi, at the confluence of rivers and crossroads of old trading paths, is an **important market town** for locals. About 30 km from China and set amidst dramatically beautiful **mountains**, Cao Bang remains remote and little visited by outsiders.

The **border** near Cao Bang was also a place of entry for the Chinese and at **Phuc Hoa** there are remains of old defences. These border lands, where one also finds the **Pac Po caves** and **Ban Gioc** beauty spots, are **off limits** at present.

To the west of Cao Bang, however, is **Ba Be**, a beautiful **national park** at the corner of Cao Bang, Ha Tuyen and Bac Thai provinces. The tourist authorities plan to develop the park which centres on an extraordinary lake, **Ho Ba Be**. This is surrounded by mountains, measures seven by three kilometres and, remarkably, has a depth of 130 metres. You can take a boat out to the islands which dot the lake.

Remote, beautiful mountain region

Deep waters

Ha Tuyen Province

Ha Tuyen, the province to the west of Cao Bang, is even **more mountainous** and **remote** than its neighbour. **Ha Giang**, the provincial capital, is on roughly the same latitude as Cao Bang and the two towns are linked by a circuitous route which cuts across mountains and follows river valleys, including that of the **Song Gam**, an important tributary of the Red.

Ha Giang is 20 km from the Chinese border. The frontier here was long disputed between the Vietnamese and Chinese until the French sorted out the matter and established the present boundary a hundred years ago. It now lies along the **Song Lo** (the River Claire), which then flows south-eastwards through Tuyen Quang, an important regional town in a **coal mining** and **lumber** district, only 100 km from Hanoi, to the Red River by the town of Viet Tri.

The **Tuyen Quang** region was a base for the **Black Flags**, a group of Chinese who had failed in their **Tai Ping Uprising** in 1865 and escaped to northern Vietnam. They formed themselves into a private army under **Luu Vinh Phuc** and terrorised the countryside. However, after the French had laid claim to the north, the Nguyens at Hue enlisted the co-operation of the Black Flags, who then channelled their aggression against the French and became a significant force in the anti-colonial resistance.

East of Tuyen Quang is the village of **Tan Trao**. For many, Tan Trao is seen as the **cradle of the Viet Minh**. In the summer of 1945 Ho Chi Minh and a hundred or so fellow resistance fighters took refuge up here and planned the independence of Vietnam. At this point, during the concluding months of World War II, the Viet Minh and the Americans viewed each other as possible allies. The Americans were fighting the Japanese, while the Viet Minh wanted to free their country of both the French and Japanese.

The Viet Minh were in need of support and supplies and the Office of Strategic Services (OSS) - the Americans' wartime version of the CIA - sent a group of men, the **Deer Team**, to Tan Trao to provide assistance and to check out this band of guerillas. Ho Chi Minh was very ill at the time and the U.S. medic on the team provided him with medicines which may well have saved his life. Within a generation Ho Chi Minh and the Americans were gravest of enemies.

A 348 km road, running along the **Lo valley**, links Hanoi with Viet Tri, Tuyen Quang and Ha Giang. It is also possible to travel sections of the Lo by boat.

Black flags against the French (margin)

Ho Chi Minh receives American treatment (margin)

Vinh Phu Province
Viet Tri, provincial capital of Vinh Phu, and nearby **Phu Tho** are both **industrial towns** processing sugar, timber and fertilisers. They are linked to Hanoi by road, rail and the Red River. Vinh Phu is a transitional province, with the **rice-dominated plains** giving way to **forested hills**. North of Vinh Yen, just to the east of Vinh Tri, is **Tam Dao**, a hill resort for Hanoi, where there is a **Tourist Office** and **accommodation**. To its west is the eleven storey (originally fourteen storey) brick **Binh Son Tower** which was built during the Ly Dynasty.

Bac Thai Province
East of Vinh Phu and Ha Tuyen provinces, and south and west of Cao Gang and Lang Son provinces respectively, is

Bac Thai, **another mountainous province**, once exploited by the French for its timber. **Thai Nguyen**, 75 km directly north of Hanoi, is the provincial capital. With access to **coal and iron deposits** nearby, it was developed into the country's major **steel making** centre.

This industrial city was capital of the former Thai Nguyen province, remembered for the 1917 **Thai Nguyen Revolt** when **Luong Ngoc Quyen**, a political prisoner, inspired an uprising in his gaol, resulting in the death of several French officers. The expected help from Chinese nationalists was not forthcoming and the group of anti-colonialists fled into the hills. They were pursued by the French, but the crippled Quyen chose to kill himself rather than slow down his fellow fugitives. His selfless actions have made him a national hero. There are a **Tourist Office**, an **hotel**, a **museum** and a **memorial to Luong Ngoc Quyen**, and of course the **steel mills**, in Thai Nguyen. A road continues north to Cao Bang. On route there is a turning to the west, to the **Ba Be park**.

On the run from the French

In 1956 these remote and mountainous provinces of north Vietnam were amalgamated by Ho Chi Minh's government to form the **Viet Bac Autonomous Region**. The inhabitants of this region, predominantly from various ethnic minorities, including the *Tho, Meo, Nung, Zao* and *Lo Lo* (see page 42), were provided with an element of autonomy within the Democratic Republic of Vietnam.

NORTH WEST VIETNAM

Ha Son Binh Province

The road south-west out of Hanoi passes through **Ha Dong** on the border of Hanoi and Ha Son Binh provinces, into the foothills and the town of **Hoa Binh**, 75 km from the capital, which stands on the **Song Da**, the Black River, a significant stream which feeds into the Red directly to the north.

As the geography changes from flatlands to hills, so does the ethnicity from *Viets* to *Muong*. This area is a traditional Muong stronghold and soon after the French established their regional headquarters 100 years ago at **Cho Bo**, just upstream from the Hoa Binh, the Muong burnt it down. The *Thai* peoples are very influential in this north-western corner of Vietnam, and, over the centuries, the Muong have adopted various aspects of their culture. They have also mixed with the Viets and, on several occasions through history, have served alongside

Mountain people

them fighting against national enemies. A visit to a showpiece **Muong Village** is one of the main tourist excursions from Hanoi and is often incorporated into the trip to Hoa Binh and Dien Bien Phu.

Prehistoric people who tamed the dog

Hoa Binh gave its name to a **mesolithic culture**, the 10,000 year old Hoa Binhian Civilisation, after stone axe heads were discovered in local caves. This prehistoric community is believed to have **domesticated the dog**.

Today, the **River Da** has been dammed and a Soviet-sponsored **hydro-electric power station** constructed near Hoa Binh. The electricity is destined for the Hanoi district as well as for the remote Hoa Binh hinterland. Increasingly, isolated tribes people will be able to leap centuries and become part of the modern world with a flick of a switch.

There is a **tourist lodge**, shaped like a traditional *Muong* house, in Hoa Binh and other accommodation is being built. The Hanoi-Hoa Binh stretch of road is good, as it had to be improved before the construction of he hydro-electric plant. An old road wends its way southwards into **Ha Nam Ninh province**, another continues westwards, into **Son La** province where you enter *Thai* territory. If on an organised excursion, you may be taken to a Thai village where the locals pass the time **panning for gold**.

Son La Province

Moc Chau is the main Thai market town in south-eastern Son La. The road passes through and follows the river valley to the town of Son La, the provincial capital, 310 km from Hanoi. Laos is the other side of the mountains on the left.

The French, having colonised Tonkin, established military and administrative outposts deep in the mountains, amongst the ethnic minorities. They caused much resentment and on many occasions the local tribes -

Tribal uprisings

the *Mung*, the *Meo*, the *Thai* and others - rose up against them. However, these were usually isolated and unco-ordinated attacks which the French were able to suppress, often very brutally.

The insurgents are remembered for their heroism and in **Son La** they tell you about the uprising against the resident French *fonctionnaire* which was later quashed, with the rebellious ringleaders - local Thais - being publicly executed in 1917.

Rising in China, the 850 km **Long Da** flows into Vietnam through Lai Chau and Son La provinces, where it runs through a remote and beautiful valley just to the north of Son La town before finding its way to the Red. Various ethnic minorities live in the valley and remain reasonably cut off from the developments further downstream. But Son La province has **timber**, **coal** and

Rich resources in Son La **other minerals**, including gold, and it is probably only a matter of time before these resources are properly exploited. The Da is navigable and maybe one day there will be boat trips along the river.

Lai Chau Province and Dien Bien Phu

The road deteriorates after Son La, though it is now under reconstruction, and forks soon after entering Lai Chau province. The main route continues north-westwards to **Lai Chau**, the provincial capital. To the left, a fairly rough road - a section of an old caravan route

---

DIEN BIEN PHU

In the autumn of 1952 **General Giap** and his **Viet Minh** occupied the valley of Dien Bien Phu and the following spring they invaded **French Laos**, returning back to their valley before the monsoons. The Viet Minh were too threatening to be tolerated and so the French captured Dien Bien Phu in late 1953, armed with a plan to turn the valley into a stronghold from where they could defend Laos and direct operations against Giap and his men.

As the French airlifted reinforcements to their base on the valley floor, the Viet Minh methodically took up their positions in the surrounding steep, wooded hills, in effect creating a cordon around the enemy, and isolating them from ground supply routes.

General Navarre, in overall charge of the French campaign, had underestimated the strength and tenacity of the Viet Minh. Moreover he had not banked on the many thousands of ordinary Vietnamese men, women and children who, laden with provisions and pieces of artillery - much of which had been bequeathed by the Chinese who feared a powerful Western force on their doorstep - risked their lives against the French land and air patrols and slogged hundreds of kilometres across densely forested mountains in order to keep the Viet Minh war effort supplied.

The French found themselves marooned on the floor of the Dien Bien Phu valley. Their pilots ran the gauntlet, dodging Viet Minh sharpshooters as they tried to fly in supplies. Furthermore, the French had a limited body of men to call upon and, by drawing troops from places around the Indochina, Navarre left himself exposed to the Viet Minh elsewhere. Initially cocksure, the French gradually realised the grim reality of their position.

Ultimately the Viet Minh held the upper hand. They had a better position, greater firepower, more men, the advantage of bad weather, which hindered the enemy more than them, and higher morale against the weary French. Battle commenced on 13th March 1954 and concluded with the French surrender to the Viet Minh on 7th May 1954.

which once stretched from China to the Indian Ocean - heads south-west through **Muong An** and **Muong Phan** to the town and valley of **Dien Bien Phu**, only 15 km from the border with Laos and 420 km by road from Hanoi.

Dien Bien Phu is a Vietnamese name. The local Thais call the place **Muong Thanh**. This remote valley, where the Thais grow rice and trade opium, was picked as the pitch for the bloody finale to French colonialism in Indochina.

The **Dien Bien Phu valley** is 19km long by 8km wide. A local guide will show you around the site of the **French camp**, including the **bunker** of the dashing **Colonel Christian Marie Ferdinand de La Croix de Castries** who was in command of the French forces here. This is currently under restoration. You can also go up to the Viet Minh bases in the hills from where the guide points

France's last battlefield

out places of confrontation and enthusiastically relates the various strategies which gave the Viet Minh victory. The local **museum** further documents the battle and maps illustrate how the French were held under siege before succumbing to Giap's conclusive on slaught.

Dien Bien Phu is being developed in a fairly low key fashion as a **national memorial**, a symbol of the Vietnamese will to overcome the foreign aggressor. There is **simple accommodation** at present, which will doubtless be improved in time.

A road leads north from Dien Bien Phu through **Muong Pon** and **Muong Lay** to **Lai Chau** town, on the banks of the Da, some 475 km by road (300 km by river) from Hanoi. Lai Chau province, spectacular with its

Remotest Vietnam

dense forests and rugged mountains, is probably the most remote in Vietnam, while its capital is the most isolated. Up until this century local government was a feudal system with the Thais at the top and a host of other ethnic minorities below them - a framework the early French colonials were prepared to keep intact.

During colonial times Lai Chau was a central piece in the French Indochinese jigsaw. In 1955, with the French gone and Indochina fragmented, the Democratic Republic of Vietnam formed what are now the provinces of Son La and Lai Chau into the **Thai-Meo Autonomous Region**, later renamed the **Tay-Bac Autonomous Region**. As in the Viet-Bac Autonomous Region to the east, it

Tribal autonomy

allowed the ethnic minorities an element of self-government and their own representation in the **National Assembly**. So, Lai Chau became relatively detached and, today, though a province like any other in the country, it is even further out on a limb than it was a hundred years ago, now being the most extreme corner of Vietnam.

Hoang Lien Son Province

An old road follows the **Na valley** north of Lai Chau town, swings east to **Phong Tho**, and then south-eastwards into Hoang Lien Son province and the hill resort of **Sa Pa**. On the provincial border the road passes **Hoang Lien Son** (Mount Fansipan), Vietnam's highest mountain at 3,143 metres, which stands at the northern end of Hoang Lien Son range, the chain dividing the Red and Black river valleys. The road improves from Sa Pa to Lao Cai, the capital of Hoang Lien Son province, 296 km north-west of Hanoi.

Vietnam's highest summit

Lao Cai, a busy market town on the Red River, has always been a place of **strategic importance**. It guards the pass between China and Vietnam facing Hekou, just across the border, and it has long served as a junction on the old **Hanoi-Kunming railway line**.

A road links Lao Chai with the **River Chay**, the other side of the mountain range to the east. This flows south-east into the **Thac Ba**, a large dammed lake. Beyond is **Ha Tuyen** province.

The more accessible southern part of present Hoang Lien Son province was closer to the action in the delta region. Throughout history this area has acted as a buffer between Viets and the ethnic minorities in the hills, with the market town of **Yen Bai** serving as a meeting point of cultures. On the 9th/10th February 1930, members of the Vietnam Nationalist Party rose up and killed ten French soldiers and officials at Yen Bai. The incident sparked off further unrest and the French reacted by bombing villages - the first time they bombed from the air. **Nguyen Thai Hoc**, the ringleader, and twelve colleagues were captured and guillotined by the French in Yen Bai that summer. The **Yen Bai Uprising** was significant as it inspired further anti-colonial revolts.

Where cultures meet

The French cultivated cash crops in Hanoi's hinterland and Yen Bai, 147 km from the capital and also on the Red, was an important centre amongst their plantations. With its forecast expansion, the **museum** at **Van Chan** (formerly Nghia Lo), an administrative town deep in the hills to the west of Yen Bai, should house a very interesting section on the local tribes.

Return from the northern provinces

From Yen Bai the road, rail and river all pass through **Vinh Phu** province before entering Hanoi province.

125

SOUTH OF HANOI

Ha Son Binh, Ha Nam Ninh and Thai Binh Provinces

Highway One and the railway lead directly southwards out of Hanoi, and clip the eastern edge of Ha Son Binh province before entering Ha Nam Ninh province and the town of **Ha Nam** (Phu Ly) on the banks of the **River Day**.

Many shrines amongst strange mountains

Further up the River Day, amongst the magnificent, strangely shaped limestone mountains of the **Huong Son** range are numerous pagodas. Such awesome, enchanting country inspired the devoted to build shrines to their gods and heroes in the many caves, on the slopes and on summits of the mountains.

The most famous place of worship is the **Huong Tich Pagoda** (Chua Hong, or Perfume Pagoda), just across the provincial border, back in Ha Son Binh province. To reach this, go up the **River Yen**, a tributary of the Day, to a staging point from where it is a walk up the hill to the large stalactited-stalagmited grotto dedicated to **Ba Quan Am**, the Chinese Goddess of Mercy. The cave has long had an attraction for the faithful. **Le Thanh Tong**, the great 15th century emperor-scholar and author of the '*Dai Viet Su Ky*', the definitive history of Vietnam, called it '*Nam Thien De Nhat Dong*' ('The Supreme Cave Under the **Pilgrim's ascent** Vietnamese Sky'). Today, thousands still tread the pilgrims' path to pay homage up at the Huong Tich Pagoda and particularly to participate in the splendid **holy festivities** which take place during the second half of the first lunar month.

Back down at Ha Nam, the railway and road turn eastwards towards Nam Dinh, the capital of Ha Nam Ninh province.

Nam Dinh, 90 km from Hanoi near the southern bank of the Red, is the third largest city in the north after Hanoi and Haiphong. It is an **industrial centre** most famous for its **textile mill** which was founded by the French at the turn of this century. Limestone gouged from the rocky outcrops which dominate the western region of the province is used as building material. Remains of a **Tran Palace** site lie just to the north near the village of **Mac**, which is notable for its early 14th century **Pho Minh Pagoda**.

Across the Red is the small, densely populated **Thai Binh** province. Its provincial capital Thai Binh, is only 20 km from Nam Dinh. Several rivers of the Red River system, including the main stream of the Red itself, meet the sea in Thai Binh province and the province has **rich**

Below sea level

The wooden
pagoda

alluvial deposits which give excellent rice yields. Some
areas of the province are below sea level and a network of
dikes and canals, like those elsewhere in the delta region,
help prevent flooding.

Both Nam Dinh and Thai Binh have Tourist Offices and
there is a museum in Nam Dinh and there are several
pagodas in the vicinity. Most notable of them is the 12th
century wooden Keo Pagoda, with over 100 rooms and a
three-storey bell tower. It is dedicated to Khong Minh
Khong, a monk who cured Emperor Ly Than Ton of
leprosy. The main attractions however, are further west,
on the other side of Highway One.

A road and the railway head south-west from Nam
Dinh, covering the 30 km to the town of Ninh Binh, a
base - with accommodation - for those travelling into the
spectacular hills nearby.

The region is historically significant, being the centre
for the Dinh and Early Le Dynasties in the late 10th and
early 11th centuries.

Having raised his army, Dinh Bo Linh, the son of a
senior mandarin, systematically defeated the Twelve
Lords who ruled Vietnam after the Ngo Dynasty.
Establishing himself as emperor and taking the name
Dinh Tien Hoang in 968 AD, he shifted the capital from
Co Loa to Hoa Lu.

Death of an
enlightened
young emperor

The popular Dinh Tien Hoang had sufficient authority
to stabilise the army, and he promoted religious
institutions, building temples and pagodas, and under
him Vietnam looked set to flourish. Tragically, though, he
was assassinated in 980 when only 26 years old.

The remains of his capital of Hoa Lu, which covered an
area of 300 hectares between the hills and the River Day
just outside Ninh Binh, can be visited. The royal family
and their immediate entourage lived in the inner citadel,
while the outer citadel was used for court assemblies and,
at its various temples and pagodas, for worship.

A hero
remembered

The famous Dinh Tien Hoang Temple at Hoa Lu was
originally built in honour of the emperor in the 11th
century, though the very fine present structure dates
from the 17th century. The temple is a symbol for the
prosperous Vietnam which existed during early years of
the Dinh Dynasty. In an inner sanctum there are statues
of Dinh Tien Hoang and his young sons, who, like their
father, were eliminated in a messy battle for the throne.

It was Le Hoan, a senior general under Dinh Tien
Hoang, who came out on top. As Emperor Le Dai Hanh,
in 980, he replaced the Dinh Dynasty with his own

(Early) Le Dynasty. Hoa Lu remained the capital and Le Dai Hanh, having suppressed a Chinese invasion and established peace with China, turned his attention towards attacking the Champa Kingdom to the South.

The shortlived Early Le Dynasty was dislodged by the more successful **Ly Dynasty** whose founder, **Ly Thai To**, moved the capital to Thang Long (Hanoi) in 1010.

After 28 years Hoa Lu's status as the centre of Vietnam was over and the city was never to regain its initial importance. Today, admirers pay homage to Dinh Tien Hoang at his temple and a festival commemorating the emperor is held here between the 15th and 20th days of the second lunar month. Emperor Le Dai Hanh and his family are also remembered at Hoa Lu, at the **Le Dai Hanh (Le Hoan) Temple**.

A few kilometres to the south of Ninh Binh a turning to the right off Highway One, leads to **Tam Coc** where local girls provide a **ferry service** in their **coracles** across a lake, along channels, and through tunnels hung with stalactites. The nearby **Bich Dong**, a hill with **three tiers of pagodas**, which was once shelled by the French who discovered it was a sanctuary for the Viet Minh, is often incorporated into excursions to Tam Coc.

Journeys through stalactited tunnels

Penetrate deeper into this dramatic limestone hill country and you will reach the **Cuc Phuong National Park**. Created in the early 1960s, the park preserves in their freedom dozens of species of animals, scores of species of birds and thousands of species of insects and plants, some of which are unique to Vietnam.

The south-east of Ninh Binh is the Catholic centre of **Phat Diem** (Kim Son), near the final reach of the River Day where, during the colonial times, aspiring Vietnamese prelates were taught the imported religion. A curious **cathedral**, with an architectural mixture of Eastern and Western styles, was built in Phat Diem earlier this century.

From Ninh Binh, Highway One and the railway pass through **Tam Diep** on their southward path into Thanh Hoa province.

An elephant statue stands guard at the Doc Pagoda in Hue.

The picturesque One Pillar Temple in Hanoi.

The Cham temple in Nha Trang.

Lush vegetation surrounds a Khmer temple in the Mekong.

TRUNG PHAN

Trung Phan, also known as Trung Bo, Turn Ky or Mien Trung, is central Vietnam, the long narrow curve stretching from Thanh Hoa province in the north to the end of the mountains in Song Be and Dong Nai provinces in the south. This is the rod which balances Vietnam's two baskets of rice (see page 86).

Vietnam's long narrow stretch

The region is dominated by the **Truong Son Mountains** which include the plateaux of the Central Highlands. In their shadow, squeezed between them and the South China Sea, is the narrow coastal plain, occasionally broken by mountain spurs protruding to the water's edge.

Rice is the main crop grown on the plains, though the soil is not as fertile as that of the Red or Mekong deltas and, by the sea, **salt** is collected in the lagoons. Up in the hills, inhabited predominantly by the ethnic minorities, are **plantations** where tea, coffee, timber and various fruits are grown as **cash crops. Da Lat** serves as a market gardening town for Ho Chi Minh City and the coastal cities. There is also some rearing of **livestock**. The tribes in the more remote regions are involved in **slash and burn farming**.

EARLY HISTORY

Cham country

Culturally, Trung Phan was once dominated by the Chams who, at the end of the 2nd century AD, created their great and highly Indianised **Champa Kingdom**. At its height this spread from present **Binh Tri Thien** province in the north to **Dong Nai** and **Song Be** provinces in the south.

The *Chams* were constantly at war with the *Viets* to their north and the *Khmers* to their south and eventually they succumbed to the Viets, who captured their capital of **Indrapura** in 1402, taking the new capital of **Vijaya** 70 years later. Confronted by this wave of Viets, the Chams continued to retreat southwards and by the end of the 17th century the Viets had colonised the entire Champa Kingdom. The Chams did retain several quasi-autonomous pockets, but these were sad remnants of a once splendid kingdom. In 1822, the last of their kings, **Po Chon**, finally ceded his throne.

TRAVELLING IN TRUNG PHAN

Vietnam's main communication artery, **Highway One**, runs along the coastal plain linking Hanoi and Ho Chi

Minh City. Another route ascends from **Hoi An**, just south of **Da Nang**, into the hills and joins the old **Route 14**, an upland road running parallel to the Highway One. This passes through Contum, Pleiku, Ban Me Thout and

Route along the central highlands

south of Da Lat before descending from the Central Highlands to **Ho Chi Minh City**. Several east-west routes link these two main roads, providing communications between coast and hills.

A **railway** follows much the same course as Highway One between Hanoi and Ho Chi Minh City, supplying an important **freight and passenger service**. The rail line from Phan Rang up to Da Lat has long been abandoned, though there is talk of restoring it for use.

While central Vietnam has no major waterway like the Red or the Mekong, it does have numerous smaller rivers which flow from the mountains eastwards, onto the plains and into the sea. They are channels for local transport. Board a **sampan** at the old imperial city of **Hue**, for example, and slowly drift down the **Perfume River** to the lagoons and the South China Sea beyond.

NORTHERN TRUNG PHAN

Thanh Hoa Province

Bim Son, the first town along Highway One you reach on entering Thanh Hoa province from Ha Ham Ninh province, has a large **cement plant** built with the assistance of the Soviets.

40 km down the road, across the **Ham Rong Bridge** over the River Ma, is **Thanh Hoa**, the **provincial capital** and industrial city, where they handle - amongst other things - the chromium deposits from nearby Co Dinh. Thanh Hoa has a Tourist Office and **accommodation**, though it is of little interest in itself. 12 km away, however, is **Sam Son**, its beach resort, with several **guest houses**. There is a temple on and fine views from **Mount Truong Le** at the southern end of the beach.

Stone age man

At **Nui Do**, a hill on the other side of Thanh Hoa, archeologists discovered stone axes and various other tools from the paleolithic era and have pronounced the **Nui Do Civilisation** as the earliest **stone age culture** in Vietnam.

Indeed, much evidence of Vietnam's earliest civilisation has been unearthed in the limestone caves in mountains around here. The most famous site is **Dong Son**, just west of Thanh Hoa city, which dates back to the **bronze ag**e and gives its name to a culture which existed between the 7th century BC and the 3rd century AD and inhabited quite a large area of northern-central Vietnam. The highly decorated, flat-topped, mushroomed-shaped **bronze drums** they used during funeral ceremonies are the most spectacular specimens of the Dong Son craftsmanship and fine examples of them can be seen at **Dong Son culture and their bronze drums** the **main museums**, along with other bronze artifacts of the age. The Dong Son peoples were part of a wider civilisation which spread from China down to Indonesia and the discovery of other such drums elsewhere in this sweep of land has helped the experts piece together various East Asian bronze age cultures.

A more recent site is the huge **Tay Do Citadel** at **Yen Ton** which was built as a major defence by **Ho Quy Ly**, the founder of the **Ho Dynasty**, at the turn of the 15th century. The Hos' rule was shortlived as they succumbed to Ming Chinese invaders, who ostensibly attacked to replace them with the Tran Dynasty, but in effect went on to annexe Vietnam as a province of China.

Chinese rule was beset with immediate hostility and it was **Le Loi**, who came from **Lam Son**, a village in the hills some 60 km north-west of Thanh Hoi city, who inspired the revolt against the Chinese. His long and bitter **Lam Son Uprising** eventually repelled the Chinese and in 1428 he became emperor, adopting Le Thuan Thien as his regal name and founding the Le Dynasty. Le Loi remains one of Vietnam's great national heroes under his more famous posthumous title **Le Thai To**.

The coastal plain in Thanh Hoa province is narrow and Highway One continues southwards through hilly countryside before re-entering the flatter lands of **Nghe Tinh** province.

Nghe Tinh Province

At **Dien Chau** a road heads westwards into the remote hills to **Do Luong** a junction of routes, follows the valley of the River Ca, then heads up to **Ky Son**, through the **Deo Noong De** (the Barthelemy Pass) into Laos and the Plain of Jars. This has long been an important trail to landlocked Laos.

Home of the resistance fighter While the Lam Song Uprising was one of the greatest revolts in Vietnam's history, Nghe Tinh province was the most fertile breeding ground of resistance fighters.

Ho Chi Minh
Ho Chi Minh, the most celebrated of all Vietnam's rebels, was born Nguyen Singh Cung - the first of his many

Ho Chi Minh's birthplace

names - on 19th May 1890 at **Sen** (Kim Lien), a village 13 km west of **Vinh**, the provincial capital.

Nearby, at **Chua** (Hong Tru), is his mother's house which can also be visited. Ho went on to study at Hue, like his father, who was a **Pho Bang** (Doctor of Literature), and then embarked on his extensive world travels in 1911. He came back to Vietnam in 1941 and returned to his native village on two occasions - in 1957 and 1961 - before his death in 1969. His old house has been restored and looks the same as it did when he was a lad. It is a place of pilgrimage for Vietnamese.

Phan Boi Chau

Born in 1867, Phan Boi Chau was another son of Nghe Tinh province and a passionate anti-colonial. He spent most of his years as an activist abroad, in Japan and China, where he organised like-minded ex-pat Vietnamese into revolutionary bodies such as the **Vietnam Quang Phuc Hoi** - the Association for the Restoration of Vietnam. He was arrested in Shangai in 1925 and sent back to Vietnam, where the government, not wanting to make a martyr of him, encouraged him to work alongside them. He refused, but by now he was politically subdued and he ended his years under a sort of house arrest near Hue, where he died in 1940.

Vinh

Like all industrial towns of the North, Vinh was badly bombed by the Americans during the Vietnam War, but Vinh, on Highway One and the **centre for routes west** into Laos, suffered particularly terrible damage. The present modern buildings are drab and give the place a shabby air. There is a hotel here, though it probably preferable to stay at **Cua Lo**, the **beach resort and fishing village** 12 km out of town, where there is accommodation by the sea along with a Tourist Office.

From Vinh the railway cuts further inland before following the river valleys and a more southward course. One crosses the **Rivers Lam and Nghen**, passes through bleak sandswept terrain to **Ha Tinh**, where a road leads

Road to the Ho Chi Minh trail

into the hills to **Khe Ve**, becoming what used to be the northernmost part of the **Ho Chi Minh Trail** (see page 136) and continuing through the **Mu Gia Pass** into Laos.

Highway One, following the coast path runs between **Cape Mui Ron** on the left and **Dong Chua** a hill on the right, and climbs gradually up **Hoanh Son Mountain**, a 1044 metre high spur of the Truong Son range, which juts out into the sea. From here, it leads through the **Ngang Pass** (Annam Quan), the Gateway to Annam. The Hoanh Son Mountain has been a natural barrier throughout history, serving as a division between the Viets and the Chams and, later, between the Trinh and Nguyen Lords. The Ngang Pass has therefore always been a significant strategic path.

The gateway to Annam

Binh Tri Thien Province
After the pass the road descends, with the sea immediately to the left, down to Binh Tri Thien province. Beyond a flat, narrow coastal plain stretches for some 275 km, ending at the **Bach Ma Mountain** which, like the Hoanh Son, has long been a geographical frontier between armies and peoples.

The **railway** crosses the provincial border only 25km east of Laos, returning towards the plains through the **Rao Nay** valley, and rejoining the path alongside Highway one at **Bo Trach**, 15 km up the coast from **Dong Hoi**, which is on the **River Nhat Le**.

Dao Duy Tu, a prominent military advisor to the Nguyen Lords in the early 17th century, built defensive walls - the **Dong Hoi Wall** and the **Nhat Le Wall** - on either side of the River Nhat Le as protection against the Trinhs. Cannons fired down onto the channel and iron chains slung between the walls hung down to the water, serving as a further defence against vessels trying to proceed upstream to the port.

Dong Hoi was badly destroyed by the Americans during the Vietnam War and today, through rebuilt, it appears to those just passing through as a drab, depressed place. Paddies, a rich green wherever they are, can often belie their true quality. Here, along this stretch of coastal plain, you realise the workers have to struggle hard in the fields to gain sufficient yields of rice. The nature of the soil aside, impoverished further by sand and salt blown from the shore, the peasants' task is made all the more difficult due to poor irrigation and the non-availability of adequate tools.

Statistics worked out after the Vietnam War revealed that the Americans had dropped half a ton of bombs per head of Vietnam's population. In Binh Tri Thien, probably more than elsewhere in Vietnam, **undiffused bombs** lie unnoticed in the fields, a hazard to the farmers. Hundreds of Vietnamese have already been killed and maimed after unwittingly detonating the explosives and the number of deaths continues to rise. But the old bombs

Hazard of undetonated mines

are also a **source of income** and people are prepared to risk life and limb to salvage them for scrap, which is taken to the coast and exported to the Japanese, who then manufacture it into cars and then sell them to the Americans. The cycle is thus completed.

Life under ground

The **subterranean tunnels** and chambers at **Vinh Moc** were built in 1965 to provide safe living quarters during the intense American bombing. Classrooms, dormitories, assembly rooms, even a mini-hospital were carved at different levels under the earth and 17 babies were born here, the locals proudly tell visitors.

The Vietnam War was merely the bloodiest and more recent of the numerous battles which have been slogged out over the centuries along the narrow neck of Trung Phan. The enemies have also been many: Viets versus the Chinese; Viets versus the Chams; Trinhs versus Nguyens, followed by Tay Sons versus Trinhs and Nguyens - both internecine conflicts; Vietnamese versus French and then the Japanese; and , finally, Viet Cong and the North Vietnam Army versus the South Vietnam Army and the Americans.

The 17th Parallel

The frontier between the two sides during the last of these conflicts was the River **Ben Hai** (the Hien Luong) which runs west to east more or less along the 17th parallel. The **Demarcation Line**, as it was known, was established on 22nd June 1954 after talks at the **Geneva Accords**. Its initial purpose was to serve as a ceasefire line between the rival factions of the North and South until elections to decide the ruler of a united Vietnam were held. There was a period during which citizens could travel in either direction to the side they preferred.

Line between north and south

The elections were never held however, and as a result Vietnam slipped into a civil war which escalated into what is known as the Vietnam War. The Demarcation Line remained the divide between North and South until the Northerners captured Saigon in 1975 and re-united Vietnam as one country.

There was a 5 km buffer zone - the **Demilitarised Zone** (DMZ) - on either side of this line. Highway One passes through the former **Vinh Linh Special Zone** (the North's half of the DMZ) and over the simple one-lane **Gio Linh Bridge** across the muddy **Ben Hai** into the old South. There does not seem to be any monument or special plaque to commemorate this historic spot and the river, the bridge and the surrounding country are much the same as the others in the region. However, it is empty and has a chilly, eerie atmosphere. So much death and maiming took place around here during the Vietnam War that this place, the most poignant symbol of this ridiculous war, will be eternally haunted.

I Corps

The Americans split the South into four military divisions - I to IV Corps - with I Corps being the northernmost region from the DMZ approximately to the 15th parallel.

The 'Frontline'

Action in I Corps intensified in 1967 and the Americans increased their military presence along their side of the DMZ, further defending their bases in **Quang Tri** region and along **Route 9**, which ran from Dong Ha inland through Cam Lo, past **Camp Carroll** - named after Captain James Carroll, an early fatality here - and **Rockpile**, a strategic look-out point, to Ca Lu, Khe Sanh and on to Laos.

Here the American Marines and other troops countered Vietnamese infiltration from the North. They built a base at **Khe Sanh** from where they could attack the Vietnamese enemy who were harbouring in Laos and, hopefully, disrupt traffic on the **Ho Chi Minh Trail**. They could defend Route 9, the road which had once served the French as their link between the coast and the Mekong in Laos and would provide the North with a path into the South should they capture it.

The American hills

Late in 1967 the North Vietnamese advanced from the west along Route 9 towards the US 26th at Khe Sanh, and from the north towards the 'Hills' - Hill 881 North, Hill 881 South, Hill 861, Hill 558, etc, - which formed a line of American defence before the Khe Sanh camp.

The North's ensuing **siege at Khe Sanh** was viewed by many as the Americans' Dien Bien Phu with the US Marines surrounded by the enemy, as the French had been fourteen years before. The fundamental difference though was, that the Americans, unlike the French, had massive military support, especially from the air. **Operation Niagara Falls** was one of the most ferocious bombing campaigns ever known in history.

10,000 of the North's soldiers died at Khe Sanh compared with only 500 or so American dead. Despite such a gigantic disparity in the death tolls, it is a moot point as to who was the victor. For the North this battle was just one episode in a far larger campaign, for it was intended to attract the Americans to this spot during the build up of the **1968 Tet Offensive** (see page 77).

For the Americans this northern quarter of the South remained very much the frontline. From 1967 onwards, half of all their soldiers killed died in I Corps and half of those fell in and around the DMZ.

South of Khe Sanh, just east of Laos border, lies **A Shau**, a valley in these rugged uplands where the Communists stockpiled munitions and other stores. In May 1969 the Americans' 101st Airbourne Division attacked the enemy stronghold entrenched on **Ap Bia**, the western ridge of the valley. They suffered heavy causalities, men were blown apart and their bodies reduced to pulp; hence the nickname, **'Hamburger Hill'**.

Excursions arranged by the Tourist Office in **Hue** take visitors via **Dong Ha**, along the old **Route 9** to Khe Sanh, now known as **Huong Hoa**, which has been neglected and abandoned to Nature. Nearby is a section of the Ho Chi Minh Trail, 'Hanoi's Road to Victory', which is viewed, understandably, with more pride.

Marginal notes: Communist base

THE HO CHI MINH TRAIL

Known today as the Truong Son Trail

This was a network of some 2000 km of roads and tracks running from the North through the densely forested, mountainous Truong Son range down as far as Son Be and Tay Ninh provinces in the South. The Trail was the crucial **North-South link** for both NVA and Viet Cong, the way along which the North could transport weapons and other provisions to their colleagues fighting in the South. The main avenue followed Vietnam's border with Laos and Cambodia, often in these neighbouring territories, and from it supply paths led eastwards to the Communist bases.

The Vietnamese started cutting the Trail in the 1950s with 75,000 men, women and children providing the labour. It was a remarkable feat of sheer manpower and endurance and it should have served as a sign and warning of the extremes these people would go to in their fight. Initially the goods were man-carried, as they had been during the Dien Bien Phu campaign. The most dextrous workers were lauded. **Nguyen Viet Sinh**, for example, became a **'Hero of the People's Armed Forces'** after lugging 45-50 kg of supplies on his back during each trip over a period of four years - 1089 working days. They estimated he walked 41,025 km and carried a total of 55 tonnes.

Later bicycles were used and then the thousands of lorries given by the Chinese and Russians rumbled along the Trail. Its many routes covered an area 800 km long by 50 km wide and they became a major target for the Americans, who destroyed the natural forest canopy, which camouflaged the roads, and expended enormous amounts of dollars on Hi-Tech devices and firepower in their unsuccessful attempt to sever this lifeline. Sophisticated warfare was foiled, damage repaired and the cause upheld - as ever.

The war over, the Ho Chi Minh Trail has been returned to Nature which is covering it with a protective blanket of foliage. The Trail may soon be lost to Man, but here in Vietnam, where death is not a conclusion, it will be immortalised in poetic legends and remembered forever.

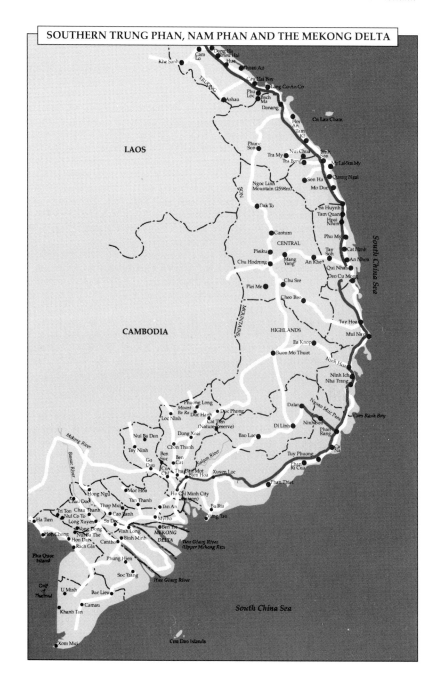

SOUTHERN TRUNG PHAN, NAM PHAN AND THE MEKONG DELTA

Cua Tung
Back on the Ben Hai, 12km downstream is Cua Tung, the
'Gate to the Sea', described by local guidebook: *'Cua Tung
. . . the "queen of beaches" in Vietnam on account of its
original beauty. Eight tongue-like strips of red basaltic land
covered with lush trees and plants jut out into the sea like the
teeth of a tortoise shell comb sticking into the supple platinum
hair of the East Sea waves'.*

Queen beach

During the Vietnam War the communications
terminated at the respective borders but today, Highway
One and the railway continue southwards through **Gio
Linh**, 10 km from the river and the first/last South
outpost on the road, with **Con Thien**, another American
post, just to the west. **Dong Ha**, a further 10 km down the
road, was an American base, as was **Quang Tri** - now
called Trieu Hai - 15 km beyond.

By the end of 1971 the number of American troops in
Vietnam was down to 140,000 and with the opposition
sufficiently weakened the North and the Viet Cong co-
ordinated a massive drive into the South. On 30th March
1972 their army crossed the DMZ and on the 1st May
they captured **Quang Tri**. The South's forces and tens of
thousands of citizens fled down Highway One which
became dubbed **'The Highway of Terror'**, as the
Communists countered retaliation from the sea and air.
These events prompted the Americans to mount their
highly destructive bombing campaign against the cities of
the North.

**South bound
exodus**

The North did not have the resources to continue their
southward thrust, and in September they lost Quang Tri.
After all the fighting, the city had been reduced to rubble.

From **Trieu Hai** (Quang Tri) Highway One and the
railway continue onto Hue.

LA VANG BASILICA

Canh Thinh, the Tay Son ruler at the turn of the 19th century, started to
persecute the Catholics after the French missionary **Bishop de Behaine** lent his
support to **Nguyen Anh** (Gia Long) in the bid to oust the Tay Son Dynasty.
The **Virgin Mary** appeared before the beleaguered **Quang Tri Catholic
community** in 1798, reassuring them that she would provide protection. Other
visions of the Virgin were seen during Minh Mang's purges and in 1900 the
faithful finally built their **La Vang Church**. However, the number of devotees
had been underestimated and in 1924 a new church was built to accommodate
the large congregation. The La Vang Basilica became a centre of worship for
Catholics from all around Vietnam, and it continues to attract pilgrims despite
being destroyed by the bombings of 1972.

HUE

Beautiful Hue

Hue is Vietnam at its most sublime and most beautiful. Situated on the banks of the **Perfume River** (the Song Huong), Hue is 680 km from Hanoi and 1075 km from Ho Chi Minh City, approximately halfway down the country. The **South China Sea** is 12 km to the north-east and **Laos**, visible as the highest mountains to the south-west, is only 55 km away.

In 1306 a Viet princess was despatched south to the Champa court where she married **King Jaya Simhavarman III**. As a dowry, she earned from her father the provinces of O and Ry. The new acquisition was renamed **Thuan Hoa** and from 'Hoa' was derived Hue.

Hue did not reach prominence until much later however. The **Nguyen Lords**, rulers of the South between 1558 and 1778, chose **Phun Xuan**, 2 km south-west of present Hue, as their seat in the 17th century, and in 1802, its real golden era began after **Gia Long** had ousted the **Tay Sons** and established it as the capital of all Vietnam.

Royal capital

Hue remained the **royal city** under the **Nguyen Dynasty**, only losing that status after Bao Dai abdicated in 1945.

The French divided Vietnam into Tonkin, Annam and Cochin China at the end of the last century and Hue became the capital of **Annam**. The emperors continued to reside in their imperial city on the north bank, while the colonials set up their administrative headquarters in grand white mansions on the south bank. Under the French, **Hanoi** and **Saigon** - capitals of Tonkin and Cochin China respectively - rapidly developed into large, thriving commercial cities. Hue did not. For the **French** it was an **administrative centre**, while most of the industry and trade of the region took place at cities elsewhere along the plains.

So Hue remained enchanting. The splendid royal structures and the lovely setting were not obscured by factories or a huge population. The **Americans** however,

Military base

turned Hue into a military base and the city and its historic monuments were badly damaged during the course of the Vietnam War.

During the **1968 Tet Offensive** the Viet Cong captured the imperial city and subsequent American retribution proved devastating. Along with vestiges of their royal inheritance, the people of Hue also lost 2800 (a U.S. figure, the Vietnamese quote a lower number) fellow citizens, aside from those killed in warfare. Assassinated and dumped in mass graves by Northern forces they were suspected, often on no evidence, of being sympathisers of the enemy. The Vietnamese may dispute the actual number, but they do not deny that the slaughter took place and they now regard it as one of the most regrettable incidents they were responsible for in the Vietnam War. On the battlefield the Communists lost over 5000 troops in the Tet Offensive, some ten times the toll suffered by the enemy - a fact commemorated by the **Ba Tanh** and **Ba Don monuments**.

Preservation by decree

Fortunately enough of Hue's historic past has survived to give the visitor a fair taste of the Nguyen emperors' royal capital and, today, these relics are protected by a UNESCO charter.

Nguyens' Hue

THE NGUYEN EMPERORS	
1802-1819 Gia Long	*1884-1885* Ham Nghi
1820-1840 Minh Mang	*1885-1889* Dong Khanh
1841-1847 Thieu Tri	*1889-1907* Thanh Thai
1848-1883 Tu Duc	*1907-1916* Duy Tan
1883 Duc Duc	*1916-1925* Khai Dinh
1883 Hiep Hoa	*1925-1945* Bao Dai
1883-1884 Kien Phuc	

The Citadel and Imperial City

'The royal city of Hue, which he (the emperor) makes his constant residence, has been the object of his greatest solicitude, for more than twenty years; during which period he has lavished immense sum, and sacrificed the lives of thousands of his subjects, by keeping them at labour, without intermission, upon its ramparts. It is situated upon a barred river, accessible to large vessels at high water only. It is surrounded by a ditch nine miles in circumference, and about one hundred feet broad; its walls are of brick, laid in cement, of which sugar is the principle ingredient, and are sixty feet high; over the arches, the pillars of the gates, which are of stone, are seventy feet high; over the arches, which are of the same materials, are towers from ninety to one hundred feet high, to which access is had by a handsome flight of stairs, on each side of the gateway inside the walls. The fortress is of a quadrilateral form, and built on the plan of Strasburg in Germany. It has twenty-four bastions,

Royal protection

each mounting thirty-six guns, and the distance between each bastion is twelve hundred Cochin Chinese perches, of fifteen feet each; the smallest guns are eighteen pounders, and the largest are sixty-eight pounders, cast in the king's own

Detail from bronze urn at the Citadel, Hue.

Bomb protection

foundry. The whole number of guns to be mounted, when the works are completed, is twelve hundred. The casements within the fort are bomb proof.

'One hundred thousand men are constantly employed upon the works, and it will require, when finished, forty thousand troops to garrison it. It is now nearly completed'. John White (1819)

Emperor Gia Long, the first of the Nguyen emperors, commenced the construction of the present Citadel and Imperial City soon after coming to the throne in 1802. Most of the building programme was completed over the next three decades.

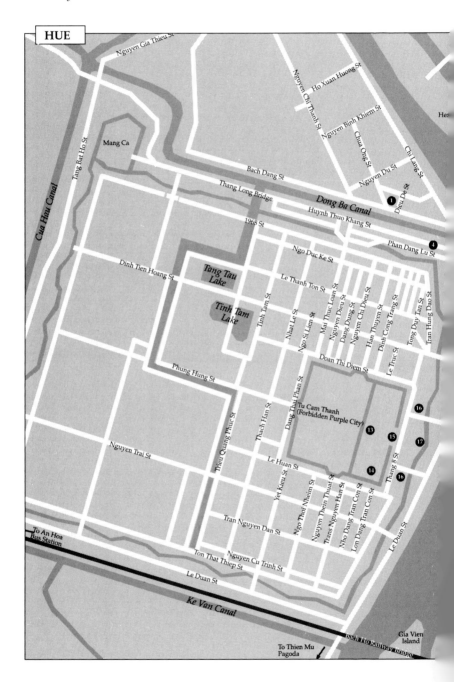

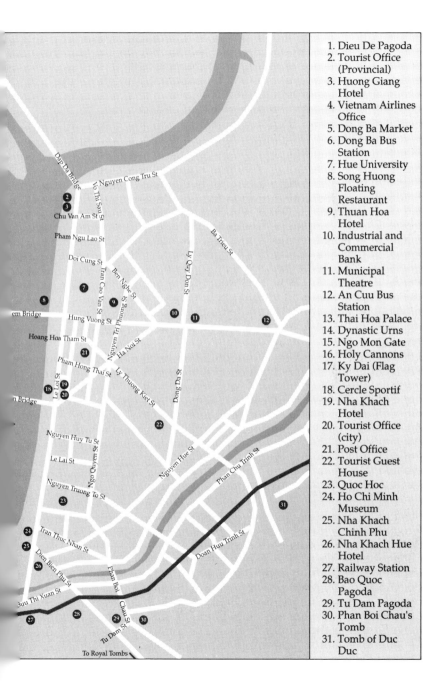

1. Dieu De Pagoda
2. Tourist Office (Provincial)
3. Huong Giang Hotel
4. Vietnam Airlines Office
5. Dong Ba Market
6. Dong Ba Bus Station
7. Hue University
8. Song Huong Floating Restaurant
9. Thuan Hoa Hotel
10. Industrial and Commercial Bank
11. Municipal Theatre
12. An Cuu Bus Station
13. Thai Hoa Palace
14. Dynastic Urns
15. Ngo Mon Gate
16. Holy Cannons
17. Ky Dai (Flag Tower)
18. Cercle Sportif
19. Nha Khach Hotel
20. Tourist Office (city)
21. Post Office
22. Tourist Guest House
23. Quoc Hoc
24. Ho Chi Minh Museum
25. Nha Khach Chinh Phu
26. Nha Khach Hue Hotel
27. Railway Station
28. Bao Quoc Pagoda
29. Tu Dam Pagoda
30. Phan Boi Chau's Tomb
31. Tomb of Duc Duc

The **site of the citadel** was originally occupied by eight villages, whose inhabitants received generous compensation from the emperor when he had them relocated. Today there are some residential quarters within the grounds.

The Citadel surrounds the Imperial City, *Dai Noi*, with its deep moat and high, solid, 10 km long **Kinh Thanh wall**. This is straight on three sides while the fourth, the south, curves to follow the bend of the Perfume. It was initially made of packed earth, but in 1818 Gia Long had the south, west and north sides lined with a layer of bricks. The wall is 2 metres thick with two dozen cannon sloops and ten fortified gates and, at the south side, the 37 metre high **Ky Dai** look-out flag tower. Surrounded by a moat 30 metres wide and 4 metres deep, it served as a formidable defence in the days before modern weapons.

Deep moat, high wall

Gia Long had the **Nine Holy Cannons** cast in 1803 from brass captured from the Tay Sons. The cannons represent the five elements of Earth, Fire, Water, Wood and Metal and the four seasons - Spring, Summer, Autumn and Winter. Their 5 metre long barrels bear the story of how the brass was acquired. Though never fired, the cannons were the symbolic protectors of the Emperor and the Nation.

The imperial complex faces south-east. Directly in front is the Perfume River symbolising the 'Clear Pond', on the left and right are the **Hen** and **Gia Ven islands** (the 'Green Dragon' and 'White Tiger' respectively). Beyond, on the far bank some 3 km away, is **Mount Ngu Binh** the 'Imperial Front Screen' which shelters the city from evil spirits and bad weather.

The symbolism of the setting

The Ngo Mon, the Royal Gate, is the main entrance, built by Minh Mang in 1834, but extensively repaired early this century. The **Ngu Phung** (Five Phoenix) **pavilion** is above the principle gate and it was from here that the emperor overlooked the official ceremonies.

Through the Ngo Mon you cross the **Emperor's Bridge** over the lotus pond and enter the **Dai Trieu Nghi**, the Great Rites Courtyard. This leads to the **Thai Hoa Palace** (the Palace of Supreme Peace) where the emperor, sitting with suitable majesty upon his golden throne, would hold audience. Only fellow royalty could join the emperor in the throne palace itself and the ministers, mandarins, generals and others were restricted to the courtyard, where they were segregated according to their position in the hierarchy, the divisions being demarcated by stellae on the palace steps. Luckily the palace survived

Golden throne

the Vietnam War undamaged and the **red lacquer and gold designs** on the ceiling, the **carved beams and poles** remain intact. The **golden throne** stands on a dais in the centre of the room.

Inner sanctum
Beyond the Thai Hoa Palace another wall encompasses the inner sanctum of the **Tu Cain Thanh**, the Forbidden City or Purple Imperial City. This was the exclusive domain of the royal family, though mandarins were admitted to discuss state affairs. This quarter of the Imperial City was the most severely bombed by the Americans and their colleagues. The remains are in different states of ruin or repair and locals can point out the Harem, the Royal Apartments, the Reading Palace, the Mandarin Lodge, the Theatre, the Flower Garden, and the various ponds. Photos on display show the palace during its pre-Tet days and the present rubble and bullet marks speak for themselves. Despite all the destruction the grounds of this inner palace, haunted by ghosts of the Nguyen emperors and the Viet Cong freedom fighters, are still worth wandering.

Grandmother's residence
Leaving the Forbidden Palace by its northern gate you reach an attractive tree-lined avenue. Following it to the left you arrive at the **Truong Sanh Palace** (the Grandmother's Palace) built by Minh Mang in the shape of the Chinese character Vuong. Next to it, the **Dien Tho Palace** (the Everlasting Longevity Palace) was constructed by Gia Long for his mother. Continuing southwards you pass the **Dien Phung** and **Hung Mieu temples** before entering the courtyard of the **Mieu (Generation) Temple**, where the Nguyens would worship their ancestors. The temple remains in good condition and houses statues and effects of various emperors.

The royal's bronze urns
In front of the Mieu Temple are nine huge bronze Dynastic Urns, the **Cuu Dinh**, which date back to Minh Mang's rule and weigh between 1500 and 2400 kg. The largest of them, standing in the centre, is dedicated to Gia Long. Ornately cast on the urns are images of the sun and moon and aspects of Nature signifying the union of the Universe and Earth under the Nguyens. Heading east you return to the Dien Thai Hoa and the Ngo Mon. The old **Museum of Hue**, opened in 1923 in Emperor Thieu Tri's palace, is just to the west of the Imperial City.

The Citadel encompasses a large area and parts of it are very attractive, notably the picturesque **Lake Tinh Tam**, a tranquil spot which was greatly enjoyed by the Nguyen Emperors.

NGUYENS' PAGODAS

In death, as in life, the Nguyen emperors were ensconced in splendour. Their tombs are palatial pagodas amidst **fragrant gardens** cut out of the luxuriant banks of the Perfume.

These mausoleums were usually designed during the lifetime of the emperor, thus allowing him to approve the plans and die reassured of a conducive resting place. They tend to have several common features.

Surrounded by a wall, the entrance leads into a **courtyard** paved with *Bat Trang*, a local brown brick. Here, standing to attention, are rows of **stone statues** of mandarins horses and elephants. The **military mandarins** are depicted with a round hat and holding a sword, while the **civil mandarins** have square hats and carry a bar to symbolise their positions. Near is the **pavilion of the stele**, where, chiselled on a piece of marble, are the emperor's achievements as told by his successor. Beyond is the **shrine** where emperor and possibly his empress are worshipped. This also includes personal effects used by him during his secular existence. Nearby are the **concubines' and servants' quarters** and finally, the tomb itself surrounded by a high wall.

In addition to this formula, which varies in style from pagoda to pagoda, an emperor may have chosen to construct other rooms, pavilions, ponds and even a theatre to keep him entertained while he supervised the building of his eternal abode.

Gia Long's Tomb

Nguyen Phuc Anh was the Nguyen Lord who fought a 15 year campaign against the **Tay Son**, finally bringing about their downfall with the aid of the French in 1802. He renamed himself Gia Long when he became **Emperor of Vietnam**. Once in power he stabilised the country and developed the administration, legal codes, the worship of Confucianism, education and literature. He died aged 59.

Gia Long's pagoda was built between 1814 and 1820 and lies 16 km from Hue, on the west bank of the **Song Ta Trach**, a tributary of the Perfume. It is now in a poor state of repair, nevertheless, it is the resting place of the Nguyens' first emperor and one of the most significant men in Vietnam's history and it has an air of strength and greatness, despite its relative simplicity. The complex is surrounded by **three dozen man made mounds** and **groves of pine**. A little far out of town and less spectacular than some of the other more accessible pagodas, Gia Long's tomb is not frequently visited by tourists.

Peace after life

Minh Mang's Tomb

Gia Long's successor Minh Mang keenly **promoted the Vietnamese culture** amongst his people, partly as a response to the increasingly influential Christian missionaries whom he purged, fearing they would undermine the nation's traditions and gain too great an authority over the Vietnamese. The emperor died at the age of 50.

Minh Mang had his mausoleum constructed 12 km from Hue, just below the confluence of the **Huu Trach** and the **Ta Trach**, the two main streams of the Perfume, and 4 km downstream from the tomb of Gia Long, his father and predecessor on the throne.

Work on Minh Mang's tomb began in 1840, the year the emperor died, and was completed three years later by his **Delightful tomb** son, **Emperor Thieu Tri**. It is the most enchanting of the imperial pagodas, not least because of its beautiful setting amongst **lotus ponds** and sweet smelling **shrubs** and **trees**. The various buildings are richly decorated but not ostentatious, typically bearing **carvings of dragons** and a menagerie of other animals. Anyway, the loveliness of the garden and the **magnificent landscape** beyond the compound - the orchards, the Perfume, the mountains in the distance - would detract from any excesses in the embellishments.

The journey itself is part of the attraction of an excursion to Minh Mang's pagoda as it entails a **sampan ride** from Hue up the Perfume River or a **car or bike ride Pleasant outing** to the village of Ben Tuan on the east bank, followed by **up the Perfume** crossing in the locals' **wooden ferry** to the tomb on the west bank. The latter route is preferable if you wish to incorporate the later imperial pagodas into your itinerary.

Thieu Tri followed similar policies to his father, Minh Mang, though his attitude towards Christianity was not so belligerent. He did, nevertheless, hold a French bishop captive in Hue and in 1847 the French navy responded by shelling Da Nang (Tourane). It was the first direct military action by the French against Vietnam.

The **tomb of Thieu Tri** is 7 km from Hue. He died at the age of 37 having reigned only seven years. The tomb is of a similar pattern to his father's pagodas, although more modest and not in such a delightful location.

Tu Duc's Tomb
Just north of Thieu Tri's pagoda is the tomb of his son, Tu Duc. It was Tu Duc who renewed Minh Mang's fervent **purge against missionaries** and thus gave the French their excuse to invade Vietnam. Faced by too great an enemy, Tu Duc gave the French possession of southern provinces, but in doing so he unsuspectingly opened the door for the complete **colonisation of Indochina**.

Tu Duc was a poet and academic and his pagoda reflects a characteristic serenity. The emperor was tormented not only by the French, whose ambitions he did try and contain, but also by **local uprisings** initiated by peasants from whom he seemed detached and whose causes he seemed not to understand. Indeed, the **expense of the lavish pagoda** Tu Duc built for himself angered many citizens who dubbed it the 'ten thousand year home', and it inspired an uprising led by three local brothers, which, though contained, did make clear the peoples' feelings. The pagoda was completed in 1867, sixteen years before Tu Duc's death at the age of 55.

Over indulging for the after life

Tu Duc would retire to his pagoda for weeks or months at a time and cut himself off from the turmoil of his kingdom. Here, within the walls, he had a **pavilion** built overlooking the water lily and lotus-filled **Luu Khiem Lake**, where he would relax and listen to the musicians who played in another smaller pavilion.

Next to the lake a flight of steps leads up to the heart of the tomb complex. There are the usual features: an **Honour Courtyard** with the carved stone figures; a **stele**, the largest in Vietnam at 4 metres high, engraved with an account by Tu Duc himself in which he admits some of the mistakes he made during his reign; the emperor's and empress' shrines - the **Hoa Khiem** and **Luong Khiem temples** respectively; the **emperor's tomb** enclosed within a wall by the **Half Moon Lake**; and on a pine-covered hillock nearby, the **tombs of his empress and of Kien Phuc**, his adopted heir.

Alongside the Hoa Khiem is the **Minh Khiem Duong**, Tu Duc's theatre where such marathon plays as the 100-day long *Van Buu Trinh Tuong* were performed. Nearby is the **Chi Khiem Duong**, the chamber dedicated to the concubines.

A sad air at Tu Duc's tomb

Tu Duc, ever conscious of his failure to halt the French, became increasingly self-deprecating and he suffixed almost every name in the pagoda with *'Khiem'* - a word meaning 'insubstantial' or 'modest' - to reflect this feeling. A Hue poet has described the mausoleum as a place where *'grief smiles and joy sighs'* and these words could be a fitting epitaph for Tu Duc himself.

The Later Nguyens

Tu Duc was succeeded in 1883 by **Duc Duc**, his nephew, who was forced to abdicate after only a few days of rule by his courtiers. His tomb is just south of Hue, between the city centre and Mount Ngu Binh, but is of minor interest. **Hiep Hoa**, Tu Duc's younger brother, was next to the throne, but the senior officials who had won him the emperorship also forced him to resign and, on 29th November 1883, he committed suicide.

Kien Phuc, Tu Duc's adopted son, became the seventh Nguyen Emperor at the age of fifteen. He fared better than his two predecessors, surviving on the throne for seven months before being pushed aside for the even more youthful **Ham Nghi**. Kien Phuc is buried in the Tu Duc Pagoda complex.

Ham Nghi's reign lasted only a year. In July 1885 he launched an attack against the French, who, though based in Hue, had not as yet claimed rights to the city. The uprising was suppressed and the **French**, viewing the incident as sufficiently provocative, moved in and **captured Hue**. Ham Nghi was forced to run and for three years he waged a battle of resistance against the French, before being betrayed to them by a local chief. He was **exiled to Algeria** where he died in 1947.

The French manipulated the line of succession and placed **Dong Khanh** on the throne in 1886. However, he died in 1888 and was buried just to the north of Tu Duc. Built in 1889, the **Dong Khanh Pagoda**, 7 km from Hue is relatively small, but it is attractive and elaborately designed in places. The emperor's personal effects are displayed alongside his shrine.

Dong Khanh was succeeded by **Thanh Thai**, the ten year old son of Duc Duc, whom the French released from prison, where he had been detained with his mother, and declared him emperor. By now the French had a stranglehold on the Vietnamese, who were forced to cede Tourane (Da Nang), Haiphong and Hanoi during Thanh Thai's reign. Furthermore the colonials forced Thanh Thai to relinquish his throne in 1907 as they found out he was plotting against them. Thanh Thai was **exiled to Reunion Island** in 1915, though he was allowed to return to Vietnam in 1947. He died in Saigon in 1954.

Thanh Thai was followed to the throne in 1907 by **Duy Tan**, his eight year old son. Like his father, Duy Tan was a nationalist and in 1916 he conspired with revolutionaries to overthrow the French. Plans of the coup were discovered on the eve of the uprising and the French were able to round up and execute the ring leaders while the young Duy Tan was **deported to Reunion Island**. The ex-emperor became a major in the Allied army during World War II and was killed in a plane crash in 1945.

Khai Dinh's Pagoda

Khai Dinh, a son of Dong Khanh, inherited the emperorship in 1916 after the departure of Duy Tan. Unlike his two predecessors he was weak and was malleable in the hands of the French, who became increasingly dominant during his nine years reign. Khai Dinh was more of a extravagant hedonist then a statesman and his pagoda, started in 1920 and completed ten years later by his son, reflects something of his character.

The Khai Dinh Pagoda, 10 km from Hue and **near Ben Tuan**, the ferry point to Ming Manh's pagodas, is grandiose, flamboyant, and ostentatious. Unlike his ancestors, who chose gracious buildings and celestial gardens for their burial ground, Khai Dinh wanted a very forthright statement of majesty.

Ostentatious even in death

Built on the side of the hill, you climb flights of steps up the **six steep tiers** to Khai Dinh's shrine. **Stone dragons** form the balustrades and the **stone mandarins** in the **Rites Courtyard** stand in rows looking like life size chess men. The exterior, while decorated with fanciful carvings, is sombre and restrained compared to the **altar and tomb chambers** at the summit of the pagoda.

Here every centimetre of the interior, from the floor to the ceiling, is decorated with colourful, highly polished inlays of glass and semi-precious stones, with lacquer, with paintings, embroidery and scripts. The designs relate to Vietnamese folklore and typically the dragon is most evident. On top of the tomb sits a life-size bronze statue of Khai Dinh upon his stately throne. These final three main halls are splendid in their excessive garishness.

Khai Dinh's was the **last of the Nguyens' pagodas**. He was succeeded in 1926 by **Bao Dai**, his twelve year old son, who became a puppet of the French and was forced to abdicate by the Viet Minh when they won independence on 25th August 1945. He later became Chief of State of South Vietnam though he lost this position to **Ngo Dinh Diem** in 1955 when the country became the Republic of Vietnam. Bao Dai left Vietnam and returned to Paris, where he had studied as a boy. He still lives in France.

The hapless Bao Dai

Other Attractions In and Around Hue

Hue has scores of pagodas and, along with those dedicated to the Nguyen Emperors, the one of greatest interest is the **Thien Mu** (Linh Mu) **Pagoda**, on the north

Sculpture at Khai Dinh tomb, Hue.

bank of the Perfume, 3km upstream of the Imperial City.

In 1601 **Nguyen Hoang**, the first Nguyen Lord of the South, was visited by an apparition of an elderly fairy who advised him to build a pagoda on this site near the bend in the river. This was a vision not to be ignored and Nguyen Hoang constructed a Buddhist pagoda using old Cham building bricks and called it Thien Mu which means **'Fairy Woman'**.

Pagoda by the Perfume

The Thien Mu Pagoda is the **oldest building in Hue**, but it began to fall into disrepair and at the turn of the 18th century **Nguyen Phuc Chu**, who was famed for **colonising of Cham and Khmer territories** and for the 146 children he fathered, had it fully restored. There are

Vietnamese children in Hue.

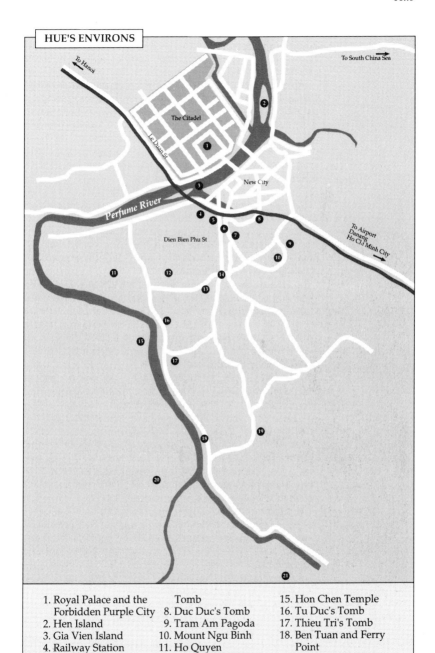

HUE'S ENVIRONS

To Hanoi

To South China Sea

The Citadel

Le Duan St.

New City

Perfume River

Dien Bien Phu St

To Airport
Danang
Ho Chi Minh City

1. Royal Palace and the
   Forbidden Purple City
2. Hen Island
3. Gia Vien Island
4. Railway Station
5. Bao Quoc Pagoda
6. Tu Dam Pagoda
7. Phan Boi Chau's
   Tomb
8. Duc Duc's Tomb
9. Tram Am Pagoda
10. Mount Ngu Binh
11. Ho Quyen
12. Tu Hieu Pagoda
13. Dong Khanh's Tomb
14. Nam Giao
15. Hon Chen Temple
16. Tu Duc's Tomb
17. Thieu Tri's Tomb
18. Ben Tuan and Ferry
    Point
19. Khai Dinh's Tomb
20. Minh Mang's Tomb
21. Gia Long's Tomb

153

many statues of Buddhas, some ancient and of great craftsmanship, and a **bronze gong** cast in 1674 by Frenchman Jean de la Croix.

From the central courtyard the three entrances of the **Cong Tam Quan gate** guarded by large colourfully painted reliefs of figures, lead to the outer garden. Here there are several **kiosks**, the **Great (2200 kg) Bell** cast in 1710 by Nguyen Phuc Chu, and **stelae**. One on the back of a marble turtle recalls the expansion of Buddhism in Hue, another tells the story of why Gia Long decided to build his Citadel at its particular site.

Dominating the whole scene is the 21 metre high octagonal **Phuoc Duyen Tower** (the Tower of Happiness and Grace) which was built by **Emperor Thieu Tri** in 1844. You can climb up the ever-narrowing stairway to the top of its seven storeys. Enshrined at each level is a small figure of a Buddha and from the windows there are **fine views over the Perfume**.

In Saigon on 11th June 1963, **Thich Quang Duc**, a 73 year old **senior Buddhist monk** from the Thien Mu Pagoda, had himself doused in petrol by a fellow monk from Hue and set alight. His **self-immolation** was a protest against the discrimination of Catholic President Ngo Dinh Diem and his family against the Buddhists. Thirty other monks and nuns followed Thich Quang Duc's example. These deaths were a major embarrassment to the Americans, Diem's patrons, and were a reason why they had the president and his brother killed on 2nd November 1963.

Malcolm W. Browne's photo of the enflamed Thich Quang Duc was one of the most poignant images to come out of Vietnam during this era. **The monk's Austin**, seen in the background, is now in a garage in the grounds of the Thien Mu Pagoda with a print of the famous black and white photo stuck on the windscreen.

A flight of steps lead from the Thien Mu complex down to the edge of the Perfume.The promenade alongside the water is a popular spot with courting couples who step out at sunset when the bend in the river glows under a golden sky.

Upstream, about halfway to Minh Mang's pagoda, is the **Hon Chen (Jade Cup) Temple**, dedicated to **Po Nagar** and the **Water God** who, surely, can have no prettier abode than this. A **festival** is held here on the 15th day of the 7th lunar month.

On the **east bank** within this bend in the river, is the **Ho Quyen**, an arena where the Nguyen Emperors would

A tower with a view

A vivid image of the war

Further riverside sights

Animal fights

pitch elephants against tigers in gladiatorial combat. There are other pagodas, temples and relics from the Nguyen era between here, the city centre and Mount Ngu Binh which lies to the east. These include: The **Tu Hieu Temple**; the **Bao Quoc Temple**; the **Tu Dam Temple**; the **Eunuchs' Graveyard**, alongside their temple, which was funded by their cult at the end of the last century to ensure their remembrance after death; the **Nam Giao** - a sacrificial altar where the emperors would perform rites to the Gods of Earth and Crops – built on a hillock by Gia Long in 1806; the **Phan Boi Chau Memorial House**,

An old fighter's prison

where Phan Boi Chau, one of Vietnam's great freedom fighters spent his last 15 years under house arrest, dying here in 1940. Finally the 103 metre high hill, **Ngu Binh**, which, like the Perfume, is a symbol of Hue, and the **Tra Am Temple** in its evening shadows. From the mount you overlook the city and surrounding country, the core around which so much of the culture and destiny of Vietnam has been shaped.

Nostalgic views of Hue

Vietnamese from all over the country and the world have a romantic vision of Hue. It is their imperial city, the place where the emperors refined culture by supporting the arts - literature, poetry, acting, cuisine, gardening, sculpture, painting, lacquerware and other crafts. Hue became the centre of Buddhism and of learning, and the **Quoc Hoc** (National Studies) in the city centre is the most famous school in Vietnam boasting a long list of illustrious alumni including presidents Ho Chi Minh and Ngo Dinh Diem. Nearby is the **Ho Chi Minh Museum** and at the other end of Le Loi and the pretty riverside corniche, is the prestigious **Hue University**.

Le Loi, a straight, wide, long, boulevard running along the south bank, is the main avenue in the **modern quarter** of town developed by the French. Their colonial administrative buildings have been inherited by the Vietnamese government and their villas by local officials.

Colonial quarter

The former **Cercle Sportif**, a sports club-cum-recreational centre on the edge of the Perfume River, is still in use. At night, the young hold dances on the moonlit rooftop verandah and at dawn, they swim in the river here on their way to school.

Cau Phu Xuan, the crossing for Highway One, and the older, more famous, frequently bombed **Cau Trang Tien** are the bridges spanning the Perfume, connecting the newer town with the Imperial City. The railway bridge **Cau Bach Ho**, is further upstream.

Just downstream of the Imperial City is Hue's main

ACCOMMODATION
The best of Hue's accommodation is on the right bank of the Perfume River and best locations are along the Le Loi waterfront. There is a minor development-restoration boom in hotels and guest houses and sampan-houseboat accommodation will possibly be introduced soon.

Huong Giang *(Perfume River), 51 Le Loi, Tel: 2122*
Modern hotel popular with the Americans during the Vietnam War. It is on the right bank of the Perfume with a splendid view along the river, especially at sunset. At night the sampans' lanterns look like floating candles. The Huong Giang's new annexe is a block up river.

Thuan Hoa *7 Nguyen Tri Phuong, Tel: 2553, 2576*
A short walk inland from the Huong Giang.

Alternatively there are a growing number of villas and former royal/colonial residences opening their doors as 'garden guest houses'. These include:

Tourist Guest House, *Ly Thuong Kiet*
Nha Khach Chinh Phu, *5 Le Loi*

Also on the long Le Loi riverfront are the **Nha Khach Hue Hotel**, (*2 Le Loi* - station end) and **Nha Khach** (*18 Le Loi*).

RESTAURANTS
There are many restaurants in Hue, but it would be a pity not to take advantage of the beautiful setting. **The Song Huong Floating Restaurant** is on the Perfume just downstream of Trang Tien bridge. Further upstream, by the Phu Xuan bridge, is the **Cercle Sportif**, while downstream, there is the top floor restaurant at the **Houng Giang Hotel**. Though not by the river, the **Thuan Hoa's** restaurant is also recommended.

TOURIST OFFICE (Provincial)
51 Le Loi (by the Huong Giang Hotel) Tel: 2369
Opening: 7-11.30 and 13.30-17.00

TOURIST OFFICE (City)
18 Le Loi, Tel: 3577
Opening: Same as above

Dong Ba Market. Of all Hue's specialities probably the best know is the **poem hat**. It is similar to the conical palm leaf and bamboo hat, the '*non bai tho*', found all over the country, but, hold it to the light and you see that designs and poems have been stencilled out of one of the layers of leaves. Beyond the market is the **Dong Ba Canal**, the old 'Sampan Alley', the traditional moorings for thousands of sampan dwellers. On the far side are the

Sampan alley

BANK
Industrial and Commercial Bank (Nhan Hang Cong Thuong)
2a Le Guy Don, Tel: 3275
Opening: 7-11.30 and 13.30-16.00
Money can also be changed at the Huong Giang Hotel.

POST OFFICE
7 Hoang Hoa Tham
International telephone calls can be made at the Huong Giang; they also have a telex service.

MUSEUMS
Opening times for Royal Tombs and sites are usually *5.30-17.00*.

TRANSPORT
Railway Station
At the bottom (upstream) end of *Le Loi; tel: 2175*. Ticket office opening hours: *5.30-17.00*

Bus Stations
An Cuu Bus Station: For transport heading southwards. Situated by the corner of *Hung Vuong* and *Ba Trieu* in the south-eastern part of town.
An Hoa Bus Station: For transport heading northwards. Situated to the west of the Citadel.
Dong Ba Bus Station: For local transport. Situated on the left bank near Trang Tien Bridge.

Airport
Phu Bai Airport is 14 km south of town. There are weekly services to Hanoi and Ho Chi Minh City on Vietnam Airlines, whose Hue offices are at *16 Phan Dang Luu (Tel: 2243)* on the left bank.

ENTERTAINMENT
There are a couple of theatres, the **Nha Hat Thanh Pho** and the **Hung Dao** in Hue and the Tourist Office has a list of their programmes. These may include *Hat Boi*, classical Vietnamese theatre. Traditional dances are also sometimes performed for tourists at the **Huong Giang,** or you can go dancing at the old **Cercle Sportif.** However, many a pleasant evening can be spent wandering the banks of the Perfume and dining at one of the floating restaurants, where they specialise in Hue's local dishes.

Dieu De Temple and the old residential area of **Gia Hoi.**

Sampans and Cycles
While the Imperial City can be reached on foot from the south bank, the Nguyens' Pagodas - and most other sights - are out of walking range. Tourist buses or taxis can take you to the places of interest, though it is more fun and less expensive to hop on sampans and cycles and

Discovery Guide to Vietnam

see what you want to see in your own time. The Tourist Office can advise you on where to find your transport and give you an idea about how much to pay. Moonlight sampan rides, sometimes with serenading musicians, were popular with Westerners in the olden days.

In Hue everybody seems to be into poetry and the **sampan oarsmen** have their own poems and songs, *ho hue*, which they chant as they row. The powerful, quick tempoed *ho mai day*, for example, is sung when the course is difficult and requires much energy, while the *ho mai nhi* has a gentler, slower beat and is sung when the pace is more leisurely.

In rhythm with the flow

Thuan An Beach and Other Beaches

Thuan An is 14 km out of town and can be reached **by road** or, preferably, **by sampan** down the Perfume. The river route meanders past islands and the small settlements along the lush banks down to a lagoon and then out to the sea. The journey takes either 30 minutes or two hours, depending on whether you take the motorised or non-motorised sampan. There is a lagoon beach and also a lovely 6 km long sandy sea beach. At present the only accommodation is the **Tan My Hotel**.

Way to the sea

From Thuan An you can continue by sampan for 30 km south-eastwards down the lagoon to the **Tuy Van Pagoda** and **Cau Hai Bay** - a large bay with a small exit to the sea. There are other beaches along the way, by the lagoon and by the sea. Cau Hai Bay can also be reached by road. Beyond the headland, 65 km from Hue, is **An Co** which also has lovely beaches.

Continuing Southwards

Highway One and the railway run alongside each other out of Hue, past the local airport, **Phu Bai** and **Cau Hai Bay** before heading for the spectacular **Bach Ma range**. Further inland about 55 km from Hue, off Highway One, is the village of **Bach Ma** which stands at an altitude of 1220 metres and was developed by the French as a small hill resort, for use in the hot summer months.

After the village of **Phu Loc**, Highway One ascends a hill, while the railway tunnels underneath, and then descends to paddies and continues on, always in the shadows of the Bach Ma Mountains, to the bay at **An Co** and the **Lang Co beach**. This is one of the most beautiful spots along the coast, an island-peninsula where the white sands of the **palm-fringed beach** stretch for kilometres eastwards out into the sea. Villagers fish, collect fruits from their **luxuriant groves and orchards,** and the food they prepare is delicious.

Road and railway follow the base of the hills, taking their own scenic paths southwards across the Bach Mas' most defiant barrier. The railway's shoreline route is more circuitous and passes through tunnels, while Highway One climbs a winding path up the **Hai Van Pass,** the 'Pass of the Ocean Clouds', a strategic avenue throughout history. Up here, the Nguyen Lords built their defensive towers, the French their pillboxes and the Americans their bunkers.

Defending the high pass

The Bach Mas once served as a boundary between Viets and Chams and, today, they divide **Binh Tri Thien** and **Quang Nam-Da Nang** provinces. The Hai Van Pass is 20 km long and from its highest point the panorama is magnificent. Towards the south you see the hill peninsula of **Son Tra** on the left, the **Bay of Da Nang,** the city itself and the rest of Quang Nam-Da Nang province stretching beyond.

QUANG NAM-DA NANG PROVINCE
Da Nang
After the spectacular Hai Van Pass, Highway One meets up once again with the railway and two routes follow the bend of the Da Nang Bay into Da Nang city.

Da Nang, 90 km south of Hue and 965 km north of Ho Chi Minh City, is **provincial capital** of Quang Nam-Da Nang. It is situated at the mouth of the **Han River,** on the shores of the Da Nang Bay, its port protected from the South China Sea by hilly Son Tra peninsula.

The city was once known as **Cho Han** (Market of the Han). The French changed this to **Tourane,** before the Japanese changed the name again to Da Nang when they occupied Vietnam in World War II.

Da Nang has the rather unfortunate distinction of being the **'Gateway of Colonisation'.** In 1847 the French naval vessel *Victorieux* under the command of **Captain Le Pierre** entered Da Nang harbour and shelled several Vietnamese ships. The reason for doing so was to bully **Emperor Thieu Tri** into releasing a French bishop who was held captive in Hue.

French point of entry

This was merely a **foretaste of French aggression,** for in September 1857 the French navy returned, captured Da Nang and went on to conquer Indochina. The city remained very French in character during the century-long colonial era, though flavoured with a dash of

Japanese in World War II. When the French went they were replaced by the Americans who intensified their involvement in Vietnam and, on 8th March 1965, they landed their first combat troops - two marine battalions - on Vietnamese soil at Da Nang, where they were assigned to protect the military air base.

Da Nang, the second largest city in the South, became an **important military base** from where the Americans launched forays into the hinterland and flew bombers deep into the North. And, as a strategic base, it was also a **target for the Viet Cong** whose most dramatic attack was during the 1968 Tet Offensive.

Seven years later as the North's army marched south towards Saigon, tens of thousands fled down Highway One fearing death at the hands of the Communists. Hue fell on the 26th March; Da Nang was the next in line. There was pandemonium as South Vietnamese tried to escape before the arrival of the Northern army. People waded out to sea and fought each other to secure places on vessels heading south and when, on the 29th March, American World Airways sent a Jumbo as airlift support, hundreds raced across the tarmac hell-bent on getting themselves out of Vietnam. Many died and numerous families were separated for ever. Da Nang was quick to fall and by the end of the 30th March the Communists had won the city.

Death while fleeing

The Champa Kingdom

The Da Nang region was also the entrance for invaders in more ancient times. This was the northern part of the great Indianised Champa Kingdom which evolved at the end of the 2nd century AD and even then **Hai Van** was the traditional border between the Viets and Chams. The Champa kingdom, encompassed a long stretch of the coastal plain which was divided into four zones: **Amaravati** - from Binh Tri Thien into Quang Nam-Da Nang province; **Vijaya** - Nghia Binh province; **Kauthara** - Phu Khanh province; **Panduranga** - Thuan Hai province.

Ancient Hindu capitals

Indrapura ('City of the Spirit of Thunder') at Dong Duong, 60 km south of Da Nang, was the Champa capital until 1000 when it proved more and more susceptible to Viet and Chinese invasion. The Chams shifted the centre of their kingdom to **Vijaya**, further to the south, and in 1402 they ceded Indrapura to the increasingly dominant Viets. The Cham archeological sites near Da Nang - Tra Kieu, My Son, Dong Duong - have yielded great riches, of which many are now housed in Da Nang's **Museum of Cham Sculpture**.

Traditional transportation on the Red River.

The railway cuts through scenic countryside north of Haivan pass.

Public transport in Vietnam.

A view of Ho Chi Minh City from the Saigon River.

THE CHAMPA SITES

Tra Kieu
40 km southwest of Da Nang in the Thu Bon River valley, this was the site of **Simhapura** (the Lion Citadel), one of the Chams' oldest capitals, which existed during Bhadravarman Dynasty towards the end of the 4th century. Nothing remains of the citadel or the temples and buildings it once enclosed, but the old trenches indicate the size of the structure and artifacts found here are now displayed in the **Museum of Cham Sculpture**.

My Son
28 km west of Tra Kieu, this is a 140 km round trip from Da Nang. My Son was a religious centre also built in the late 4th century by the Bhadravarman kings. Being a highly Indianised culture, the Chams prayed to Hindu gods and this complex was dedicated to **Shiva**, their 'patron god'. The site was known as **Srisanabhadresvara** and scores of structures were erected over the century. During the Vietnam War however, this area was held by the Viet Cong and the Americans deemed it a free-fire zone; their bombs destroyed many of the old buildings. The most impressive remaining example of Cham architecture is the tall 10th century **My Son Tower** and its surrounding half dozen smaller towers. My Son is a bit of a slog to get to, but this is one of the best Cham sites, despite American destruction, and it gives an idea of the civilisation's art over the centuries. The Tourist Office can advise on and arrange excursions.

Don Duong
60 km south of Da Nang, this site covers a large area and includes the broken vestiges of shrines, temples, and monasteries including the **Monastery Laksimdra-Lokesvara**, the divine guardian of the king.

The Champa Museum

Cham remnants

Artifacts from Champa sites are displayed at the **Museum of Cham Sculpture**, near the river on **Duong Tran Phu**. This was founded by the *Ecole Française d'Extreme Orient* in 1916. Some 300 pieces of sculpture succinctly reveal the rise and fall of Cham art showing the impact of outside influences at different eras. A booklet *'Museum of Cham Sculpture'* produced by the Foreign Languages Publishing House in Hanoi is available at the museum and serves as an excellent guide to the different galleries. Opening hours: *8.00-11.00 and 13.00-17.00 daily.*

Champa Art
• *Early Tra Kieu Style* (late 7th century)
The earliest Cham stone art dates back to the 7th century. Previous works may have been fashioned out of wood which disintegrated over time. Tra Kieu was in **Amaravati** and most of the pieces were discovered in this

Tales from the sub-continent

northern region. The Chams had been 'Indianised' long before and the **carved sandstone altar** depicting the great Hindu epic, the *Ramayana*, reveals the extent of the Indian influence. The altar depicts in detail famous scenes from Princess Sita's wedding: Prince Rama being granted Sita's hand by her father; the envoys informing Rama's father of the event; the wedding itself - which, besides the Rama-Sita union included the marriage of Rama's three brothers to Sita's three cousins; and the *asparas* (dancing girls) presenting flowers to the couples.

• *An My Style*
The An My site is in present Tam Ky district, some 30 km south of Tra Kieu, and the artifacts found here show a fusion of Indian, Cham and other South-East Asian styles such as the Mon-Dvaravati. They show the **transition** from the Early Tra Kieu to the later My Son El eras. A hallmark of An My type is the human statue with spiralling tumbling hair, almond-shaped earrings, wide open eyes curved at the corners, thick lips and long straight noses.

• *My Son El Style* (8th and 9th centuries)
The Cham regions and clans united in the 8th century, to the benefit of their art, and the My Son El style is a combination of the previous early Tra Kieu and An My styles. For a time craftsmen were influenced by Mathura-Gupta Indian, Khmer and Thai styles, but then the Indian model gradually made way for the more indigenous, southern-generated Cham style, though the **Hindu symbols** still remained very evident. The 60 cm high sandstone **Ganesh** (the Hindu elephant god), is an interesting example from this period. Some pieces show faces with slanting eyes, heavy brows, big nose and thick lips which altogether seems a curious physiognomic melange.

Indian influence

• *Dong Duong Style* (late 9th and early 10th century)
The Champa rulers had shifted the capital to the southern Panduranga region in the late 8th century, however **King Indravarman II** moved it back to **Indrapura** in the late 9th century and here he built his **Laksmindra-Lokesvara Buddhist monastery**. By now Buddhism had spread and was becoming increasingly accepted in South-East Asia. The Chams adopted the *Mahayana* sect of the faith and combined it with their belief of Shiva and ancestor worship. Their statues of this period reveal both Hindu

and Buddhist aspects, with the latter style becoming more dominant by the 10th century. There are also **sculpted figures** of deified Cham kings and **stone altar carvings** depict the life of Prince Siddharta (the Buddha) from his birth in the gardens of Lumbini. The most refined and elegant piece however is the 114 cm high **bronze statue of Lokesvara**, the spiritual guardian of King Indravarman II.

• *Khuong My Style* (early 10th century)
Sculpture during this period adopted some of the old Tra Kieu and My Son El styles, as well as characteristics of Khmer and Indonesian art. For example there is influence from the Khmers' **Koh-ker** style where the faces are heavy, the men have moustaches, the lips are thick and eyes are wide and open. The head-dress is fancy and the costume is a *sampot* with a frontal flap hanging from the waist to the feet.

Khmer influence

• *Late Tra Kieu Style* (late 10th century)
By now, the Chams had developed relations with the **Javanese** and copied aspects of their art, though once again they turned mainly to their much cherished Early Tra Kieu and My Son El art for inspiration. The Late Tra Kieu era became something of a golden period in Cham sculpture and the most celebrated pieces from this time are the beautiful **sandstone dancing girls** with sensual, supple figures bent in the *tribhanga* position; their headdresses with the *Kirita-Mukuta* are quite unique. The carving of **stone animals** also returned to vogue, with deer being frequently represented.

Revival of animal art

• *Chanh Lo Style* (11th century)
The Chanh Lo style inherited many of its traits from the Late Tra Kieu period. However, these were unsettled times and art did not flourish. Chanh Lo, the site where many of the artifacts from this period were found, is 150 km south of Da Nang.

• *Thap Man Style* (12th to 14th centuries)
The Champa capital was moved south to **Vijaya** in the 11th century and, during this era, there was a fusion of the different styles of art as the Chams, Viets and Khmers were each influenced by the others' works. Two aspects of the Thap Man Style which feature off and on throughout Cham history are the portrayals of **animals in stone** and the Chams' founding goddess **Uroja** (meaning female's breast).

• *Yang Mum Style* (late 14th into early 15th century)
Cham art had started to decline in the 14th century,
however, the Yang Mum style appeared briefly. **Statues**
found in the highlands of **Gia Lai-Contum region** reveal
a strong Khmer influence. One distinguishing feature of
these sculptures is the placing of the legs which are
hidden behind the flap of the *sampot*.

Decline of Cham art

After the Yang Mum Style Cham art waned and during
the 18th century it disappeared almost completely.

Around the corner from the museum, south down
Duong Phan Chu Trinh, is the **Tam Boa Pagoda**. Continue
and you reach *Duong Nguyen Van Troi* which leads onto
the busy bridge of the same name which crosses the Han
to the thin spit of land between river and sea. The road
branches to the left and leads up to the **Son Tra**
peninsula, with the radar screens on top of the hill, while
the right fork goes to the **Ngu Hanh Son** and the **Marble
Mountain**, some 8 km from Da Nang.

Ngu Hanh Son Mountains
A cluster of five limestone mountains, the Ngu Hanh Son
are known as the Five Ritual Elements: **Mount Thuy**
represents water; **Moc** is wood; **Tho** is earth; **Kim** is

Craftsmen at the Marble Mountains

metal and **Hoa** is fire. At the foot of the hills craftsmen
chip at chunks of stone and marble, shaping them into
figures of gods and heroes. It is an ancient occupation in
these parts and the final pieces are on sale to visitors.

Two steep-stepped paths ascend Mount Thuy. The
longer of the two leads to **Tam Tai Pagoda**, the other to
the **Linh Ung Pagoda**, an ancient shrine which was
restored by Minh Mang in 1826 and further renovated in
1975. Here devotees worship **Quan Am** - the Goddess of
Mercy; **Pho Hien** representing forgiveness; and **Van Thu**
- signifying wisdom.

Many of the grottos in the Ngu Hanh Son serve as
shrines and the most spectacular is the vast, 30 metre
high **Huyen Khong Cave** in Mount Thuy, near to the
Tam Tai Pagoda. Originally a Brahamanic temple during
the Cham times, it was later dedicated by the conquering
Viets to the Buddhist deity, **Sakya Muni**. More
impressive than works of holy art is the **cave** - a
geological masterpiece in itself. A guide uses a torch to
illuminate the statues of the revered, though the best time
to visit is the late morning when maximum light
penetrates the darkness of the grotto.

Freedom fighters used these caves as a refuge during
their wars and they are remembered by plaques and by

guides who reverentially read anecdotes about their
heroes' courageous deeds against superior enemies.
Down below, within easy view of the hills, American
soldiers would take a break from the war to go
swimming in the sea.

Grottoes and pagodas aside, it is a pleasant climb up
Mount Thuy and, from various vantage points, there are
fine panoramic views over beach and sea.

Da Nang's **main beaches** are on this stretch of shore,
between Ngu Hanh Son and Nui Son Tra. They are **Bai
Tam My Khe** and **Bai Tam Non Nuoc** which has a hotel.
The more sheltered **Bai Tam Thanh Binh** is on the other
side of town in the Bay of Da Nang.

*Down to the
beach*

Downtown Da Nang

The French developed the **docks at Da Nang** at the end of
the last century after it became evident that the old port
of Hoi An, just down the coast, could no longer
accommodate the larger ocean-going vessels.

There is a section of the port on the western bank of the
Han, near downtown Da Nang, and it is an interesting
stroll along the **riverside promenade**, which has been
named *Duong Bach Dang* after the river near Haiphong
where the Vietnamese scored a couple of their greatest
ever victories. The wide, tree-lined corniche with its
decaying colonial buildings and old shipping and
chandlers' offices evokes the city's French past. The
Tourist Office is on Duong Bach Dang, near the ferry
crossing, and there are **several restaurants** overlooking
the river.

*Colonial
corniche*

The city's main market, **Cho Han** (Da Nang's early
name) occupies a block off Duong Bach Dang and backs
onto *Duong Tran Phu*, a main downtown thoroughfare
with the imposing all-white **cathedral**. Built for Da
Nang's French community in 1923, medieval in style and
complete with stained glass saints, this is a stark symbol
of Catholicism, forerunner to colonialism, here in the
town which was the first to fall to the French. Today, the
cathedral serves several thousand local Catholics.
Opposite is the **Hai Chau Hotel** and a short walk further
down are the **Tu Do** and **Kim Do** restaurants. Elsewhere,
in the neighbouring streets, are the previously named
Orient and **Pacific** - the best hotels in town, the city's
theatre, other restaurants and most of the shops. **Cho
Con**, another **important market** is near the railway line at
the other end of Duong Hung Vuong from Cho Han.

*Monument to a
foreign belief*

DA NANG FACTS

ACCOMMODATION

Da Nang's two best hotels, American favourites, the Pacific and the Orient, stand opposite each other in the heart of town. There is other downtown accommodation as well as lodgings which are scattered further afield, especially to the north of the city. Alternatively there is a beach hotel on the way to Marble Mountain.

Phuong Dong Hotel (The Orient), *99 Phan Chu Trinh, Tel: 22654, 21266*

Thai Binh Duong Hotel (The Pacific), *80 Phan Chu Trinh, Tel: 22137, 622921*

Hai Chau, *Duong Tran Phu, Tel: 22722*
A couple of blocks down from the Orient in the direction of the river. Recently built and less expensive than the big two.

Song Han, *26 Duong Bach Dang, Tel: 22540*
A quieter, more pleasant location by the River Han, a few blocks north of the waterfront Tourist Office and the city centre.

Non Nuoc, *Non Nuoc Beach, Tel: 21470*
A modern beach hotel on the old China Beach (American name for Non Nuoc Beach) near Marble Mountain.

RESTAURANTS

Besides the hotel restaurants there are the popular **Tu Do** at 180 Duong Tran Phu (down the road from the Hai Chau) and the nearby **Kim Do**. There are also other downtown restaurants. Alternatively, on the Duong Bach Dang waterfront are the **Seaman's Café** and the **Thanh Lich**, both a short distance downstream from the Tourist Office.

TOURIST OFFICE (Da Nang Tourism)
48 Duong Bach Dang, Tel: 21423
Opening 7-11.30 and 13-16.30, Monday to Saturday

POST OFFICE
46 Duong Bach Dang
Telephone and telex services available. Opening: *5-20.30 daily.*

BANK
Foreign Trade Bank, *48a Le Loi*
Opening: *7.30-11.30 and 13-15.30 daily except Thursday, Sunday and Saturday afternoon.*

TRANSPORT
Bus
The terminal for long distance buses is a few kilometres to the west of town.

Train
The railway station is northwest of the city centre, on Duong Haiphong.

Air
Three flights a week, in each direction, between Hanoi and Ho Chi Minh City stop at Da Nang airport. **Vietnam Airlines** are at *35 Duong Tran Phu (Tel: 21130).*

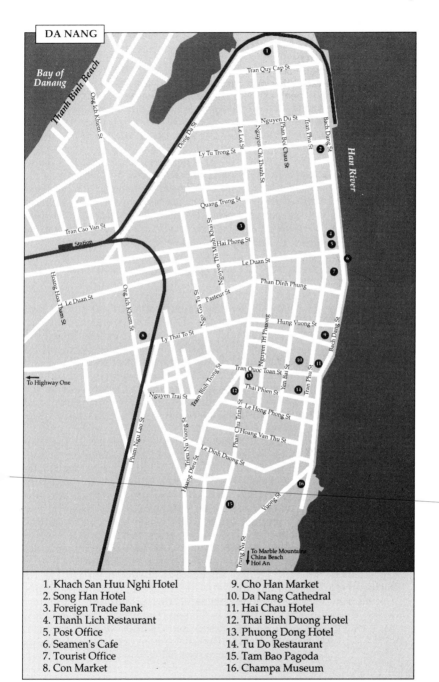

| DA NANG |

Bay of Danang

Thanh Binh Beach

Han River

Tran Quy Cap St

Nguyen Du St

Tran Phu St

Bach Dang St

Phan Boi Chau St

Le Loi St

Nguyen Chu Thanh St

Ly Tu Trong St

Dong Du St

Ong Ich Khiem St

Quang Trung St

Nguyen Thi Minh Khai St

Hai Phong St

Le Duan St

Phan Dinh Phung

Tran Cao Van St

Station

Hoang Hoa Tham St

Le Duan St

Ong Ich Khiem St

Pasteur St

Ngo Gia Tu St

Hung Vuong St

Bach Dang St

Ly Thai To St

Nguyen Thi Phuong

To Highway One

Tran Quoc Toan St

Yen Bai St

Tran Phu St

Nguyen Trai St

Tran Binh Trong St

Thai Phien St

Le Hong Phong St

Phan Ngu Lao St

Phan Chu Trinh St

Hoang Van Thu St

Trieu Nu Vuong St

Le Dinh Duong St

Hoang Dieu St

Vuong St

Trung Nu St

To Marble Mountains
China Beach
Hoi An

1. Khach San Huu Nghi Hotel
2. Song Han Hotel
3. Foreign Trade Bank
4. Thanh Lich Restaurant
5. Post Office
6. Seamen's Cafe
7. Tourist Office
8. Con Market
9. Cho Han Market
10. Da Nang Cathedral
11. Hai Chau Hotel
12. Thai Binh Duong Hotel
13. Phuong Dong Hotel
14. Tu Do Restaurant
15. Tam Bao Pagoda
16. Champa Museum

Hoi An

'The Chinese and Japanese drive the chief trade of Cochin-China which is managed at a fair held yearly at one of the ports of this kingdom, and lasting about four months. The Chinese, in their vessels they call junks, bring the value of four or five millions in plate; and the Japanese in their ships called sommes, an infinite quantity of very fine silk and other commodities of their country. The King has a vast revenue from this fair by customs and imports, and the whole country receives great profit . . . Here the king of Cochin-China assigned the Chinese and Japanese a convenient spot of ground to build a city for the benefit of the fair. This city is called Fai-fo (Hoi An), and is so large, that we may say there are two, one of Chinese, the other of Japanese; for they are divided from one another, each having their distinct governor and the Chinese living according to the laws of China, as the Japanese do according to the laws of Japan.'

Ancient port

Christopher Borri, one of the earliest Catholic missionaries to visit Vietnam, (1620).

30 kms down the coast from Da Nang, **Hoi An**, formerly known as Faifo, was once a highly **cosmopolitan port**. It was a trading centre during the Cham era, though it reached its height during the rule of the early Nguyen Lords in the 17th century. Chinese and Japanese merchants set up shop in Hoi An and brought with them aspects of their cultures. So, too, came the pioneering European seafarers, the Portuguese and Dutch, who were later followed by other inquisitive Westerners.

Chinese and Japanese connections

Hoi An was badly destroyed during the **Tay Son Uprising** in the 1770s-80s. It recovered, however, only to be abandoned by the French a little over 100 years later after its river, the **Thu Bon**, and its harbour filled with alluvium. The waters were too shallow to take the new larger vessels and Hoi An's position as prime port was duly inherited by Da Nang which had a better natural harbour.

Seafarers forgot about Hoi An and so too, it seems, did Vietnam. The old town survives as a remnant of a greater era. The **Chinese influence** is still dominant and Hoi An has distinct quarters for the different Chinese ethnic groups, each one having its own pagoda and community centre, as they do in Cholon. The narrow lanes are lined by rows of two-storey houses made mostly of wood. During the floods, the whole family would take refuge on the top floors to escape the rising waters.

Still a port of the past

The 16th century **Japanese Bridge** is covered and made of wood. At one end are statues of monkeys and at the other end there are dogs, which, according to local folklore, tells us that work on the bridge commenced in the **Year of the Monkey** and was completed in the **Year of the Dog**. Sailors and merchants would pray at the pagoda on the north side of the bridge and thus secure safe passage and successful business.

Cuong De is an interesting street with a **market** and several unusual Chinese pagodas. These include: the **Chua Ong Pagoda**, built in 1655; the **Fuckien Pagoda**, which enshrines the Heavenly Lady, who is the protector of seafarers; the 17th century **Le Nghia Pagoda**, which is built on the site of an earlier 15th century temple. This street is traditionally the centre for the Chinese community as a whole.

Old Chinese community

While the maritime trade died a long time ago, it has been replaced to some extent by a brisk business in **cotton and silk weaving** and many of Hoi An's inhabitants are now employed behind the loom.

Cu Lao Cham, a small volcanic island 12 km off Hoi An's coast, was where the 8th century Chams would cast their criminals. The locals, who are Cham in features, are **fishermen** who also collect swallows' nests which they sell in Hoi An market. There is a ferry to the island from a point between Hoi An and Da Nang.

Swallows' nests

From Da Nang, Highway One and the railway continue their southward course along the coastal plain. **A road westwards** from Hoi An crosses Highway One and following the old Route 4, cuts further inland, up the Cai river valley, before eventually taking a southward route along the **old Route 44**. This leads through the hills near the Laos border into Gia Lai-Contum province. Further down Highway One another road turns inland and meets the first route at the small town of **Phuoc Son** (Kham Duc) which was one of the battlefields during the **1968 Tet Offensive**. Viet Cong hid throughout these hills and were supported by the offshoots off the Ho Chi Minh Trail and, as a result, this area became a target for the Americans.

Viet Cong hideout

Highway One and the railway pass next through the town of **Tam K**y and, now close together, they skirt the edge of the **An Hoi lagoon**. Immediately inland are the large **Phu Ninh Lake** and **Nui Chua** which, at a height of 1360 metres, was once earmarked as a hill resort by the French. From here, road and rail cross into Nghia Binh province.

SOUTHERN TRUNG PHAN

Nghia Binh Province

The northern part of the coastal province of Nghia Binh used to be **Quang Ngai province**, scene of some of the vilest atrocities performed by the Americans during the Vietnam War.

On entering the province from the north you pass through fields of sugar cane and **Binh Son**, a sugar processing town, from where a road leads up into the hills, along the Tra Bong river valley, to the old Viet Cong camp of **Tra Bong**. In the other direction, towards the coast, are the village of **Son My** and its neighbouring hamlet of **My Lai**.

My Lai

In Quang Ngai the Americans were faced by resolute Viet Cong who had the sympathy and support of the mass of ordinary citizens. From ground, air and sea they indiscriminately bombarded the settlements, notching up some 50,000 casualties a year in this province alone. In 1967 an independent observer made a survey of 450 hamlets in Quang Ngai and recorded that 70% of them had been destroyed by US fire power.

Task Force Oregon - a particularly hardened contingent of soldiers - was despatched to suppress America's opponents in Quang Ngai. They abandoned the gentler pacification programmes such as herding villagers into Strategic Hamlets or trying to convert allegiance through propaganda which were sometimes used in a bid to sever the peasants' links with the Viet Cong. Their philosophy, it seems, was *'To win 'em you've got to kill 'em'*. And that meant destroying all - ordinary folk as well as the guerillas.

On the morning of **16th March 1968** the men of Task Force Oregon descended on Son My and its hamlets and meted out a hellish **massacre**. The worst of this crazed orgy of slaughter was led, by example, by Lieutenant William Calley Jnr., a platoon leader in the 23rd Infantry Division (American), who attacked the people of My Lai.

Men, women and children of all ages were butchered along with their animals. Their bodies dumped in wells to pollute the water and homes and crops were set ablaze. 347 inhabitants of My Lai died in this incident and a total of 504 died in the Son My village district. In the West the **My Lai affair** has been featured as the symbol of America's carnage in Vietnam. It was, however, by no means a unique case of excessive uncontrolled violence.

High death toll (margin note)

Vilest war crime (margin note)

The town of **Quang Ngai**, 10 km south-west of Son My on the **River Tra Khuc**, served as an American base and was a target for the Viet Cong during the 1968 Tet Offensive. The town is a **market** for the locally grown rice, sugar, corn and groundnuts and is famous for its large **bamboo and wooden waterwheels** which are used for irrigation. In the medieval past this was all Cham territory, until the Viets conquered the region during their southward expansion. **Emperor Ho Qui Ly**, who had fought many a battle against the Chams, built a couple of forts in the region at the turn of the 15th century, but it was not until the Southern Nguyen Lords started colonisation in the 16th century that Quang Ngai came fully under Viet control. In the early 1800s **Emperor Gia Long** built the old **citadel** in Quang Ngai town.

Viets move southwards [margin]

A road leads to the cinnamon plantation hills following the course of the Tra Khuc part of the way to **Son Ha**. From there it turns south along the **River Re**, before bearing westwards again into neighbouring Gia Lai-Contum province and to the provincial capital of Contum (see page 173).

Back in **Quang Ngai**, the southbound route of Highway One and the railway pass through the **tobacco plantations** around **Moc Duc**, from where another road branches off into the interior, and meets the sea at the small port of **Sa Huyen** where hectares of **salt fields** produce some 65,000 tons of salt per annum. Archeologists have discovered **tombs** at Sa Huyen dating from the 1st century AD and after analysing the artifacts, they now believe this area was a colony of the **Bronze Age Dong Son culture** which was based in present Thanh Hoa province.

Tobacco and salt [margin]

Continuing on, the route runs close to the shore, passing through **Tam Quan Hoai Nhon** (Bong Son), **Phu My**, **Cat Hanh**, a village particularly badly damaged during the Vietnam War, **Phu Cat**, and **An Nhon** (Binh Dinh). The names of these small towns just inland from the coast would be familiar to ex-servicemen who were stationed in **II Corps**, the Americans' military zone which covered the section of Vietnam from Tam Quan south to Phan Thiet.

Vijaya, in the southern part of present **Nghia Binh**, was capital of the Champa Kingdom from 1000 AD until, in 1471, the southward bound Viets conquered the city, killing 60,000 and capturing 30,000 of its people. The defeat was a death knell to the Chams' culture. They abandoned Vijaya and fled further south into the hills.

And destroy an ancient culture [margin]

171

Broken down vestiges of the Champa Kingdom are scattered throughout this region. Some are being preserved and restored, others are ignored. Locals and guides can point you towards the best and most accessible of the sites.

Road to the hills

Just before Qui Nhon a road, the **old Route 19**, leads west into the hills and, via the **An Khe Pass**, into Gia Lai-Contum province and the town of **Pleiku**. To the east a turning heads off Highway One for the last few kilometres into Qui Nhon.

Qui Nhon

Qui Nhon, 400 km south of Hue and 680 km from Ho Chi Minh City, was developed as a **fortified administrative centre** under the **Nguyen Lords**, and was fought over by the **Tay Son** rebels and **Nguyen Anh** (who became Emperor Gia Long) during a series of battles at the end of the 18th century.

Two hundred years later, the Americans turned Qui Nhon, with its **deep natural seaport**, into an important **military centre** and a **supply base** for Pleiku up in the hills. Quite typically, the bars and bordellos - local style, though with American names to make clients feel at home soon sprung up and, not so usual, an **ice cream factory** was set up by Meadowgold Dairies who made sure their product had the all-American taste.

Qui Nhon is protected by a long peninsula of land which extends from the north and forms a natural barrier in front of the city. Today the harbour remains important and **shrimp breeding** is amongst the local industries. The **main beach** is long and sandy and early each morning many hundreds come here for their pre-work dip, Tai Chi exercises, a 'work out' Vietnamese style, and coffee. The main hotel, the **Qui Nhon**, *8 Nguyen Hue (Tel: 2401)*, overlooks the beach but is a kilometre or two from the centre of town. There are several downtown hotels.

Home of Vietnamese opera

Qui Nhon does not have much to offer the tourist, though it is home to the traditional **Vietnamese opera** which can be seen at the city's theatre. **The Tourist Office**, *Tran Hung Dao* (the beach, or eastern end near the Qui Nonh Hotel, *Tel: 2329*) will have details of programmes.

Highway 19 from Qui Nhon passes through **Tay Son** (Phu Phong), some 55 km from Qui Nhon. This is the homeland of the three **Tay Son brothers** - Nguyen Hue, Nguyen Nhac and Nguyen Lu who inspired and led a popular uprising against the Nguyen Lords in the 1770s-

80s. (Nguyen is a common name in Vietnam and the Nguyen brothers should not be confused with the Nguyen Lords/Emperors who were their enemies). It proved to be a prolonged struggle with the advantage alternating between the sides over the years. However, the Tay Son boys were eventual victors, beating the Nguyen Lords in the South. Nguyen Anh, the incumbent Nguyen Lord, fled and prepared to fight another day.

Revolution to unite Vietnam

The Tay Sons went on to conquer the Trinh Lords of the North. Having won the whole country they had, for the first time in history, united Vietnam under one banner.

The Tay Sons divided the country into three administrative regions. Nguyen Hue (who became **Quang Trung**, first emperor of the **Tay Son Dynasty** in 1788) took charge of the north; Nguyen Nhac controlled the centre with his capital at Qui Nhon, or rather at the now ruined city of **Hoang De** just to the north of Qui Nhon; and Nguyen Lu was designated the south.

The Tay Son Dynasty had great promise and Emperor Quang Trung, the most effectual of the brothers, increased his popularity and consolidated his position after his outstanding defeat of the Chinese at the Battle of Dong Da during the Tet of 1789. His reign and his dynasty were shortlived however, he died in 1792 and his lineage lasted only another ten years. Tay Son authority began to crumble in the mid to late 1790s and this heralded the opportunity for **Nguyen Anh**, whose right to rule Vietnam had French support, to return. In 1802 he put an end to Tay Son aspirations, won the throne and crowned himself **Emperor Gia Long**, the first of the Nguyen Emperors.

Further west, up **Highway 19**, the remnants of a **Tay Son fort** provide an unspectacular legacy of the great movement led by three local lads.

The **An Khe Pass** is the border between Nghia Binh and Gia Lai-Contum provinces and there is another pass, the **Mang Yang**, before the final run into Pleiku.

Gia Lai-Contum Province

Gia Lai-Contum province which is more or less the amalgam of the old Kontum and Pleiku provinces, borders Laos and Cambodia to the west. This is part of the **Central Highlands**, a very different land to the coastal plains, where cattle, timber, tea, coffee and other plantation crops are the main revenue earners. The inhabitants come primarily from the ethnic minority tribes such as the Jarai, Bahnar, Rhade, Sedeng and

A different world up in the hills

Rengao; they share their **beautiful jungles** with elephants, tigers (apparently) and a host of other exotic animals.

Jungle under fire

Like elsewhere, however, it was an area dappled with Viet Minh and then Viet Cong strongholds which suffered French domination, followed by a fair pounding from the Americans.

Highway 14 passes through Gia Lai-Contum province from north to south via **Dak To, Tan Canh**, and **Pleiku**, where it meets **Highway 9**, before entering Dac Lac province. All these settlements along the way served as **American military bases** and this whole area suffered much fighting and bombing over the years. Dak To, Tan Canh, Contum and the Rocket Ridge - the hills immediately to the west - served as frontline outposts against the ever-threatening Northern army, which, with 35,000 troops under the command of **General Hoang Minh Thao**, camped at **Base 609**, at the junction of Laos, Cambodia and Vietnam, and launched an offensive at the end of March 1972.

The master strategy

This attack was part of the Communists' major **Easter Offensive** which co-ordinated a series of incursions from the north down the coastal plain and from the west across the Central Highlands. The Americans held off the initial assault from their bases in **Rocket Ridge**, but, within a month they had lost **Dak To** and **Tan Canh**. Curiously the Communists did not pursue their obvious advantage and continue down Highway 14 to Contum which they, doubtless, would have captured.

As it turned out **Contum** did not fall until the Communists' final surge towards Saigon. The town was 'liberated' on 17th March 1975. The following day Pleiku, some 45 km down Highway 14 also fell.

On north-south Route 14, and linked to **Qui Nhon** on the coast by Route 19, **Pleiku** and nearby **Camp Holloway** became a highly strategic and significant base for the South. Once an administrative centre and military outpost for the French it served as a springboard for the American forays against the Ho Chi Minh Trail and the Viet Cong and Northern army who lay encamped in the surrounding countryside.

Peace brings remoteness

Both Contum and Pleiku are now rather more remote and the busy routes which used to feed them are, today, off the beaten track. The few Western visitors to these towns tend to be ex-servicemen returning to old battlefields. There is simple accommodation at both Contum and Pleiku.

One of the earliest set battles of the Vietnam War was fought in the forested **Ia Drang** valley and **Chu Prong** hills south-west of Pleiku and west of **Plei Me**, near the Cambodian border. Here, in November 1965, the U.S. 1st Cavalry Division clashed with the Communists. The exact death toll is unknown, but it was high; 233 Americans were killed in four days, well over half of them in one ambush, but the number may have totalled over 300, while an estimated 1300 and 2000 NVA and Viet Cong died in the action. The Americans were shaken by their losses, but many saw it as a victory by virtue of the ratio of the body count.

The body count ration equals victory

A road west out of Pleiku leads into Cambodia. To the south Highway 14 passes by the two pronged mountain of **Cu Hodrung**, the 'navel of the world' according to the local Jarai mythology, because it was here, after the Earth was created and subsequent floods, that the Jarai man and woman were washed ashore. At **Chu Sre** a branch takes a more easterly course and follows the **River Ba** via **Cheo Reo** into Phu Khanh province, while the main southbound route crosses over into Dac Lac province. To the east of Pleiku, Highway 19 serves as the connection to **Qui Nhon** and **Highway One**.

From the junction outside Qui Nhon, Highway One follows its southward path. The terrain immediately becomes hilly and the highway climbs the scenic ascent, passing through the **Cu Mong Pass** into Phu Khanh province. The railway, however, is forced to take a gentler inland course along a river valley before crossing the provincial boundary.

Phu Khanh Province

Phu Khanh is a hilly coastal province. The **Truong Son** range edges down to the sea and Highway One, closely followed by the rail track, takes a path along the narrow stretch of flatlands, over passes and between hills. The shore has many lagoons and beaches, and peninsulas and headlands jut into the sea.

Mountains meet sea

This area was Cham territory until the first Nguyen Lord, Nguyen Hoang, ever keen to push southwards, annexed these lands in 1611. Over the subsequent centuries Cham influence diminished as Viet migration into the region increased.

Tuy Hoa

The small port of Tuy Hoa, on the northern bank of the **River Da Rang** (the lower reach of the Ba), 560 km north of Ho Chi Minh City, is the **first main town** in the northern part of the province. During the colonial era the Viet Minh 'liberated' Tuy Hoa and neighbouring countryside and the French, unwilling to expend resources trying to win the place back, left Tuy Hoa as a Viet Minh enclave. After the departure of the French the majority of Viet Minh abided by the 1954 Geneva Accords and regrouped in the North to await the general election (which was never held).

Tuy Hoa notched up a moment of fame when, in 1955, the South's **President Ngo Dinh Diem** came here *'to meet and talk to the people'*. It was his first such major trip into the former enemy countryside and he was uncertain what to expect. He was received by a huge and rapturous crowd of up to 100,000 locals who, it transpired, were more excited by the carnival-like occasion than the man himself. However, though the majority were probably oblivious to Diem's anti-communist tirade, they cheered when prompted to do so and a delighted Diem and his equally elated American colleagues returned to Saigon believing in this show of popularity.

Tuy Hoa has earned further fame for its **bridge** over the River Da Rang which is one of the largest in Vietnam.

A road cuts inland from Tuy Hoa up to **Cheo Reo** and **Pleiku**. Highway One continues southwards over the **Ca Pass** near the picturesque **Mui Nay**, once known as Cape Varella, where an outcrop of rock silhouetted atop a hill has been interpreted as the 'Mother and Child' awaiting the father's return from sea. Nearby is the fine stretch of **Dai Lanh beach**. The road then crosses the **Co Ma Pass** before reaching the flatter land and **Xuan Tu beach**. There are thermal springs in the hills near **Ninh Hoa**. A road, the old Route 21, leads westwards to **Ban Me Thout**.

After Ninh Hoa, Highway One goes through the **Ro Tuong Pass** to the village of **Ninh Ich**, where, up in the hills, are the three **Ba Ho** waterfalls. Each fall has a pool and they say that if you immerse yourself in each one all your ailments, mental and physical, will be cured. From Ninh Ich, Highway One runs a further 20 km over the Ru Ri Pass to **Nha Trang**. On the outskirts of the town are the **Hon Chong Rocks**, a dramatic group of boulders by the sea which have been deemed a 'tourist sight'. Sadly, though, they have been defaced with graffiti. Entrance into Nha Trang is by the **Xom Bong bridge** over the River Cai. There are **Cham ruins** located on the right just before the crossing.

The President's tour

Waiting for father

Defacing nature

Nha Trang

Nha Trang, on the **River Cai**, and 445 km north of Ho Chi Minh city, is Vietnam's most famous and best established **beach resort**. The whole area was part of the Champa Kingdom until 1653, when Nguyen Lord Phuc Tan won the stretch of land from the Ca Pass down to Phan Rang. The **Po Nogar Temple** complex on the edge of Nha Trang is amongst the finest remains of this ancient civilisation. The Tay Sons conquered the region during their rebellion in the 1770s, but were ousted by Emperor Gia Long in 1793. Realising the need to defend the place, he ordered the construction of the **Dien Khanh citadel**, 10 km west of present Nha Trang. Sections of wall still stand.

R&R hot spot The **French** established the resort at Nha Trang which was later enjoyed by the **Americans** who used it as a local R&R (rest and recreation) centre for their off duty troops. As in other sea towns Nha Trang saw tragedy in spring 1975, as the Communists rolled down Highway One, thousands of ordinary citizens grappled to secure a place on a rescue vessel. Down at the wharf locals point out where people died as they shoved and were squashed in their crazed desperation to escape the Northerners.

Still a place for fun At the weekends Nha Trang's lovely 6 km long, straight sandy **beach** is packed. However, there is not yet a tourist in sight. The locals - young, old, couples and families - flock here, park their bicycles on the sand and spend their time sitting around, swimming, exercising, playing football or other games. A wide palm-treed **promenade** follows the length of the beach and has café-bars, snack stalls and vendors offering fish specialities, beers, freshly squeezed juices, tropical fruits and whatever else may be on the menu. **Beach Road** (Tran Phu) runs alongside, lined with relatively low rise seafront buildings, hotels, offices, institutions, villas which date mainly from the colonial era.

With the Americans came the raucous lifestyle, and the **Cyclo Races** described by the wife of an American major in her book on Vietnam under Nha Trang's 'Other Entertainment': *'Cyclo races - Great fun at night. Hire your cyclo and agree on the price in advance. Have your friends do the same. Fastest cyclo driver gets a bonus at the end of the long four-lane beach road. Most people race from one beach bar* **Races on the corniche** *to the next, which are numbered 1 to 14 instead of named. Some Americans like to put the driver in the seat and drive the cyclos themselves !'*

At the southern end of the beach is the small port of **Cua Da** and the impressive **Institute of Oceanography**

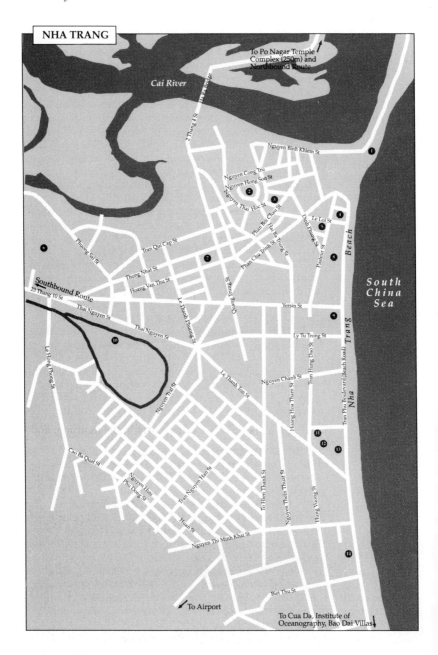

NHA TRANG

To Po Nagar Temple
Complex (250m) and
Northbound Route

Cai River

Nguyen Binh Khiem St

Nguyen Cong Tru

Nguyen Hong Son St

Nguyen Thai Hoc St

Le Loi St

Dinh Phong St

Phan Boi Chau St

Hai Ba Trung St

Pasteur St

Beach

Phan Chu Trinh St

Tran Qui Cap St

Phuong Sai St

Quang Trung St

Thong Nhat St

Hoang Van Thu St

Le Thanh Phuong St

Yersin St

Southbound Route

23 Thang 10 St

Thai Nguyen St

Thai Nguyen St

Ly Tu Trong St

Le Hong Phong St

Nguyen Trai St

Le Thanh Ton St

Nguyen Chanh St

Hoang Hoa Tham St

Tran Hung Dao St

Tran Phu Boulevard (Beach Road)

Nha Trang

South China Sea

Cao Ba Quat St

Nguyen Hieu

Phu Dong St

Tran Nguyen Hai St

To Hien Thanh St

Nguyen Thien Thuat St

Hung Vuong St

Huan St

Nguyen Thi Minh Khai St

Biet Thu St

To Airport

To Cua Da, Institute of
Oceanography, Bao Dai Villas

```
┌─ KEY TO MAP OF NHA TRANG ─────────────────────────┐
│                                                     │
│   1. Nha Nghi Hotel            8. Pasteur Institute │
│   2. Dam Market                9. Thong Nhat Hotel  │
│   3. Lac Canh Restaurant      10. Railway Station   │
│   4. Post Office              11. Hung Dao Hotel    │
│   5. Thang Loi Hotel          12. Tourist Office    │
│   6. Giant Buddha             13. Hai Yen Hotel     │
│   7. Binh Minh Restaurant     14. Khach San Hotel   │
│                                                     │
└─────────────────────────────────────────────────────┘
```

An abundance of dead fish which was founded in 1923 by the French and houses tens of thousands of (dead) species of marine life, as well as a **modest aquarium**. It remains an important centre for aquatic research. A row of **cafés** serve fresh fish dishes and **handicrafts** made from shells are for sale.

From the jetty you can take a local ferry or water taxi to one of the many off shore islands. **Hon Mieu** (also know as Tri Nguyen), is about fifteen minutes away and is one of the nearest islands. Here they have made an **open air aquarium** by building a pen around an area of sea and filling it with South China Sea fish. **Hon Yen**, 17 km off Nha Trang, is famous for its swifts' nests (*salangame*) which are harvested and used in soups and a variety of traditional medicines.

During their time the Americans used to water ski, scuba dive, snorkel, take boats out to the islands and go for a swim, a fish and a picnic; Nha Trang must have been like heaven after the hellish warfare up in the hills.

The main **fishing port** is at the northern end of town at the mouth of the River Cai. On the northern bank is the busy **fish market**, in full swing early in the morning, and

Beach at Nha Trang.

179

across the road - Highway One - is the cluster of Cham towers, Po Nagar.

Po Nagar

Cham temples

Po Nagar - or **Po Yang Ineous Nagar**, (Goddess Mother of the Kingdom), as is her full title - is wife of Shiva and one of the Chams' most venerated deities. She must be worshipped as it is she who taught the Chams how to farm and it is she who controls the rice harvests each year. Po Nagar is also the goddess of women in the guise of **Pata Kumei**, the Queen of Women, and she has many daughters, some evil, some good, all of whom are also revered. Even the Viets adopted Po Nagar as a goddess, naming her **Ba Chua Ngoc** and they hold a **festival** for her at Nha Trang in the second and eighth lunar months. Additional feasts are also held for her and her daughters at other times.

Eight Cham towers built between the 7th and 12th centuries AD once stood on this site, which must have been a lovely peaceful location before Highway One and the crowds arrived. Today the **four towers** which remain reveal the strong **Hindu influence** so dominant in Cham art, architecture and religion. The main **North tower**, dedicated to Po Nagar, was built by King Hari Varman I in 817 with characteristic large brick slabs. It stands 23 metres high and is typical in design, having four walls tapering into a pyramidal roof. The ten-handed effigy of Po Nagar was decapitated by the French who despatched the head to a Paris museum; she has subsequently been repaired.

The **Central tower** honours **Cri Cambhu**. This was originally built in the 8th century, but was destroyed by Malay pirates in 774, rebuilt ten years later and then fully restored in the 12th century. Young couples come to pray at the tower's **'fertility shrine'** in the hope of being blessed with children. The **North-west tower** commemorates **Shiva/Sandhaka** and the **South tower** honours **Ganesha**, the Hindu elephant god.

Modern Buddha

A more recent religious monument is the **giant Buddha** which was built in Nha Trang in 1963 in memory of the Buddhists who protested, sometimes martyring themselves for the cause, against President Diem's opposition to their faith.

South of Nha Trang, Highway One and the railway pass between two hills - **Cau Hin** and on the left and **Se Gai** on the right - before taking separate paths into **Thuan Hai province**. Just north of the provincial frontier

NHA TRANG FACTS

ACCOMMODATION
There are half a dozen hotels evenly spaced along the Tran Phu beachfront. A further cluster of hotels are inland in the downtown.
Three of the best waterfront hotels (north to south):

Thang Loi, *4 rue Pasteur, Tel: 22226*
A block inland from the seafront, on the corner of Le Loi.

Thong Nhet, *18 Tran Phu, Tel: 22966*

Hai Yen, *40 Tran Phu, Tel: 22928*

At the very top of the beach, there is the **Nha Nghi**, *48 Nguyen Binh Khiem, Tel: 22216*.

At the lower end, are the:

Hung Dao, *3 Trang Hung Dao* (behind the Hai Yen Hotel), *Tel: 22246*

Khach San, *58 Tran Phu, Tel: 22997*.

Continue a few kilometres further along the seafront and, on the hills near the village of Cau Da, are **Bao Dai's 1920s holiday villas**. They have recently been converted into guest houses for tourists *(tel: 22449)*. Other fine old residences are being refurbished for the growing number of visitors.

RESTAURANTS
Along with the beach, seafood is Nha Trang's greatest claim to fame. There are restaurants at most of the waterfront hotels and good local places to eat in the Dam market area on the way to the fishing port, notably the **Lac Canh**, and in the downtown area, the **Binh Minh**.

TOURIST OFFICE (Province)
Hai Yen Hotel, *40 Tran Phu, Tel: 22753*
Opening: *7.00-11.00 and 13.30-17.00 Monday to Saturday*

TOURIST OFFICE (City)
Hung Dao Hotel, *9 Tran Hung Dao, Tel: 2123*
Opening *7.00-11.30 and 13.00 to 17.00 Monday to Saturday*.

NIGHTLIFE
Cyclo racing along the corniche is something of the past, for the present at least. Popular with the locals are the evening stroll, and cycle, or moped 'cruises' up and down the beachfront. Besides the **cafés** on the promenade there are some **restaurants** in the gardens of the villas and hotels and these are pleasant places to spend the evening. Other restaurants are at the ports or in the heart of the city, the busy quarter which extends beyond the smarter streets immediately behind the Beach Road.

Highway One runs close to the coast at Cam Ranh Bay.

Cam Ranh Bay, considered to be the best **natural harbour** in the world after Sydney, was developed by the Americans into a massive **naval and military base** in the mid 1960s. After the Vietnam War the Soviets inherited the complex and it was their largest naval base beyond their shores. Now, with so much detente and good will flowing between the old enemy superpowers, the future of the harbour is uncertain.

Redundant in peacetime

Dac Lac Province

The large hilly inland province of Dac Lac, bordered by Phu Khanh province to the east and Cambodia to the west, is the heart of Vietnam's **game country**. Here **Emperor Bao Dai** and the French used to arrange shooting parties and many have claimed these forests to be amongst the richest **hunting grounds** in the world. This is the home of elephants, tigers and a multitude of other exotic species, as well as a host of ethnic minorities, most conspicuously the Rhade and M'nong.

Highway 14, the main north-south route through the Central Highlands, is met by **Highway 21**, the east-west (coast-interior) road from Ninh Hoa, at **Ban Ma Thuot**, the 'capital' of the hills. The French administered the hill tribes and plantations from here and, like the Americans later, defended their interests against the Vietnamese freedom fighters.

On the morning of 10th March 1975 the North's army blasted **Ban Ma Thout**; the town had fallen by dusk.

Wildlife and **tribes people** are still the main attractions of the region. Once elephants were deployed in battle where their bulk and strength must have been a formidable asset, and served as majestic transport for emperors during state occasions. Today there is an **elephants' training school** at Ban Ma Thout, where the elephants are taught how to serve the locals as beasts of burden. The last emperor used to hunt the creatures in the surrounding forests, but they are now protected by governmental decree. According to the shopkeepers at least, poaching is not a major problem and the ivory trinkets for sale in Ho Chi Minh City's Dong Khoi Street and elsewhere have been made from the tusks of elephants which have died naturally. Be warned however, that there is now a strictly enforced, **worldwide ban on the import of ivory** and confiscation of the article is the minimum penalty.

The local **Tourist Office** proposes to organise

Warrior elephants

photographic safaris atop elephants as well as specialised wildlife excursions deep into the jungle, although, as yet, these are still in the planning stages.

Tribal Visits
Ban Me Thuot's **museum** displays the material culture of the various tribes of Dac Lac. Traditions enshrined in this gallery are still alive in the surrounding countryside, but who knows how long it will be before they fade into extinction. The Tourist Office arranges **visits to villages** - currently to **Tua**, 12 km south-east of Ban Ma Thuot, and **Don** some 45 km to the north-west. Gongs are symbols of the *montagnards* struck at various rituals and inhabitants may well perform their customary **gong festival** or their **rice wine-bamboo pipe ceremony**, the pipe serving as a straw to drink the wine.

Going native

Traditionally outsiders are greeted politely and are expected to partake in the usual welcome - a ritual described by Norman Lewis in the mid 1950s after his visit to a village in the regions: *'From the sheer multiplicity of the rites, all of which require alcoholic consumption, the intriguing side-issue emerges that respectability and drunkenness are allied. The upright man gives evidence of his ritual adequacy by being drunk as often as possible, he is respected for his piety, a pattern held up to youth. The words 'nam lu' uttered in grave welcome to the stranger in a Moi (tribal) village, and meaning let us get drunk together, have all the exhortatory value of an invitation to common prayer. Moi villages are said to be one of the few places in the world where the domestic animals, dogs, pigs and hens, having fed in the fermented mash from the sacred jars, are to be seen in a state of helpless intoxication. Conviviality is the rule; a norm of polite conduct. Passers-by begged to join in Moi orgies of eating and*

Polite drunks

drinking and it is bad taste - that is offensive to the spirits - to eat or drink less than is provided by the fearsome liberality of the hosts. To prevent any possibility of the visitor's unwittingly committing this kind of discourtesy, or remaining in a state of disreputable sobriety, an attendant squats at his side keeping a careful check on his consumption and ensuring that he drinks at least a minimum measure of three cow's horns'.

Today's tourist may not be expected to knock back a minimum of *'three cow's horns'* worth of alcohol, however, the spirit of the tradition still survives.

While the sharing of a drink - alcohol or otherwise - is a universal gesture of friendship, other customs and beliefs up here are more esoteric and more difficult to comprehend. An American ethnographic study noted that: '*Sneezing has a special significance amongst the Rhade. They believe sneezing irritates the spirits, and after a sneeze by a person or an animal, one must remain still until the spirits recover from their anger. An early morning sneeze before going to work insures good luck for the rest of the day. A sneeze, however, during a trip or upon starting a trip or departing from a person's home, required a short delay to prevent misfortune.*'

Sneeze for luck

And '*The M'nong believe that spirits make their wishes known through dreams and omens. For example, during the selection of a house site, it is considered a good omen if the owner of the new house dreams about fruit, rice, a paddy, a tomb, hunting, or swimming. If the dream is about buffaloes, killing deer, or the breaking of teeth, it is considered a bad omen. Seeing flames devour the loincloth of a person is a dream predicting that person's death.*'

Despite the devastation of the Vietnam War Dac Lac's vegetation is luxuriant. Forests include many species of precious **hardwoods** and a wide variety of **other flora**. While timber is lumbered commercially and wild plants are gathered by locals and traded in the markets, the main cash crops are **coffee**, **tea** and **rubber** which are grown on plantations and are then sent down to the plains from where they are exported.

The Central Highlands are famed for their picturesque scenery and a popular beauty spot in the forests just out of Ban Ma Thout is the **Drai Sap Waterfall**. Down Highway 14 is the pretty **Dac Lac Lake** where Emperor Bao Dai had a small palace. Many of the Emperor's former residences around the old south are being converted into guest houses; the same fate probably awaits this place. For the moment accommodation is limited to the simple **Thang Loi Hotel** in Ban Ma Thuot and a couple of lesser hotels which the Tourist Office regards as unsuitable for foreigners.

Emperor's country home

Highway 21, east out of Ben Ma Thout, passes through **Ea Knop**, heads into Phu Khanh province and down to **Ninh Hoa** near the coast. **Highway 14** continues its southward path, running close to the Cambodian border before turning into Song Be province, while **Highway 27** - also southbound - passes Dac Lac Lake on its way into Lam Dong province.

Lam Dong Province
Highway 27 from Ban Ma Thout enters Lam Dong province and meets the **Ho Chi Minh City - Dinh Linh -**

Da Lat road near the **Lien Khang Waterfalls**. To the right the road continues to follow a southerly direction, while to the left it takes a northerly path for the final 30 km up to the town of Da Lat.

From the coast roads lead up from Nha Trang and, more commonly used, from **Phan Rang**. This is the old Route 11, now **Highway 20**. Just beyond the provincial divide, is Ngoan Muc Pass at **Don Duong**, a lake created by the **Da Nhim River Dam**, which provides water for hydro-electric production. The Da Nhim power plant was funded by Japanese money as part of a war reparations deal. It is a further 36 km from here to Da Lat.

Da Lat

Da Lat is Vietnam's most famous **hill resort**. It lies 300 km north-east of Ho Chi Minh City, 105 km inland from Phan Rang and some 200 km south of Ban Ma Thout.

Cool retreat

Its creation was due to **Alexandre Yersin**, a French doctor who came to Indochina in the 1880s and spent most of the rest of the next years in Vietnam, dying here in 1943 aged 80. Yersin, highly respected by both his compatriots and Vietnamese, had his base in **Nha Trang** where he founded the **Pasteur Institute**. Between 1890 and 1894 he travelled extensively around the Central Highlands, gathering information about the medicinal value of plants. On one of his journeys he discovered a lovely site with hills and lakes, pastures and pine forests and, at an altitude of 1500 metres, a refreshing temperature ranging between 4°C in December and January and 26° C in March and April. He recommended to senior colonial officials that a hill resort be built here - a sort of Alpine sanctuary where the French could retire from the heat of the plains. His suggestion was approved and Da Lat came into being at the turn of the 20th century. Its official birthday was in 1889, though the inauguration was in 1912.

A paradise is created

The name Da Lat is derived from either '*Da*' meaning 'Stream' and '*Lat*' a local sub-group of the region's Koho peoples (thus 'Stream of the Lats') - or, as some people maintain, from an acronym of the first letters of *Dat Aliis Laetitiam Aliis Temperiem* meaning 'Joy to One Happiness and Health to Another'. Either way the name evokes a pleasing image and one which Vietnamese everywhere cherish, whether they have been up here or not. It is pictured as a cool, temperate paradise - Vietnam's little Alpine Switzerland - an escape from the hot, dusty, crowded cities, a place where waterfalls cascade through

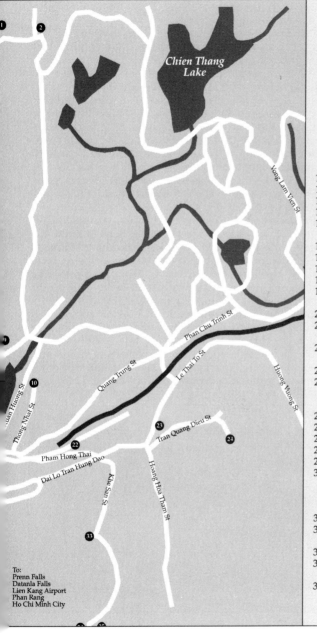

1. Lake Thong Nhat
2. Da Thien Village and the Valley of Love
3. Cemetery
4. Cam Ly Airport
5. Da Lat University
6. Chua Linh Son
7. Museum of hte Ethnic Minorities and the Revolution
8. Golf Course
9. Orchid Gardens
10. Old Grande Lycée
11. War Memorial
12. Cam Ly Waterfall
13. Lam Son Hotel
14. Vietnam Airlines Office
15. Central Market
16. Anh Dao Hotel
17. Ngoc Lan Hotel
18. Bus Station
19. Thanh Thuy Restaurant
20. Duy Tan Hotel
21. Thuy Ta Restaurant
22. Old Railway Station
23. Lam Vien Hotel
24. Palace No. I (Chateau Bourgery)
25. Post Office
26. Tourist Office
27. Palace Hotel
28. Da Lat Cathedral
29. Da Lat Hotel
30. Palace No. II (Governor General's Residence)
31. Pasteur Institute
32. Palace No. III (Bao Dai's Residence)
33. Minh Tam Hotel
34. Thien Vuong Pagoda
35. Minh Nguyet Cy Sy Lam (Chinese) Pagoda

scented forests and the air hangs heavy with the perfume of flowers and sweet romance.

Romantic resort

This imagery has become part of the local culture and Da Lat continues as a retreat, traditionally popular with young couples and honeymooners.

The town is spread over several valleys and hills. The boomerang-shaped **Lake Xuan Huong** is the resort's focal point. A road and promenade skirt its banks and two restaurants, the **Thuy Ta** and the **Than Thuy**, have excellent locations on the lake shore. The park on the north side is the **Da Lat Golf Course** which is currently being redeveloped. Next to it are the **orchid gardens**. Numerous varieties of orchids, as well as other flowers, including the favourite **calistemon** (bottle brush), grow up here in these hills, giving the resort its slogan: *'Da Lat - the Flower Capital of Vietnam'*.

Dying for love

Beyond the Xuan Huong area, to the north and east, roads and tracks lead to scenic spots. Some 3 km to the north-east is the picturesque **Lake Than Tho** (the Lake of Sighs) where, according to local legend, Hoang Tung would rendezvous with Mai Nuong, his young sweetheart. He had to go to war however, and on the couple's penultimate meeting he sighed at the thought of leaving. Mai Nuong interpreted this as his suspicion of her fidelity and so, to prove her faithfulness, she, the next day took a draft of poison and lay down by the lakeside to die, as she awaited her lover. Another tale relates how a young girl used to come to the lake and sigh as she saw the smartly uniformed young officers out exercising. The

Old steam engine at Da Lat.

Beret and Gauloise in Da Lat.

stories may seen contrived, but romance is an integral part of Da Lat and such tales are well loved.

Continuing northwards along *Duong Vong Lam Vien*, you pass between two lakes, the larger **Chien Tang** is on the right, before reaching the **Valley of Love** which was once Emperor Bao Dai's hunting grounds. It is an attractive place and, as the name suggests, a popular place with lovers. A dam was built in 1972 to create the lake which was named after **Da Thien**, a respected local Catholic priest. A village on the southern shore also bears his name.

Beyond this, 7 km north of the town, is **Nui Ba**, a mountain also enshrouded in a love story. In a *'Romeo and Juliet'* type tragedy two young lovers from rival tribes had a clandestine relationship. The two families were aghast on discovering the affair and demanded it came to an end. Nai Vien, the girl, fled up into the hills. The boy, Lam, followed, but on reaching the summit he found Nai Vien had pined to death. A tearful Lam returned to announce the death to the clans, who, horrified at the tragedy caused by their differences, united and made a pilgrimage up the hill. But instead of finding Nai Van's body they discovered a mountain in the shape of a sleeping woman, the two peaks being her breasts. Today, trekkers climb Nui Ba which is also known as **Lam Vien**, derived from the couple's name. Confusingly *'Lam '* means Forest and *'Vien'* means Garden, offering another plausible root for the name. They say that on a clear day you can see Nha Trang and the coast from the 2163 metre high summit.

More tales of love (margin)

On the north side of Da Lat stand the main **cemetery**, essentially a Buddhist burial ground, and Da Lat's principle pagoda, the **Chua Linh Son**. Built in 1942, this houses a **statue of Buddha** measuring 1.80 metres in height, weighing a remarkable 542 kgs. Nearby, at the north end of the old golf course, is **Da Lat University**, established in 1958, and to the south of the pagoda is the **Museum of the Ethnic Minorities and the Revolution**, where the material culture of the local tribes such as the Koho is displayed along with more ancient relics of the Chams' whose kingdom once extended this far inland. There are mementos of the struggle against the French and Americans.

Focus on local tribes (margin)

A **soldiers' cemetery** and a **monument**, completed in late 1979 and dedicated to those who gave their lives to the resistance movements stands on the western outskirts of Da Lat near the old military airport. Da Lat's major embroilment in the Vietnam War was during the 1968 Tet Offensive when the town became one of the centres of the Communists' insurgence.

Just south of the museum, in the heart of town, is the large and very interesting **market** where an abundance of local produce is up for sale. Da Lat is an important **market gardening** centre, supplying Ho Chi Minh City and the coast with its goods. This main indoor market is on different floors and, packed in another enclosure across a back street, are many food stalls serving local dishes to the workers. The downtown area around the market is Da Lat at its busiest and here you find the bus depot, many cafés, restaurants and the cheaper hotels.

Pushing a little further south, past the western edge of **Lake Xuan Huong**, you reach *Dai Lo-Tran Phu*, the main thoroughfare on which you will find the old **cathedral**, the **Da Lat Hotel**, the **Post Office**, the **Tourist Office** and the famous **Palace Hotel**.

Continue west along *Dai Lo-Tran Phu* and you ascend into a salubrious quarter of French-built villas, many of which are now occupied by government bodies and institutions. These include the **Pasteur Research Centre**. A road heading further up a pine-covered hill leads to **Palace Number Three**, once Bao Dai's residence and later inherited by the South's presidents.

Bao Dai had the large, though not too extravagant white villa built in the 1930s as a country home and lodge. The 'palace' and its gardens have been kept as they were during the erstwhile emperor's period of tenure.

The most prominent officials also had retreats up in Da Lat. The notorious **Madame Nhu**, President Ngo Dinh Diem's powerful sister-in-law, resided in **Lam Ngoc** (Forest Jewel), a specially built, heavily guarded villa which had escape tunnels running underneath the swimming pool to a neighbouring house.

Follow *Dai Lo-Tran Phu* eastwards into *Dai Lo Tran-Hung Dao* and, up on the right, you pass **Palace Number Two**, originally the residence of Admiral Jean Decoux, the Governor-General of Indochina between 1940 and 1945. This later became the home of **Ngo Dinh Nhu**, Diem's younger brother and Madame Nhu's husband. **Paintings** by **Do Trong Nhon**, a pre-Liberation artist famous for capturing Vietnam's daily life, hang in the 'palace'.

This route is lined with smart French-styled Alpine villas dating from the 1930s, 40s and 50s. A track, *Tran Quang Dieu*, up to the right leads to **Palace Number One**,

Fruit and veg for the cities

Royal residence

Home of the notorious Madame Nhu

Alpine villas

the somewhat grander Chateau Bourgery which has the appearance of being abandoned, though, apparently, a local institution makes use of it several times a week. Down the hill is the **Lam Vien Hotel**. *The palaces are open to the public between 7.30 and 11.00, and 13.30 and 16.00 daily.*

Roads leading southwards off *Dai Lo Tran-Hung Dao* have panoramic views over the valleys. One such path, **Duong Khe Sanh**, leads to the **Chinese Pagoda**, as much a place of worship as an excuse for an excursion to this scenic spot.

Local Transport

Beyond the heart of Da Lat, the attractions are spread out over a large area. The **French style, language and relics** seem to have lingered longer in Da Lat than elsewhere or, at least, these French legacies appear more conspicuous up here. Old Peugeot 203s, for example, still serve as local taxis. Alternatively there are lambrettas, bikes for rent or horse landaus, which are particularly popular with couples who hire them for a circuit around **Lake Xuan Huong**. Also popular are the **horse rides**. Holidaymakers don cowboy gear, mount Da Lat ponies and are led around the lake with photographers on hand to take souvenir snapshots.

The **railway station** to the east of the lake was once terminus for the now redundant cog-and-rack line to

One of Da Lat's waterfalls.

DA LAT'S WATERFALLS

Waterfalls are promoted as Da Lat's main attraction. Most are in the countryside beyond the main resort area. The flow of water varies according to the season and the best time to visit is shortly after the end of the monsoon, when the flood water is still providing the most spectacular cascades. Of the 30 falls in the region the following are the best known:

Cam Ly
3 km west of Da Lat, on the way to the war memorial. 15 metres high, and 20 metres wide, Bao Dai's father-in-law, Nguyen Huu Hao, is buried on a nearby hill.

Da Tanla
6 km south of Da Lat. Tall falls cascading down tiers.

Prenn
13 km south of Da Lat. These were named after the Queen of Thailand during her visit here in 1959. You can walk underneath/behind the falls.

Ankroet
17 km northeast of Da Lat. It is a pretty ride out of town to the small falls and the lake, which has been dammed and provides water for hydro-electricity.

Lien Khang
30 km south of Da Lat and - like the Prenn - off the road to Ho Chi Minh City.

Also alongside the highway to Ho Chi Minh City are the **Gougah Falls** (40 km from Da Lat) and the **Pongour Falls** (50 km from Da Lat and 7 km off the main road). These are the widest of all cascades mentioned. Locals say they are 150 metres across.

Wrecked steam trains Phan Rang. It still stores a few old **steam engines** and maybe one day the service will be revived to cater for the tourists. For the moment however, the road offers the only transport down to the coast, to **Ban Ma Thout** to the north and **Ho Chi Minh City** to the south-west.

The **Tourist Office**, opposite the Da Lat Hotel at *12 Tran Phu (Tel: 2125)*, provides information about buses, long distances taxis and flights. The **airport** is 27 km south-west of Da Lat at **Lien Khang**. They also organise tours around Da Lat and can give details about new guest houses, visits to the 'Palaces', trekking, bicycle hire, trips to the Koho villages and so forth.

Highway 20 from Da Lat to Ho Chi Minh City, nicknamed the **'Lumber Route'** due to its timber carrying traffic, follows a south-westerly course. It passes various **waterfalls** enroute. At **Lien Khang** the turning to the right leads north to **Ban Ma Thout**, and at **Di Linh** there is a junction with one road north and another to the south and **Phan Thiet** on the coast.

Beyond Di Linh lies the **Di Linh plateau**, one of the main **coffee, tea** and **fruit** growing regions of the Central Highlands. It is possible to visit **farms** around **Bao Loc** in the main market town area, together with the **tea factory, agricultural college** and the **silk worm centre** with its mulberry plantation where they breed the worms and

Plantations and silk worms

DA LAT FACTS

ACCOMMODATION
As a hill resort, Da Lat has many hotels. Best is the now rather faded, grand Palace. Not so agreeable are the cluster of inexpensive lodgings in the centre of town. Scattered around Da Lat are numerous royal and colonial villas, the holiday homes of various former indigenous and foreign rulers. Suites are even available at **Bao Dai's summer palace** and the old **French Governor's residence** (ask at the Tourist Office).

• **Palace Hotel**, *2 Tran Phu, Tel: 2203.*
Large white colonial pile dating from the early 1920s with lawns leading down to Xuan Huong.

• **Da Lat Hotel**, *7 Tran Phu, Tel: 2363*
Large and old, but without the colonial 'grand charm' of the Palace; the Da Lat is opposite the Palace.

• **Duy Tan**, *83 Duong 3/1, Tel: 2215*
Modest, pleasant honeymooners' hotel on the western side of town.

Around the corner at *5 Hai Tnuong* is the **Lam Son Hotel** *(Tel: 2124)*. Near the market and bus station are the **Anh Dao** and the **Ngoc Lan** catering for trippers from Ho Chi Minh City.

Out of town, to the east, is the **Lam Vien**, a hotel under renovation. This is a pleasant area of French and post-colonial villas, some of which are being converted into guest houses. The example is the 1890s **Monh Tam** on *Duong Khe Sanh*, 3 km from town, formerly home of the 'Dragon Lady', president Diem's sister-in-law; it is a quiet location with attractive views over the forested hills and valleys.

RESTAURANTS
Being a centre of fruit and veg, Da Lat has an abundant market. The best places to eat are the stalls inside the markets. Alternatively there are many good restaurants in the town centre which are popular with trippers from Ho Chi Minh City. With attractive settings on Lake Xuan Huong are the **Thuy Ta**, below the Palace Hotel, and the **Thanh Thuy** on the far bank. The main hotels also have restaurants.

gather the silk. Traditionally this is Koho and Ma territory, however, a large community of northern Vietnamese settled here after the 1954 partition.

The road continues from **Bao Loc**, through the **Bao Loc Pass** and descends the forested highlands at the southern end of Lam Dong province. From here it leads through the Truong Son mountains to Trung Phan through the **Chuoi Pass** and into Dong Nai province, the flatlands of the south and to Nam Phan.

Thuan Hai Province

Thuan Hai province is the main homeland of the remnants of the Chams whose splendid civilisation once flourished in the central coastal plains of Vietnam. They constitute about 10% of the province's population.

Last of the Chams

Phan Rang lies 320 km north of Ho Chi Minh City, and 760 km south of Hue on the **River Cay**. It is the first town in the province and, just before entering, you pass two ruined **Cham Towers** alongside the road.

Phan Rang is known by the Chams as **Panduranga**, which was capital of their empire for spells in the 8th, 9th and 15th centuries. As the Viets pushed southwards during the Nam Tien, Panduranga and nearby **Thap Cam** and **An Phuoc** became pockets of resistance against the colonisation. Today, these are still the main centres for the descendants of this ancient culture.

Winding ascent into the forests

Highway 20, heads inland from Phan Rang along the flat lands before making a steep, winding wind ascent up into the forested hills, past the hydro-electric pipes, into Lam Dong province and on to Da Lat, a total of 110km from the coast. A **railway line** follows the same direction, from **Buu Son** near Phan Rang. Trains once provided an important supply service between Phang Rang and Da Lat running the gauntlet of Viet Minh and then Viet Cong ambushes. The line was abandoned, but you can still see the path of the old track, despite the efforts of the lush vegetation. Archaic **steam engines** - some rusting and neglected, others caringly preserved - lie unused in yards at Buu Son and Da Lat, still bearing bullet holes in their armoured plate as a reminder of their services in war. There is talk amongst tourism developers of reviving the route.

The **Cham Cultural Centre** in Phan Rang is run by a body of Chams dedicated to preserving knowledge, at least, of their traditions. This can provide information on the several ancient Cham sites in the vicinity and also offers directions to the present Cham villages. Amongst the remnants of a happier, richer past are the last 13th century **Po Klaung-garai** complex and the 17th century **Po Rome** buildings. Today's humbled Chams live in villages such as **Bau Truc, Huc Duc** and **Ching My** where they retain elements of their cultural identity.

Phang Rang is not really a place where tourists stay, as most wish to continue their journey to Da Lat, Nha Trang, or - if southbound - to Phan Thiet or beyond. The town's accommodation is simple, comprising the **Thong Nhat, Huu Ngi** and **Ninh Chu Hotels**, the last being by the beach.

Ninh Chu, near the fishing village of **Tri Thuy**, is Phan Rang's **main beach** and is to the south of the town centre. A further 30 km down Highway One and you come to **Ca Na**, another beach, but more famous for its **salt fields** which have long provided Vietnam with large yields of salt, much of which is exported.

Salt for profit

Highway One, followed fairly closely by the railway, continues southwards through **Tuy Phong**, and the fishing port and Cham centre of **Phan Ri Cua** before turning inland, returning to the coast at Phan Thiet.

Phan Thiet, 200 km north of Ho Chi Minh City and 880 km south of Hue, is another Cham town as well as being a significant **fishing port**. *Nuoc Man*, the pungent fermented fish sauce so popular in Vietnam, is a local speciality. As elsewhere along this stretch of coast, Phan Thiet has a sizeable Cham community and there are **temples** and **defences** scattered around the area.

Phan Thiet also has **beaches** and, as it's within reasonable range of Ho Chi Minh City, it will probably develop its tourist facilities for weekenders. For the moment, there is the **Vinh Thuy** *(tel: 2622)*, a newly built hotel by the sea; alternatively there is the **Phan Thiet** *(tel: 2573)*, a local Tourist Department hotel. The provincial **Tourist Office** is at *82 Trung Trac (tel: 2474)*. Road number 724, formerly Route 88, heads north out of Phan Thiet and into Lam Dong province, where it meets other routes which connect it to **Highway 20** and to Da Lat. Highway One and the railway bear west from Phan Thiet and travel into Dong Nai province.

NAM PHAN AND THE MEKONG DELTA

Vietnam south of the Truong Mountains is known as Nam Phan (or Nam Bo or Nam Ky or Mien Nam). It is a flat plains region dominated by the greater Mekong Delta. Over eons the torrid waters of the **Mekong** have gathered silt from along the river's lengthy course and deposited it to create the present delta. The process continues and the ever-expanding delta grows some 80 metres a year.

Fast expanding delta

Just to the north of the branches of the Mekong the smaller **Vam Co**, **Saigon**, and **Dong Nai** rivers have shaped their own delta areas. Reference to the (greater) Mekong Delta usually means the combined delta regions of all these rivers - a total area of 67,340 sq km.

EARLY HISTORY

The Funanese, Khmers and Chams once occupied Nam Phan, each living as a politically independent group. **Hun Chen**, a Brahmin from India, arrived towards the end of the 1st century AD and conquered, then married **Queen Lieu-ye** (Willow Leaf) of **Funan**. He was responsible for the Indianisation of the region and, over the following centuries, the **Hindu culture** penetrated deeper to become all pervading amongst the Funanese. The capital of the kingdom was **Vyadhapura**, near present **Banam** in Cambodia; the main port was **Oc Eo**, 190 km to the south, in the present **Kien Giang province** of Vietnam. There were **maritime trading routes** linking up with China, South East Asia, India, Arabia and even possibly with the Mediterranean, as archeological discoveries such as a Roman gold medallion dating from 152 AD would suggest.

Fan Man's victories

General, and subsequently **King Fan Man** embarked on a colonisation spree in the early 3rd century, conquering a greater portion of Vietnam and parts of Siam, Laos and the Malay Peninsula, and laying the basis for Funan's most illustrious epoch in the late 5th century. The decline, though, came shortly after. The *Khmers* of **Kambuja** (or Chen-La, according to Chinese history) were vassals to the north who conquered and absorbed Funan in 535. From the fusion of the Khmers and Funanese evolved the great **Khmer Kingdom**, with its capital at **Angkor Wat**. Nam Phan became an outlying province of the Khmer Empire.

The *Chams*, concentrated along the coastal strip north of Nam Phan, periodically launched campaigns against the neighbouring Khmers, including a **successful naval mission** up the Mekong in 1177 which effectively sacked Angkor Wat. But the decisive thrust came from the Viets, who, completing their long southward march from the Red River Delta, overwhelmed the Khmers in the 18th century to win the Mekong Delta and establish the boundaries of present Vietnam.

Cham's assault on Angkor Wat

The lower Mekong Delta was known as **Cochin China**, so named by the early Portuguese traders because they wanted to distinguish 'Cochin in China' from their colony of Cochin in India. *'Cochin'* may have been derived from **Kiao Tchi** (Giao Chi) as the Han Chinese named their province of Vietnam. Through history 'Cochin China' has meant different things to different people. At one time it constituted half the country, being divided into Upper and Lower Cochin, while under the early colonial French, Cochin China more or less corresponded to Nam Phan.

TRAVELLING IN NAM PHAN AND THE MEKONG DELTA

By Water

From the air the Mekong Delta looks beautiful, a vast, flat expanse with large areas covered by neat squares of paddies, some a waxy green, others submerged by water and glistening.

You realise that there are more waterways than there are roads, from the narrow irrigation canals to the wide muddy brown branches of the Mekong and a greater volume of water traffic than road traffic - shallow draft ocean vessels, barges, ferries, river taxis, sampans and fishermans' houseboats.

From ancient times travellers have used this network of waterways to traverse the Mekong Delta. The Chinese even used to talk of *'sailing across Funan'* (the kingdom which occupied the delta some 1500 years ago). For today's traveller, catching a boat is the most interesting way of seeing the Mekong Delta, especially as the channels penetrate into regions inaccessible by road. **Board a boat at Ho Chi Minh City** and travel up the **Saigon** or the **Dong Nai** or downstream into the **mangrove forest** where the river splits into many channels before reaching the sea to get the best feel of what this area is all about. There are no official tourist cruises at present, although this is bound to change as the

By boat to penetrate the Mekong

Travelling in the Mekong Delta.

tourist industry expands. For the time being, however, the traveller has to sort out his own river transport, though the local **Tourist Office** will provide some assistance.

By Road

Having run the length of the country from Hanoi, Highway One and the railway enter Nam Phan from Phan Thiet and proceed to **Xuyen Loc** and **Bien Hoa** before reaching **Ho Chi Minh City**. Highway 20 from Da Lat connects with Highway One between Xuyen Loc and Bien Hoa.

The most important road to penetrate the Mekong Delta is the extension of **Highway One** which runs from Ho Chi Minh City south-west to **My Tho**. There is no bridge over the Mekong and the ferry across its **Tien Giang** branch is upstream to My Tho. Another road links My Tho to **Cao Lanh**.

Ferries across the Mekong's streams

From **Vinh Long** the Highway One extension continues on to **Can Tho**, which is reached by the ferry across the **Hau Giang**. From Can Tho a road follows the river upstream to **Long Xuyen**, **Chau Doc** and Cambodia. Just before Long Xuyen, a turning southwards leads to **Rach Gia** from where there is a road up the coast to **Ha Tien** and Cambodia.

199

The Highway One extension heads south-west from Can Tho to **Soc Trang** and to **Bac Lieu** and **Ca Mau**. Lesser roads lead off this main avenue, though the quality of their surface is often poor. The **bus service** into and around the Mekong Delta is expanding and improving and in addition to the large buses there are now mini buses. For information about these routes contact the local **Tourist Office**.

Highway 22, north-west out of Ho Chi Minh City, is the **main road into Cambodia**. The **tunnels** of **Cuu Chi** are 35 km out of town on the right hand side of the road. At **Go Dau** the road divides into two; one branch leads west to the Cambodian border, only a few kilometres away, and on to Phnom Penh, the other goes north to **Tay Ninh** and then on to Cambodia.

Road to Cambodia

Highway 19 heads directly north out of Ho Chi Minh City into Song Be province, the rubber country and the heartlands of Viet Cong resistance. At **Chon Thanh** it meets **Highway 14**, the Truong Son's north-south route.

NORTHERN NAM PHAN
Song Be Province

The first town in Song Be province on Highway 14 is **Duc Phong** (Bu Dang). Some 35 km to its south, on the banks of the **Dong Nai River** and around the junction of Song Be, Dong Nai and Lam Dong provinces, is the rich and remote **Cat Tien nature reserve**, habitat for a wide variety of animals including elephants, tigers, bears, leopards and the Vietnamese rhino, a species believed to be almost extinct.

Last of the Vietnamese rhino?

The road continues south-westwards through **Duc Hanh**. Phuoc Long, where the French exiled their dissidents, is up the road to the right at the foot of **Mount Ba Ra**. From here, it leads to **Dong Xoai** and **Chon Thanh**, 265 km from Ban Ma Thout and 80 km north of Ho Chi Minh City on the old Ho Chi Minh-Loc Ninh rail line and Highway 19, formerly Route 13.

There were many **Viet Cong bases** amongst the paddies, forests and rubber plantations of Song Be, a province born from an amalgam of former Phuoc Long, Binh Long and part of Binh Duong provinces. **Loc Ninh**, near the Cambodian border, 60 km north of Chon Thanh, was a **major terminus for the Ho Chi Minh Trail** and the 2000 km pipeline from the North which fed oil to the resistance movement.

Loc Ninh and its surrounding area were the headquarters of the **Communists' Central Office for**

South Vietnam (COSV) - a Viet Cong control centre which became a prime but elusive target for American operations such as **Operation Burning Arrow**, which dropped 1250 paratroopers and sent in a battalion aboard helicopters in what proved to be a failed attempt to find and capture the COSV base.

Highway 19, a significant avenue into Saigon for the Communists during their final 1975 offensive, passes through **Ben Cat**, the north-eastern corner of the **Viet Congs' Iron Triangle** (see page 229), before reaching **Thu Dau Mot**, Son Be's provincial capital, 30 km north of Ho Chi Minh City.

Thu Dau Mot and **Lai Thieu**, about 12 km south, on the way to Ho Chi Minh City, are famous for their **handicrafts** particularly their **ceramics** and **lacquerware**, which is amongst the finest in Vietnam and the world. Potteries and workshops in surrounding villages such as **Tuong Binh Hiep**, 6 km north-west of Thu Dau Mot, can be visited. The finished products are for sale.

Amongst Thu Dau Mot's pagodas is the **Ba Ho Quoi**, the tomb of a noble who was buried with two of his - live - *montagnard* servants who accompanied him to heaven so they could attend to their master's needs.

Celestial servants

Highway 19 continues from Thu Dau Mot via **Lai Thieu** which is famed for its **orchards** and into Ho Chi Minh City.

Dong Nai and Vung Tau-Con Dao Provinces
Highway One and the railway cross paths at **Xuyen Loc** in the middle of Dong Nai province. Highway 20, having descended from the Central Highlands, passes through the northern part of the province, not far from the area where **rhinos** have recently been sighted on the banks of the **Dong Nia**, and joins Highway One west of Xuyen Loc. A road south of Xuyen Loc leads the 77 km down to Vung Tau.

Vung Tau
Vung Tau, along with its immediate hinterland and the islands of Con Dao, some 195 km to the south-west, constitute Vung Tau-Con Dao, the **smallest province** in Vietnam, covering only 249 sq km. It has been classified as a **'Special Development Zone'**.

Europeans at the mouth of the Saigon

Vung Tau stands on a headland called **Cap St Jacques** by Portuguese seafarers and the French colonists. It juts into the sea near the mouth of the **River Saigon** and the town has long been a port, serving as a shipping outlet

Choice resort

for Ho Chi Minh City. The French saw beauty in the sand and Vung Tau's fine beaches and proximity to Saigon, 120 km south-east of the city, also made it an obvious choice for a resort.

For the Americans Vung Tau was a playground where soldiers took time off to enjoy their Rest and Recreation (R&R) on the beach and at bars with names like the Honolulu. It was also a training camp for the **Political Action Teams** (PATS), the pro-South Vietnamese commandos who were then sent to infiltrate the Viet Cong and North Vietnamese forces.

Day trippers

Nowadays, over the weekends, families and groups of youngsters take day trips from Ho Chi Minh City and Bien Hoa, to Vung Tau although few stay overnight, except during the longer holidays. Soviet oil workers have constituted the bulk of foreign tourists since a joint Viet-Soviet venture set up rigs 150 km from this coast in the 1980s.

Downtown Vung Tau lies between two hills on the western coast of the peninsula, overlooking **Bai Truoc** (Front Beach). To the north, around the promontory, is the more peaceful **Bai Dau beach**; to the south, skirting the other hill, are the **Roches Noires** and the more exposed **Bai Dau beach**. On the other side of the headland, facing eastwards, is **Bai Sau** (Back Beach), a 5 km long stretch of sand. The sea here can be good for surfing, but is also dangerous. 15 km up the coast is **Long Hai** which also has a sandy beach.

Christ over the South China Sea

Opportunities for water sports will increase as the tourist business is rapidly expanding. Alternative activities are limited to taking walks up and around the two hills from where there are fine views. Up on the southern hill **(Nui Nho)** are a **colonial lighthouse** and a giant American-built **statue of Jesus**. Also, looking across the South China Sea, on the north side of the town centre, is **Bach Dinh** (White Villa), the early 20th century, colonial-style residence of emperors, later the home of President Thieu.

The most famous of Vung Tau's pagodas is the **Niet Bau Tinh Xa**, one of the largest temples in Vietnam, built in 1971 on the southern end of the peninsula on the hillside overlooking the South China Sea. Visitors pose for holiday snaps alongside the serene 12 metre long **reclining Buddha**. Statistics of enormity, such as the weight of the **bronze bell**, which tips the scales at 5000 kg, are proudly documented.

The **Thich Ca Phut Dai**, dedicated to **Sakya Mouni**, the

Buddhist God of Mercy, is also an impressively proportioned temple with a 20 metre high stupa. Its **urns** contain earth gathered from the Buddha's four most sacred places. Built in 1962, it is near Bai Dau beach.

In contrast to these modern shrines is the century old **Linh Son Temple** with its even more ancient - possibly pre-Khmer - **statue of Buddha**. Nearby is a **temple** dedicated to the whale, object of worship for local fishermen since the days of the Champa Kingdom. A **festival to the whale** is held on the 16th day of the 8th lunar month.

10 km north of Vung Tau is the **tomb of Chau Van Tiep**, the Viet general who won this region from the Khmers in the 18th century. Locals point out the place

---

VUNG TAU FACTS

ACCOMMODATION
The French colonials, American soldiers, Soviet oil worker, all types of Vietnamese and, most recently, Western tourists have retreated to Vung Tau for fun. Over the years many hotels have been built to accommodate them. Central and close to Front Beach are:

Hoa Binh, *11 Nguyen Trat, Tel: 2265*
One of the largest and probably the best Hotel in town. The **Thien Thai** and **Hanh Phuoc** hotels are both nearby on *Nguyen Trai.*

A few hundred metres to the north is a cluster of other hotels including:

Thang Loi, *1 Duy Tan, Tel:2135*

Song Hong, *12 Hong Dien, Tel: 2137*

There are also, rather confusingly, the **Song Huang** *(tel: 2491)* and the **Song Hau** *(tel: 2589)* in Truong Vinh Ky and Duy Tan respectively.

International, *4 Thuy Van, tel: 2666*

Along the waterfront, to the right and to the left, there are bungalows for rent by the night or for longer at **Thanh Liem Bungalows** and the **Rung Duong Bungalows**.

The **Tourist Office**, *59 Tran Hung Dao*, (inland from Front Beach), *tel: 2138*, can recommend suitable lodgings and restaurants of which there are quite a few, and give information on local entertainment and boat and air services to **Con Dao**, as well as transport to **Bien Hoa** and **Ho Chi Minh City**.

where the Khmers built a reservoir which served as a watering hole for their elephants and horses.

There are several **fishing communities** dotted around the peninsula and they sell their catch at various **markets**; the main one near the town centre. Locally gathered and crafted **seashells** are sold as souvenirs.

Con Dao Islands

The Con Dao (Con Son) Islands lie 195 km south-west of **Vung Tau** and 80 km off **Hau Giang province**. The Group comprises fourteen islands covering a total of 67 sq km. There is one large island, on which **Con Dao City** - the capital - stands. Poulo Condore as the Con Dao Islands were previously known, have long had a place in the annals of Western seafarers. According to **William Dampier** who sailed to the islands in the late 1680s:

'*These islands lie very commodiously in the way to and from Japan, China, Manila, Tunquin, Cochinchina, and in general all this most easterly coast of Indian Continent; whether you go through the Streights of Malacca, or the Streights of Sunda, between Sumatra and Java: the one of them you must pass in the common way from Europe, or the other parts of the East-Indies.... Any ship in distress may be refreshed and recruited here very conveniently; and besides ordinary accommodations, be furnished with masts, yards, pitch and tar. It might also be a convenient place to usher in a commerce with the neighbouring country of Cochinchina, and forts might be built to secure a factory; particularly at the harbour, which is capable of being fortified.*'

A factory was built on **Poulo Condore** by the English in the early years of the 18th century. However, it did not last long. **Captain Alexander Hamilton**, who travelled this region soon after, recounted the fate of the English and their factory:

'*Pullo-condore had once the honour of an English colony settled on it, by Mr. Allan Ketchpole, in anno 1702, when the factory of Chusan, on the coast of China, was broke up, he being then director for affairs of the English East India Company in those parts.*

He made a bad choice of a place for a colony, that was producing nothing but wood, water and fish for catching. He got some Maccassers to serve for soldiers, and help build a fortification, and made a firm contract with them to discharge them at the end of three years, if they were minded to quit his service, but did not perform what was contracted, which was to cause his own ruin, and the loss of the colony; for these Eastern desperadoes are very faithful where contracts and covenants are

Maritime crossroad

Erroneous judgement

duly observed when made with them, but in defailance, they are revengeful and cruel. Mr. Ketchpole having detained the Maccassers beyond the time of the agreement, still entrusted them with a guard of his own person and garrison, and then taking the opportunity of the night, when all the English were in their beds, they inhumanely murdered them all.'

In June of 1819 **John White**, the American sailor, reached Poulo Condore:

'On the 6th the island of Pulo Condore was descried, with its lofty summits towering to the clouds. The English had formerly a fort and factory on the island, to facilitate the intercourse with China and the neighbouring coast of Cambodia, which in the year 1705 were destroyed, and all the English massacred by the Macasser soldiers in their employ, who composed a chief part of the garrison; since which time no attempt has been made by an European power to establish a colony there, nor indeed would any advantage arise from such an establishment, as the island is very unhealthy and unproductive, abounding in noxious reptiles, and affording no good fresh water, although it possesses an excellent harbour, and a fine landlocked basin, fit for careening. There are a few miserable inhabitants on the island, governed by a mandarin, tributary to the king of Cochin-China.'

Macassers on the rampage

Nguyen Anh fled to the islands, during the **Tay Son Uprising** in the 18th century. He struck a deal with French missionary **Pigneau de Behaine** serving as mediator, whereby, in return for military help, Vietnam would cede to France various territories, including Poulo Condore.

During the French rule of Vietnam, Poulo Condore became a notorious **prison** for anti-colonial agitators. Cells were holes in the ground, covered by an iron grill to prevent escape, but to allow in the full blast of the sun or monsoonal downpour. The prison is now a **national monument**, commemorating those revered Heroes of Vietnam who served time and died here.

Penal colony remembered

Today Con Dao has a population of several thousand and the inhabitants **fish** and **dive for pearls**, and also gather *salanganes* (birds' nests) which are found in caves and are regarded as a delicacy in the Vietnamese cuisine.

Fish, pearls and birdnests

Parts of the islands are a **National Park** and there are **beaches** which, one day, may be developed for tourism. But for the moment Con Dao remains too far off the beaten track for most visitors.

There are **ship and plane services** between Vung Tau and Con Dao City.

Twenty-two km out of Vung Tau, the main road north

reaches a junction at **Ba Ria**, at the foot of the **Nui Bao Quan**. One road continues north to Xuyen Loc, another east along the coast and a third - **Highway 51** - heads north-west to Bien Hoa.

Bien Hoa

On the east bank of the **Dong Nai River**, 25 km north-east of Ho Chi Minh City is Bien Hoa, **capital of Dong Nai** province. It is best known for its **Industrial Park**, an industrial zone within easy access of Ho Chi Minh City, and for its old **U.S. air base**.

The French developed Bien Hoa into a colonial administrative centre and built the first airstrip outside the town. The Americans, in their capacity as 'advisors' in the 1950s, expanded this into a significant military air base. It soon attracted communist terrorists and on 8th July 1959 guerillas burst into a recreational room on the base and shot several U.S. army officers - the first Americans to be killed in what developed into the Vietnam War. On 30th October 1964 Viet Cong blew up six B-52 planes and, during the 1968 Tet Offensive, the base became one of their main targets.

First American war victims [margin note]

Present Bien Hoa was founded in the 1680s by Chinese migrants preceding the main wave of Viets' southward expansion, though old pottery unearthed in the vicinity reveals that this site had been settled over 2000 years ago. **Pottery**, **ceramics** and **decorative bricks** are still made in workshops and factories in Bien Hoa and neighbouring towns such as **Di An**, 8 km to the south-west. Visitors are welcome. These crafts and others, old and new, are exhibited in the local **museum**.

Ceramics centre [margin note]

The large **Thanh Long Pagoda**, housing the Buddha with eighteen hands, is the most famous pagoda in Bien Hoa. There is another, the **Dai Giac Pagoda**, on Dragon Island, an old Fukienese Chinese district on the outskirts of town. The pagoda of **Buu Phong** (Precious Peak) is on a hill at **Buu Long**, 7 km out of Bien Hoa, and is reached by a flight of 99 steps. It was built by Emperor Gia Long on the site of a more ancient temple. Also near here is an 18th century **Taoist temple**, the **Chua Bien Phong**, or simply Chau Ba, meaning the Ladies Temple, because of the goddesses worshipped within.

Before the arrival of the Viets, this area was the disputed border between the old Khmer and Champa Kingdoms and, today you often come across legacies of these two once flourishing civilisations. In the 15th century a Champa king donated a **statue of Vishnu** to a temple near the banks of the Dong Nai along with a **stele** which documented, in Sanskrit, his battles against the Viets and the Khmers. The Khmers later took the statue and hid it in a tree trunk, but it was discovered in the 18th century by Viet farmers who subsequently built the **Buu Son Pagoda** to house the god, whom they adopted as their 'patron saint'.

The land around Bien Hoa is **agriculturally productive**.

The French developed rubber in this region and those plantations, still in operation, can be visited. **Other cash crops** in the province include coffee, rice, tobacco, sugar cane and, amongst a wide variety of fruits, the grapefruit-like *trai buoi* or pamelo, a local favourite. A conspicuous cottage industry around here, as in many places in Vietnam, is the **weaving of raffia** into fans, hats, baskets, mats, windbreakers, indeed, into anything a customer may request.

There are **hotels** in Bien Hoa, however, being so close to Ho Chi Minh City, tourists are unlikely to stay here.

The final drive into Ho Chi Minh City is along a four-laned stretch of Highway One, while entry into the city itself is over the **Bien Hoa Bridge** which spans the River Saigon. The Southern army made a token last stand here against the Northern force on 30th April 1975.

HO CHI MINH CITY (SAIGON)

Ho Chi Minh City lies on the west bank of the meandering **River Saigon**, 75 km upstream from the **South China Sea**.

The site was probably first settled by the Khmers and there was certainly a small, thriving port here in the 16th century. The place has had many names. First known as **Ben Nghe** ('the landing stage of the buffaloes'), because the barking crocodiles sounded like buffaloes; it later became **Dong Nai** ('the field of roses)' and later still was transformed into **Ben Thanh** ('the landing stage near the citadel').

Meaning
behind
the name

The Viets took the town in 1698 during their southward march and they subsequently 'Vietnamized' it. Nguyen emperor Gia Long built his **Gia Dinh Citadel** here at the turn of the 19th century and it was briefly his capital before he moved to **Hue**. Gia Dinh remained the regional capital, but it was razed to the ground in 1835 as a result of royalist-peasant fighting. A year later **Emperor Minh Mang** constructed his own citadel on the same site but this was destroyed by French shelling 24 years later. The citadels stood in the present **Gia Dinh-Binh Thanh**

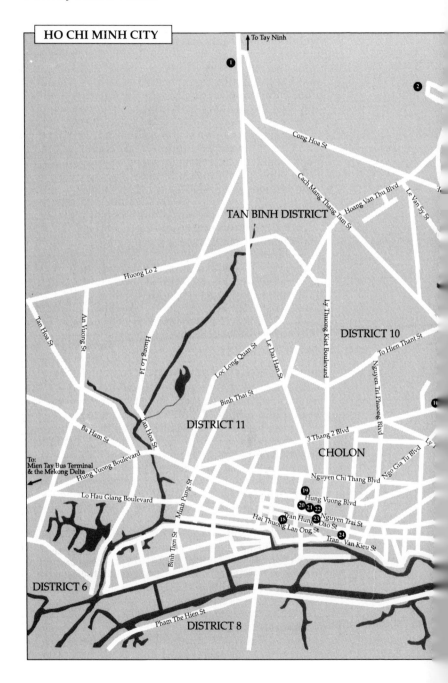

HO CHI MINH CITY

To Tay Ninh

Cong Hoa St

Cach Mang Thang Tam St

Hoang Van Thu Blvd

Le Van Sy St

TAN BINH DISTRICT

Huong Lo 2

Tan Hoa St

An Vuong St

Huong Lo 14

Loc Long Quan St

Le Dai Han St

Ly Thuong Kiet Boulevard

DISTRICT 10

To Hien Thanh St

Nguyen Tri Phuong Blvd

Binh Thai St

Ba Ham St

Tan Hoa St

DISTRICT 11

3 Thang 2 Blvd

CHOLON

Ngo Gia Tu Blvd

Ly T

To:
Mien Tay Bus Terminal
& the Mekong Delta

Hung Vuong Boulevard

Nguyen Chi Thang Blvd

Lo Hau Giang Boulevard

Minh Pung St

Hung Vuong Blvd

Nguyen Trai St

Nguyen Dao St

Tran Hung

Hai Thuong Lan Ong St

Tran Van Kieu St

Binh Tien St

DISTRICT 6

Pham The Hien St

DISTRICT 8

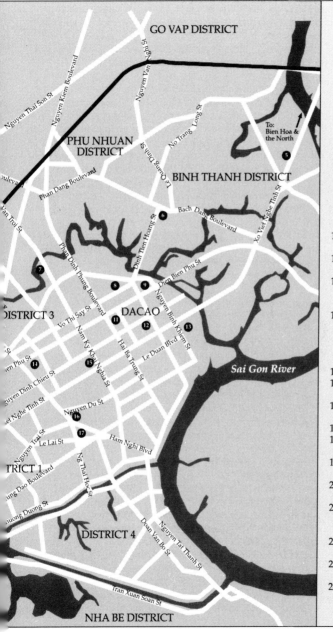

1. Tay Ninh Bus Terminal
2. Tan Son Nhat Airport
3. Nha Khach Viet Kieu Hotel
4. Tan Son Nhat Hotel
5. Mien Dong Bus Terminal
6. Le Van Duyet Tomb
7. Vinh Nghiem Pagoda
8. Tran Hung Dao Temple
9. Emperor of Jade Pagoda
10. Hoa Binh Theatre
11. Cambodian Consulate
12. Vietnam Airlines (Domestic)
13. National Museum, Botanical Gardens and Zoo
14. Xai Loi Pagoda
15. Museum of War
16. Immigration Police
17. Le Lai Hotel
18. Nui Phu Hoi Quan Pagoda
19. Phuc An Hoi Quan Pagoda
20. Quan Am Pagoda
21. Cung Chua Thien Hau Pagoda
22. Nghia An Hoi Quan Pagoda
23. Tam Son Hoi Quan
24. Thien Hong (Arc-en-Ciel) Hotel

district of north-east Ho Chi Minh City, but today, evidence of their existence is limited to archeological discoveries.

John White, the American sailor, had the following to say about Saigon on his arrival there in 1820:

'Toiling under a scorching sun, through a street strewed with every species of filth: besest by thousands of yelping, mangy curs: stunned alike by them and the vociferations of an immense concourse of the wondering natives, whose rude curiosity in touching and handling every part of our dress, and **Curious natives** *feeling our hands and faces, we were frequently obliged to* **chastised with** *chastise with our canes, (which, however, made no impression* **canes** *of fear on the survivors,) and the various indefinable odours, which were in constant circulation, were among the amenities which were presented us on our first excursion into the city. At the end of the first street, however, the scene changed to one of a more pleasing nature. Our route lay through a serpentine covered way, walled with brick, and cut nearly a quarter of a mile through a gentle acclivity, covered with venture, on our arrival at which, the native canaille, biped and quadruped, left us, and we soon arrived, by a handsome bridge of stone and earth, thrown over a deep and broad moat, to the south east* **The beautiful** *gate of the citadel, or more properly, perhaps, the military city;* **ancient Saigon** *and of immense thickness, enclose a level quadrilateral area, of nearly three quarters of a mile in extent, on each side. Here the viceroy and all military officers reside, and there are spacious and commodious barracks, sufficient to quarter fifty thousand troops. The regal palace stands in the centre of the city on a beautiful green, and is, with its grounds of about eight acres, enclosed by a high paling. It is an oblong building, of about one hundred by sixty feet square, constructed principally of brick, with verandahs enclosed with screens of matting: it stands about six feet from the ground, on a foundation of brick, and is accessible by a flight of massy wood steps.'*

Saigon, possibly derived from **Cay Gon**, the Vietnamese for the ubiquitous **Ceiba tree**, became the name commonly used by the French in the mid 19th century. By then the town, together with nearby **Cholon**, had a combined population of 80,000, had become the entrepot for the Mekong rice, and was linked to the royal capital of Hue by the **Mandarin Road**. **Vice-Admiral Rigault de Genouilly**, in command of the campaign which sailed up river in 1859 and laid siege to Saigon, realised its importance: *'Saigon is the rice granary which partially feeds Hue and the Annamite (Vietnamese) army: the rice is due to be carried to the North in March. We must stop the rice'.*

The French eventually won Saigon in 1861. A year later a peace treaty with the emperor granted them rights to the neighbouring Bien Hoa, Gia Dinh and Dinh Tuong provinces, and the offshore islands of Poulo Condore.

French Rule

The French proceeded to develop the town, which had by then been abandoned by most of the native population and had fallen into terrible disrepair. Over the next 50 years Saigon was recreated a **French city** in the tropics, with wide-tree-lined boulevards, a railway line to **My Tho** and a city tram system, zoo and botanical gardens displaying one of the finest collections of fauna and flora in the East. Municipal buildings were constructed and, after a nationwide competition in France, a Parisian architect, **Ferre**, won the honour of designing the **Saigon theatre** in 1897. The *Café de la Rotonde*, at the bottom end of *Rue Catinat* (Dong Khoi Street), run by the celebrated **Madame Perrier**, became the fashionable rendezvous, while along the riverfront promenade the Signal Mast Pier gained the nickname *Pointe des Blagueurs* (Jokers' Point), as the spot to pick up tit-bits of local gossip. Colonial heroes had statues built in their likeness and the streets and squares were given their names.

Increasing yields of **rice** and **rubber** were brought to Saigon for export from the Cochin China hinterland. The population grew rapidly and Saigon became the administrative and commercial hub of Indochina, with Cholon as the main native district. An image of exotic Saigon evolved as a splendid French capital in the Orient. More realistically, Saigon seems to have been a very parochial colonial city of limited chic.

'Saigon is a French town in a hot country. It is as sensible to call it - as is usually done - the Paris of the Far East as it would be to call Kingston, Jamaica, the Oxford of the West Indies. Its inspiration has been purely commercial and it is therefore without folly, fervour or much ostentation. There has been no audacity of architecture, no great harmonious conception of planning. Saigon is a pleasant, colourless and characterless French provincial city, squeezed to a strip of delta-land in the South China Seas. From it exude strangely into the surrounding creeks and rivers ten thousand sampans, harbouring an uncounted native population. To the south, the once separated China-town of Cholon has swollen so enormously as to become its grotesque Siamese twin. There are holes in the urban fabric roughly filled in with a few thousand branch and straw shacks, which are occasionally cleared by

French create their France of the Orient

Gossip on the corniche

Another man's view of 'Paris of the Far East'

211

accidental fires. The better part of the city contains many shops, cafés and cinemas, and one small, plain cathedral in red brick. Twenty thousand Europeans keep as much as possible to themselves in a few tamarind shaded central streets and they are surrounded by about a million Vietnamese and Chinese.'

Taken from Norman Lewis' 1950s account of Saigon in *A Dragon Apparent.*

Remnants of an Era

Saigon became the headquarters for the **Americans** during their occupation of Vietnam. Troops taking a break from the battlefield packed the numerous bars and bordellos, preferring to risk the constant threat of a Viet Cong bomb attack than squander their R&R. Today, there are only a few relics of the American presence such as the tank and helicopter in the forecourt of the **Museum of War**. And while some modern buildings were erected in the 1960s, the Americans were not here to develop the country and the old French structures still dominate the city, housing the ghosts of colonialism.

After marching into Saigon on 30th April 1975, the Vietnamese government renamed the city **Ho Chi Minh City**, in honour of their late leader. The name is a mouthful and Saigon is still commonly used.

Behind Ho Chi Minh City's old French facade there remain further legacies of the past. Baguettes are sold on the street corners, old men wear berets and smoke cheap imitiation Gauloises. At night, upstairs at Maxim's they dance the fox-trot, Twist and dated 'Disco' to the music of the live six-piece band dressed *en Smoking.* The twenty thousand Europeans may have gone and the Vietnamese and Chinese population has multiplied many fold, but

Charming for being French Ho Chi Minh City is an anachronism. And the fact that it is still *'a pleasant . . . French provincial city'* stuck in a time warp out in the tropics gives it its very colour and character 40 years on.

Now, however, as Vietnam opens up, development is likely to be rapid. Already the video sets and latest electrical gadgetry assembled in Japan, Korea and Taiwan are for sale in the market. They say Ho Chi Minh City, rather than Hanoi, will be South East Asia's ' new Bangkok. At present it may seem a far-fetched vision as the lights go out at 11pm sharp at Maxim's and the city's other few nightclubs. But the downtown area has a strong heritage as a playground - for the Americans twenty years ago and the French twenty years before them - and it will be quick to change if allowed to do so.

Downtown Sightseeing

A city shaped
by foreigners

Ho Chi Minh City might have neither ancient nor spectacular sights, but it is not without interest. Once a thriving colonial city, a national capital, a military HQ for the world's greatest army, a squalid Fun City for its soldiers and a refugee 'camp' for millions; this was once the focus of world attention which suddenly fell into obscurity. Ho Chi Minh City's peoples and street life as much as it buildings reflect the city's history.

The city is divided into *Quan* (Q) (quarters). Q.1 is the downtown area, while Q.3 to its north and west is the smart residential area. Q.4 (south) is dockland, and Q.5 and Q.6 (to the south west) comprise the Chinese district of Cholon.

Dong Khoi

The heart of Q.1 is **Dong Khoi**. (a recent name meaning 'Uprising'). This road from the river to the **Gia Dinh Citadel** was once known as Palanqua Street, before it was renamed Rue Catinat by the French and then Tu Do (Freedom) by the Vietnamese. It has long been the city's busiest street.

New names for
new areas

At the top end, architect Bouvard's red brick and granite **Cathedral of Notre Dame**, also known as the Queen of the Peace, stands in solitary splendour in the centre of a spacious shady square. It is not a grand monument, but ever since its completion in 1880 the cathedral, with its 40 metre twin towers, has served as a conspicuous city landmark. Today its doors are almost always locked. The road has gradually encroached upon its neat surrounding garden and now the cathedral stands marooned, serving as a roundabout island for the multitude of cyclists who never give it a second glance. A bronze statue of **Pigneau de Behaine**, the bishop who fostered French-Vietnamese relations almost 200 years ago, once stood in front of the cathedral.

A cathedral as a
centre piece

The large, domed **Post and Telegraph Office** to one side of the square has more character. It was built shortly after the cathedral by **Villedieu**, who went on to take charge of the Civil Building Office in Tonkin. Inside, a large smiling portrait of Ho Chi Minh keeps a watchful eye on the proceedings; most of the fixtures and fittings date from the colonial times.

Continuing on, you come to the **Hai Au Hotel** (the Continental) at the corner with *Lam Son*, which is the conclusion of *Le Loi*. Also in this square, is Ferre's theatre, the **City Theatre**, a colonial landmark at the end of Le

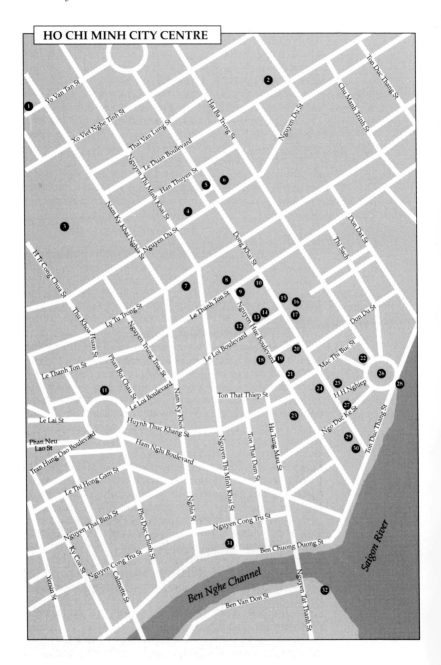

HO CHI MINH CITY CENTRE

Loi. The **circus** which is held in the theatre is worth a visit. The **Tourist Office** has the full programme of events.

Leafy downtown

The **Doc Lap Hotel** (the Caravelle) stands on the other side of Lam Son. When in full leaf the boughs of the trees in *Dong Khoi* form an umbrella over the streets and, looking down from the roof terrace of the Doc Lap, all you see is a green path leading down to the River Saigon. This stretch of *Dong Khoi*, from the Doc Lap to the river is

Caravelle Hotel, Ho Chi Minh City.

where most of the Western shops and cafés stood in the past and is still the busiest. The side streets are also full of action; those to the right lead into **Nguyen Hue**, those to the left constitute a less salubrious district.

There are many shops selling laquerware and other handicrafts. The persistent hawkers offer maps, cigarettes – for sale individually or by the pack, chewing gum and old Republic of Vietnam money. There are the flotsam of the Vietnam War, the beggars with 'hard luck' stories about the annihilation of their family or of runaway American lovers. Women stir steaming cauldrons on the roadside and serve up delicious snacks. There are restaurants, bars, notably **Brodards**, and a couple of mid-range hotels. At the lower end is **Maxim's** and finally the **Cuu Long Hotel** (Majestic) on the corner.

Tearful tales

Ton Duc Thang
The wide Ton Duc Thang runs alongside the river. Vietnamese terrorists were publicly executed here by the early French colonists, near where the **statue** of 13th century hero **Tran Hung Dao** now stands. The **waterfront promenade** is not as elegant as it was in the past, nevertheless it is worth taking a walk down by the Saigon. The **sampans** are still there, huddled along the river bank while stubby, rusty **ferries** carry passengers across the river. There is a tradition of converting old ships into bars and mooring them along this stretch of the river. In the past, these were targets for terrorists. Today, the luxurious **Saigon Floating Hotel** is berthed opposite the Tran Hung Dao statue, icons of the future and past.

Life on the water

Nguyen Hue
Nguyen Hue (previously Charner Boulevard), is Ho Chi Minh City's wide, grand, well ordered central avenue. It is not as interesting as the more intimate Dong Khoi and, in contrast, it seems rather too empty - except during Tet when it is covered in flowers and packed with people. At the top end stands the grandiose former **City Hall**, now the Peoples' Committee Office. Frenchman **Ant Brebion** had this to say about it soon after its completion:

'The City Hall of which the Boulevard forms the solemn approach, is a costly building overburdened with ornate cornices, mascarons and false colonettes in stucco, topped by a truncated belfry on the pattern of these pavilions whose style is associated with the names of Vespasian and de Rambuteau, two large terraces provided with balustrades support the main body of the monument to the height of the first storey. The whole*

Bad taste in wedding cake architecture

HO CHI MINH CITY FACTS

TOURIST OFFICES:
Vietnam Tourism, *69-71 Nguyen Hue, Tel: 92442, 90775, Fax: 84-90775*

Saigon Tourism, *55 Dong Khoi, Tel: 93444, Fax: 84-98540*

Immigration Police, *161 Nguyen Du, Tel: 99399*
Opening: *8.00-11.00 and 13.00-16.00, Monday to Saturday morning*

Chamber of Commerce (Vietcochamber), *69 Dong Khoi, Tel: 25504*

Post Office, *Top end of Dong Khoi*
Opening: *6.30-19.30 daily*

BANK
Bank of Foreign Trade, *25 Ben Chuong Duong, Tel:94223*
Opening: *7.00-11.30 and 13.30-15.30, Monday to Saturday (closed Saturday afternoon)*
There is also an exchange desk at the airport.

AIRLINES
Vietnam Airlines (domestic), *27b Nguyen Dinh Chieu, Tel: 99910*

Vietnam Airlines (International), *116 Nguyen Hue, Tel: 92118*
Bookings on other airlines can be made here.

Air France, *130 Dong Khoi (Caravelle Hotel), Tel: 9098*

Philippine Airlines, *4a La Loi, Tel: 25538*

Aeroflot, *4h Le Loi, Tel: 93489*

RAILWAY
1 Nguyen Thong (District 3), Tel: 45585
Opening times for tickets: *7.30-11.00 and 13.00-15.00 daily*

BUS TERMINALS
Mien Tai Terminal: 10km west of the city in An Lac district, for transport to the south.
Mien Dong Terminal: 5 km north of the downtown area in Binh Thanh district, for transport to the north.
Tay Ninh Terminal: 7 km north west of the city, near the airport, for transport to Tay Ninh and the north west.

ACCOMMODATION
As in Hanoi, the refurbishing of the colonial hotels is under way. The difference is that Ho Chi Minh has a greater number of the old places to restore and a larger clientele to fill them. Furthermore here in the south they respond faster and more effectively to market demand and there is a greater urgency in the redevelopment programme. The old names are in brackets.

Saigon Floating Hotel, *Ton Duc Thang, Tel: 90788, Fax: 84-8-90783*
Hardly one of the old colonial hotels, but currently the most luxurious and modern accommodation in town. This lavish houseboat was towed from Australia in 1989 and it has remained moored here on the River Saigon ever

since. On board facilities include a swimming pool, saunas, a tennis court, a gym, as well as the best international business services and communications in Ho Chi Minh City.

Ben Thanh Hotel (Rex), *141 Nguyen Hue, Tel: 92185, Fax: 84-8-91469*
The city's grand hotel since the time of American occupation. There is a swimming pool and lovely roof top terrace with bar and views over Nguyen Hue.

Hai Au (Continental), *132 Dong Khoi, Tel: 94456, Fax: 84-8-90936*
Saigon's legendary rendezvous immortalised in books such as Graham Greene's *The Quiet American*. With the recent refurbishment at great expense, the old colonial hotel is once again the place to stay for that combination of character and comfort.

There are several other hotels down Dong Khoi; continuing down Dong Khoi from the Hai Au:

Doc Lap (Caravelle), *19-23 Lam Son, Tel: 93704, Fax: 84-8-99902*
Another famed lodging from the war days. The high rise hotel, particularly strong in French character, was where many of the war correspondents resided. There is a pleasant roof top terrace.

Bong Sen (Miramar), *117-119 Dong Khoi, Tel: 91516*
Also known as the Lotus (bong sen). Another high rise, but less expensive and less stylish then the Doc Lap, though also in the heart of the action. There is a small roof top terrace.

Huong Sen (Astor), *70 Dong Khoi, Tel: 91415*
A little smaller and of roughly the same mid-range standard as the Bong Sen which is across the road.

Dong Khoi, *8 Dong Khoi, Tel: 92178*
Another of the old favourite colonial haunts, currently inexpensive as it awaits refurbishment.

Cuu Long (Majestic), *1 Dong Khoi, Tel: 95516, Fax: 84-8-91470*
Once the most elegant of the French hotels. Overlooking the River Saigon it has a prime location and it, too, is very much part of local folklore. Its pavement cafe was a rendezvous for the likes of Graham Greene. Unless it is lavishly refurbished it will remain a pleasant 'off beat' hotel, away from the mainstream businessmen.

There are also a few hotels on the parallel Nguyen Hue:

Kim Do, *133 Nguyen Hue, Tel: 93811*
Thang Long (Oscar), *69a Nguyen Hue, Tel: 93416*
Both inexpensive central hotels.

Huu Nghi (Palace), *56-64 Nguyen Hue, Tel: 97284, Fax: 84-8-99872*
One of the tallest buildings in Vietnam, Saigon's favourite former Palace is popular for its weekend dances. There is a pool and terrace on the 15th floor from where there are some of the best views in town. It is much the same standard and style as the Doc Lap.

Elsewhere in town:

Le Lai, *76 Le Lai, Tel: 95147, Fax: 84-8-90282*
A smart hotel just beyond the market. There is less expensive accommodation in the immediate vicinity.

Thien Hong (Arc-en-Ciel), *52 Tan Da, Tel: 52550*
The best of the hotels in Cholon.

Hotels near the airport:

Tan Son Nhat, *200 Hoang Van Thu, Tel: 41079*
Nha Khach Viet Kieu, *311 Nguyen Van Trot, Tel:40897*

NIGHTLIFE
There were 500,000 prostitutes in South Vietnam at the height of American occupancy, a ratio of one for every US serviceman. After the reunification in 1975 entertainment took on a new aspect, however the communist government purged the decadence and having fun suddenly became a rather serious affair. The vision of the fashionable world was blocked and Saturday night out meant ballroom dancing to a formal dance band. Now, as Vietnam emerges from the darkness, the young have caught sight of the West and focused on Madonna, Michael Jackson and the like. The formality shrouding enjoyment is lifting and, tonight, Vietnamese can let their hair down on the dance floor at the most of the top hotels, as well as nightclubs such as **Maxim's** on *Dong Khoi*.
Saturday evening though, should start with bike cruising. There is a set circuit: clockwise down *Dong Khoi*, then up *Nguyen Hue* and around again and again for an hour or two. Thousands on bicycles or motorbikes take part in this Saturday ritual which is no more than a promenade on two wheels. It is a happy throng going around in circles tinkling their bells and hooting their horns.
Alternatively there are the **Municipal Theatre** on Dong Khoi and the **Hoa Binh Theatre** in District 10 both of which stage Vietnamese plays, concerts and other entertainment.

RESTAURANTS
The best of the hotels mentioned above have good restaurants and serve Vietnamese, Chinese and Western dishes; often the restaurants are on the top floor and aperitifs are served on the adjoining roof garden overlooking the city. Beyond the hotels there are two celebrated favourites: **Maxim's** *13-17 Dong Khoi (Tel: 966760)*, in the heart of the downtown with live music while you dine and dancing upstairs to help with the digestion, and **La Bibliotheque de Madame Dai** (Madame Dai's), *84a Nguyen Hue*, near Notre Dame, where there are half a dozen tables for diners in the library of the home of Nguyen Phuoc, a former lawyer and senior representative of the old South. Elsewhere there are many restaurants, especially in and around *Donh Khoi* and the **market areas** where there are also the informal food stalls serving local dishes to locals. Delicacies for the not so delicate include snake, bat, porcupine and even wilder choices and can be had at places such as **Nha Hang** in *Me Linh (Tel: 22628)*, not far from the Saigon Floating Hotel; dog, a northern speciality, is less appreciated in the south. Cholon, 'China Town', has the greatest selection of Chinese food. Ask locals for current restaurant recommendations.

construction is in very bad taste. So we shall refrain from mentioning the names of the two architects who had to spend nearly ten years 1900-1908 to complete the designs for this edifice'.

There are **shops, offices** and **several hotels** on Nguyen Hue. A colourful **market** is clustered in the lanes on the south side of the boulevard, where locals sell meat, fish, live animals, vegetables, spices, imported cigarettes and beers and the latest electrical gadgets. Infamous Bamboos (the old Indochinese slang for brothels) stood here a hundred years ago and were patronised by soldiers and sailors until their all too public notoriety led to them being closed down. A few simple **restaurants**, serving excellent food, can be found in these backstreets. The Le Loi thoroughfare leads to the **Ben Thanh**, the city's main market, topped by a famous **clock tower**, which comprises numerous stalls inside a large colonial hall. The junction of major avenues in front of the Ben Thanh is traditionally an assembly point for public rallies.

Modern market in place of old brothel

Further Out

The sights beyond the downtown area are reasonably spread out and it is wiser to take a cyclo or hire your own bike if you want to visit them.

Cyclo tour

The **Thong Nhat Hall**, surrounded by **extensive gardens**, is a few blocks north-east of the Ben Thanh. It stands conspicuously at the end of *Le Duan*, a short walk from the Cathedral Square. In 1872 the French built for their Governor General a vast and - according to some French sources of the day - pretentious pile in these grounds, an appropriate symbol for a colonial power. Later, convict labourers took a year to complete the landscaping of the lawns.

The Palace

After the departure of the French, the residence became the Presidential Palace and home of **Ngo Dien Diem**, President of the Republic of Vietnam, though, in February 1963 the place was badly bombed by disenchanted Southern airforce officers. The new palace, typically Sixties in style was completed in 1966 and called **Independence Palace**.

Just before 11am on 30th April 1975, Northern tanks rumbled down the boulevard leading to the palace. They smashed through the gates, one of the soldiers jumped down and ran up the palace stairs and hoisted the Viet Cong flag. Inside, in the State Room on the second floor, the South's President, **General Minh**, and his cabinet calmly awaited the Communists. This was the final moment of the war and, after all the carnage, the surrender was surprisingly peaceful. General Minh, known as 'Big Minh' because of his size, was allowed to emigrate to France in 1983. The palace was renamed **Hoi Truong Thong Nhat** (Reunification Hall).

Big Minh surrenders

Thong Nhat Hall is still used for government business, however you can visit some of the rooms including the **State Room**, where the Southern government conceded defeat in 1975, the **Banquet hall**, the **Golden Room** – one of the main reception rooms – and various private chambers of past presidents.

Entrance: 105 Nguyen Du; Tel: 90629
Opening Hours: 8.00-10.00 and 13.00-17.00 hours daily

Le Duan

Originally called Norodom Boulevard in honour of **Norodom I, King of Cambodia**, who came here on a state visit in 1867, this is the long, straight avenue leading from **Thong Nhat Hall** to the **Botanical Gardens**. Neat lawns straddle the first stretch of Le Duan, beyond the cathedral square on the right, the boulevard is lined by government buildings. The old elegant **French Embassy**, now the **Consulate**, is here, as is the **former American Embassy** which now houses offices for a government petrol company. It was from here the last of the American subjects made their dramatic roof top helicopter evacuation on the 29th April 1975. The one time **British Embassy**, now looking very neglected, is further down the boulevard. The French used rubble from **Minh Mang's citadel** - which they destroyed in 1859 - to build the final section of Le Duan. The **citadel**, like Gia Long's citadel before, was centred on the area to the left of lower Le Duan. The city's smart **residential district**, originally created during colonial times and comprising luxury villas and consulates, spreads out on the eastern side of Le Duan.

Embassy rows

At the bottom end of Le Duan is a large park, which includes the **Botanical Gardens and Zoo (Thao Cam Vien)**. It was created by the French in 1864 and covers 33 hectares and thus 'balances' the Thong Nhat Hall estate up at the top end. The **National Museum** is near the entrance of the park.

The most direct way back to the city centre is to return up Le Duan until you reach the cathedral and Dong Khoi on your left.

Ho Chi Minh City's Pagodas

The city's more famous pagodas are spread around the Quan 3 district, north-west of the downtown area. Opening times vary, some keeping normal business hours, others staying open all day.

Vinh Nghiem Pagoda in *Nam Ky Khoi Nghia:* A large modern-style Buddhist pagoda built in the mid-1960s. A major festival is held here on the 15th day of the first lunar month.

Xa Loi Pagoda in *Ba Huyen Thanh Quan,* off *Dien Bien Phu:* A modern-style many-storied Buddhist pagoda which, according to devotees, houses a sacred relic of the Buddha. Buddhist monks immolated themselves here in reaction to President Diem's purge on their faith.

Buddhists' drastic protest

Emperor of Jade Pagoda in *Mai Thi Luu,* near *Vo Thi Sau,* in the Dakao district: Built in 1900, this includes a statue of the Chinese **Quan Am**. Quan Am was rejected by her husband and family and, disguised as a monk, took refuge in a temple. A woman accused her, obviously wrongly, of fathering her son. Nevertheless, Quan Am adopted the boy, only to be denounced by the rest of society. On her death the truth of how she had been so unjustly maligned was revealed and she was pronounced **Guardian of the Mother and Child**. This is a Taoist and Buddhist pagoda and it also used to be a meeting place for various Chinese secret societies. The Hall of Hell has a relief showing the thousand tortures of Hell.

Tran Hung Dao Temple in *Vo Ti Sau,* near *Dien Bien Phu Street:* A temple, built in 1932 and renovated in the 1950s, dedicated to **General Trang Hung Dao**, the revered 13th century soldier, who scored an heroic victory against Kublai Khan. The more famous Keip Bac Temple, in the north of the country, was erected in his honour on his death in 1300.

Medieval hero

Two key figures in Vietnam's history, both close associates of **Emperor Gia Long**, were buried in the **Gia Dinh**. The first, **Pigneau de Behaine**, the French missionary who served as the catalyst in what became the colonial French-Vietnamese relationship, died in 1799. The second, **Le Van Duyet**, was a prominent general under Gia Long during his battle against the Tay Son Uprising. After his death in 1831, **Emperor Minh Mang** posthumously accused him of treason and then had his tomb in Gia Dinh destroyed. However, Le Van Duyet's mausoleum and honour were restored by **Emperor Tu Doc**, Minh Mang's successor. Address: *Dinh Tien Hoang.*

Museums
National Museum (Bao Tang Lich Zu)
The museum, immediately to the left on entering the **Thao Cam Vien park**, was built in 1928 with assistance from the French School of the Extreme Orient. **Archeological finds and artifacts** from Vietnam's various ancient and more recent civilisations are on display. These, accompanied by maps and diagrams help put in context the country's different historical eras although, unfortunately, there are few captions in English.

One of the main collections of discoveries is from the **The Dong Son** **Dong Son** civilisation, the Bronze Age culture which **and their** reached its peak around the 3rd century BC and stretched **bronze drums** from the Chinese border south of present Nghia Binh province. The name is derived from **Dong Son Village**, near Thanh Hoa in Thanh Hoa province, which was one of the first and most important sites unearthed by archeologists. **Sa Huynh**, in Nghia Binh province, proved to be another significant dig and the settlement was probably a colony of Dong Son. Highly decorated **bronze drums**, large, mushroomed-shaped with a flat top and handles on the side, are the most famous of the Dong Son artifacts. The drums were used in burial ceremonies and similar examples have been found in lands from China to Indonesia. The Vietnamese have adopted the drum as a symbol of their ancient culture. Also amongst the Dong Son collection are **arrowheads**, **agricultural implements**, **pottery**, **bracelets**, and **ornaments**, most of which show the Chinese and Indonesian influence.

The Indianised kingdom of **Funan** flourished in present southern Cambodia and Vietnam between the late first and mid-sixth centuries AD. the capital was on the Mekong in Cambodia, but the main port, **Oc Eo**, was in **Oc Eo and its** the present **Kien Giang province** of Vietnam. Items **international** originating from the other side of the world have been **connections** found at the Oc Eo site, giving further credence to the notion that the port was on the China-India-Middle East-Europe trade route. Some of the discoveries are on display in the museum.

Statues of Hindu gods gathered from the ancient Khmer and Cham sites are also on exhibition. The Khmers, successors to the Funanese occupied southern Vietnam and the Chams held the coastal territory immediately to the north. Both were Indianised, politically independent civilisations who survived alongside each other for centuries, until the Viets, on their southward march, absorbed their cultures during the 17th and 18th centuries.

The southward march retold

Typically, the history of the Viets is well documented from their cradle in the Red River Delta onwards. Objects from the Viets' history, whether their own or foreign, are also on display.

Opening hours: 8.00-11.30 and 13.00-16.00 daily, except Monday

The **Memorial Temple**, opposite the museum and also built in 1928, honours past heroes. Traditionally, the heads of government would come here to pay homage to the illustrious ancestors before taking office.

The Park, Botanical Gardens and Zoo (Thao Can Vien)
The park is pretty and a popular place for couples to stroll and for families to picnic. At the far end, it leads down to the **Thi Nghe**, a tributary of the Saigon. There is a simple **Amusement Park** for kids, apparently both the Botanical Gardens and Zoo are undergoing an ongoing facelift. Fifteen years ago the **Gardens** had just short of 2000 different species of **medicinal** and **ornamental plants**, over 100 varieties of **orchids** and 40 types of **water lilies**, thus constituting one of the finest collections of such plants in the world; present statistics are unknown. The **Zoo** which comprises cages and enclosures scattered around one section of the park, had sad-looking elephants and various other species of indigenous fauna on show.

Ho Chi Minh's Wharf (Nha Rong - The Dragon House)
On the 5th June 1911 Ho Chi Minh left Vietnam from the Saigon docks. It was 30 years before he returned home. The wharf from where he departed is on the lower side of the confluence of the River Saigon and the Rach Ben Nghe. The **Nha Rong**, the mid-19th century building standing on this spot, is the city's **'Ho Chi Minh' museum**, housing memorabilia relating to Uncle Ho.

Uncle Ho remembered in the south

Opening hours: 8.00-11.30 and 14.00-18.00 hours daily, except Monday and Friday.

Museum of War
In *Vo Van Tan Street*, parallel to the larger *Xo Viet Nghe Tinh*, the museum occupies the former Information

A stall in the Hanoi market.

Ducks and chickens for sale in the Hanoi market.

The mangosteen is an unusual-looking fruit grown in Vietnam.

Rice paddies are a common sight in Vietnam.

**The native view
of the war**

Service Office of Saigon University. Concentrating on the
North-South war between the **Communists** and the
American-Southern forces, the displays - photographs,
diagrams, commentaries, weaponry and other war
paraphernalia - simply, but effectively, show the brutality
of the war, albeit from one side. They recount the
relentless American offensives, the injustice of the
Strategic Hamlets, the instances of torture inflicted by
U.S. soldiers - such as the case of the captured Viet Cong
suspect who had his liver cut out while still alive.
Outside, in the **forecourt**, are the **larger weapons** like
tanks, a helicopter and a fighter jet. There is also a
guillotine brought over by the French at the beginning of
this century which was taken around the country and
used to decapitate Vietnamese agitators.
*Opening times: 8.00-11.30 and 13.00-16.00 daily, except
Monday.*

Museum of the Revolution (Vien Bao Tang Cach Mang)
Another **display of war**, though this is more of an
illustrated history, of the struggle and final victory of the
Vietnamese against the French and the Americans, rather
than merely images of brutality. Appropriately the
museum is housed in a palatial, late 19th century colonial
building, an ostentatious symbol of the regime Ho Chi
Minh wanted to overthrow. A Soviet tank and an
American helicopter stand in the lawns.
*Opening times: 8.00-11.30 and 14.00-16.30 daily except
Monday.*
Address: 27 Ly Tu Trong (Tel: 99741)

Drug Addicts, Orphans, Lacquerware and Orchards
Drug addiction amongst younger people became a
serious problem during the Vietnam War and its
aftermath. A **rehabilitation centre** was established in
1975 and today it is featured on tourist itineraries. The
Vietnamese claim to have invented a novel cure for
addicts known as BM1, which is a 'medicinal sweet'
made of natural herbs and containing no narcotic
antidote. **Drug Treatment Tours**, packages comprising
treatment and tourist excursions are available for
foreigners. The contact address is *39 Le Thanh Ton Street,
Ho Chi Minh City, Tel: 95000, Telex: 8 275 HOTCL, Fax: 84-
98540.*

Cure for junkies

Orphans were another sad result of the war and a visit
to an **orphanage** can also be arranged. To quote the
tourist brochure: *'School of young buds: The war has created*

*so many orphans whose care and education show the pre-
eminence of a socialist state. You will be greeted by songs, and
dances as fresh and innocent as young shoots.'* Several times a
week orphans, and youngsters with relations living
abroad, are assembled at the airport and, each one tagged
with name and destination, are despatched by the plane
loads through the **United Nation's ODP** (Orderly
Departure Programme) to their new or long lost parents
in the West (see page 115).

Vietnamese excel in two crafts in particular. In these
they are reputed to be the best in the world. One is
embalming, the other is **lacquerware (see page 20)**. Visits
to lacquerware factories in nearby **Thu Dau Mot** can be
arranged through the **Tourist Office**. The final product
can be bought direct from the craftsmen or in the shops in
Dong Khoi and elsewhere in Ho Chi Minh City.

Vietnamese have a great love and respect for **flowers**
and, during the season, families will arrange outings
specially to see and breathe the new blossoms.
Excursions to gardens, the hamlets and orchards, where
they grow mangosteens, rambutans, durians, jack fruit,
and chom chom, are offered to tourists.

Cholon

Lying 5 km apart, Cholon and Saigon used to be know as
the Twin Cities. As the two centres grew however, they
merged to form the present conurbation. Cholon, initially

a cluster of villages referred to as **T'aigon**, was founded
in the late 18th century by Chinese immigrants. The
Chinese community lent their support to the Nguyen
Lords during the **Tay Son Uprising**, but they backed the
wrong side. The Tay Son gained the upper hand and, in
1782, a vengeful faction of the rebels went on the
rampage through the streets, destroying Cholon and
killing 10,000 Chinese.

The Chinese community were quick to rebuild and,
being sharp in business, the city developed into a very
significant **commercial centre**. Indeed, after the French
took control of Saigon, many mercantile families forecast
opportunities and moved down from their traditional
trading base of Hoi An, near Da Nang, to Cholon.

Today, Cholon is the **main Chinese centre** in Vietnam
and one of the largest Chinese communities outside
China. It remains a 'Little China', distinct in character
from the rest of Ho Chi Minh City, largely due to the very
nature of the Chinese who wish to remain detached.

The **French** and **Americans** were wary of Cholon and

viewed it as a volatile, troublesome area. Viet Minh and Viet Cong terrorists would go into hiding here and the district also spawned its own agitators. Amongst them were the infamous **Binh Xuyen**, thought of more as a band of gangsters than a political group though they did align themselves to legitimate national movements. Their victims included a group of 150 French women and children whom they slaughtered in 1945. They were later reconciled with the French and the Binh Xuyen gained seats in the National Congress during Bao Dai's government. However, they continued their Mafia-like activities and were subsequently purged into political extinction.

A Binh Xuyen hotbed

The Chinese population is made up of various ethnic groups which originated in different parts of China (see page 43). These groups have their own communities and each has built its own places of worship, restaurants, social clubs and so forth. You get an interesting insight into the character of the Chinese community by wandering around the streets of Cholon, especially in the company of a local who can point out the idiosyncrasies of the different groups.

Understanding the Chinese

Getting to Cholon: The best way from central Ho Chi Minh City is to follow either *Le Loi* or *Xo Viet Nghe Tinh* which lead into *Tran Hung Dao* and *Hung Vuong* respectively. Both these avenues cut through the heart of Cholon.

Cholon's Pagodas

Cholon's main sights are its many pagodas. The following are amongst the most central and better known. Locals can direct you to others and provide you with fuller information.

Cung Chua Thien Hau Pagoda in *Nguyen Trai:* Built in the late 1820s though subsequently renovated, the pagoda is known by many names including, simply, the **Cantonese Pagoda**, after the community which constructed it. The pagoda is dedicated to **Thien Hau Thanh Mau** (A Pho), the Holy Mother and protector of seafarers, whose statue, topped by a wooden crown, stands on the **main altar**. Lesser divinities also have shrines and ceramic friezes, silk paintings and red lacquerware depicting symbols and legendary tales adorn the complex. The huge **conical incense spirals** which hang in the **inner courtyard** can burn for three months and, during that time, safety will be granted to the person to whom it is dedicated. Worshippers burn their **votive paper** in honour of the deity and pop the flaming talisman into the **ovens** erected here for this purpose. Characteristically the **God of Happiness** and the **Door Mandarin** guard the entrance. Splendid **festivals** are held here, especially the one on the 18th day of the 3rd lunar month. This is probably the best known pagoda in Cholon and the one usually shown to visitors.

Interesting Chinese worship

Nghia An Hoi Pagoda in *Nguyen Trai:* Built by the Chinese in dedication to, amongst other, **Thien Hau,** protectress of the seafarer.

Minh Huong Gia Thanh Pagoda in *Tran Hung Dao:* Built in 1788 this is one of the earliest of Cholon's pagodas. It was constructed by **descendants of the Ming supporters,** of Fukienese origin, who fled China for Vietnam when the Ming Dynasty fell in the late 17th century. It is dedicated to **Tran Thang Tai**, a venerated devotee of the Mings, and decorated with **dragons** - the royal emblem.

Nui Phu Hoi Quan Pagoda in *Phung Hung:* A **Confucianist** temple built by the **Fukienese** community in 1835, it is dedicated to the deity of Happiness and Virtue.

Tam Son Hoi Quan Pagoda (or Chua Ba Chua) in *Trieu Quang Phuc:* Another **Fukienese** pagoda, built in 1835, it is dedicated to the **Goddess of Fertility and Newborns** and is visited by pregnant women, would-be-mothers and mothers with young children.

Maternal protection

Chua Quan Am Pagoda in *Lao Tu:* Mysteriously, although its exact origins are unknown, this is one of the older and most ornately decorated pagodas. The roof is adorned with different **mosaic objects** and elsewhere there are **lacquerware panels**. An effigy of **A Pho**, the Holy Mother, is honoured on the main altar; other statues stand in attendance. Amongst the other shrines there is one dedicated to a cat.

Phuc An Hoi Quan Pagoda in *Hung Vuong:* Built at the turn of this century, this ornate pagoda is dedicated to **Quan Cong,** the horse and protector of travellers.

Further afield, to the north-east of downtown Cholon, are other pagodas, notably the 19th century **Phung Son Tu Pagoda** on boulevard *3 Thang 2,* the more modern **Khanh Van Nam Vien Pagoda** on *Lo Sieu* and, beyond, the **Giac Vien Tu** and **Giac Lam Pagodas.**

China Market

Cholon means 'Great Market' and **Cho Binh Tay**, the main market, on *Hau Giang*, beyond the turn of the century **Cha Tam church** and bus station, has all the Chinese specialities and has a different atmosphere to the Vietnamese markets elsewhere in the city.

NORTHWEST OF HO CHI MINH CITY

The Cuu Chi Tunnels

The Parrot's Beak, a spur of Cambodian territory jutting into Vietnam lies only 50 km west of Ho Chi Minh City. The area in between was formerly **Hau Nghia Province**, a land once rich in Viet Cong which served as a nerve centre and base for Communists operating in Saigon.

This strategic region, a terminus at the southern end of the Ho Chi Minh Trail and within striking distance of Saigon, had been a communist stronghold under the Viet Minh and, in the build up to the Vietnam War, was inherited by the Viet Cong. It was precisely this growing, malignant Communist infiltration in the environs of Saigon which alarmed the Americans and led them to lend their support to the Southern regime.

The core of the growth was an area northwest of Saigon know as the **Iron Triangle** with **Ben Suc** and **Ben Cat** as its northern points and the Cuu Chi district at the southern end of the wedge, pointing at the capital.

In the mid 1960s, soon after the arrival in Vietnam, the American army launched **Operation Crimp**, a savage campaign designed to root the Viet Cong out from the region. They went on to create their own elaborate bases in this enemy territory so as to keep in check the Viet Cong and hence, hopefully, hinder communist development in Saigon.

As the Americans continued to smother the region with their Hi-Tech destruction, razing forests which were potential enemy cover, they began to appreciate the tenacity of the Viet Cong, who, armed with makeshift weapons and their huge will to win, were prepared to challenge the most sophisticated armies and fight until the other gave up the battle. In Cuu Chi the Viet Minh had built a series of **subterranean passages** as their hideout from the French. The Viet Cong burrowing away with nothing more elaborate than hoes, extended the tunnel network, eventually creating over 200 km of underground corridors and chambers.

Above ground the Americans gained a dominant presence, but, from their secret warren, the Viet Cong

Different arsenals, same war

were able to conduct a highly effective guerilla campaign and maintain control of the area. **Tunnel entrances** were excellently camouflaged, usually under natural foliage, sometimes under a bed or cooking hearth in a sympathiser's hut. When the Americans did discover a tunnel they would often send men down into this dark, dank underworld in search of the enemy. And once in this hellish labyrinth, combat was reduced to the most basic, and a man's wits, courage and stealth were as important as any piece of weaponry.

Underground warfare

The Viet Cong lived in these tunnels, popping up to fight and returning to their lair after the mission. Their underground sanctuary was a remarkable feat of engineering. Passages linked sleeping-eating chambers, stock rooms, arsenals (sometimes 5 metres high), surgeries, temporary morgues, and conference areas, which were occasionally used by the morale boosting actors' troupe as a theatre. The more elaborate mazes were built on different levels, connected by trap doors with escape routes leading to exits in a river bank. The Viet Cong also stored weapons here many of them captured from the enemy, including a tank, which had its own room specially made and served as a reinforced command 'bunker'. The tunnels even housed their rice rations, military documents and plans, printing presses and the other things required to maintain their war effort.

Maintaining the morale

The Americans had various methods of flushing out the elusive Viet Cong from their subterranean nest, chucking grenades down the tunnel entrances or detonating even more powerful explosives on the shaft walls. They pumped gas, smoke and water down the passages and their B-52s dropped bombs which penetrated the earth before blasting at tunnel level. These elaborate and highly expensive tactics had varying success rates, although the B-52s' destructive cargo was probably the most effective. By the end of the Vietnam War some 12,000 Viet Cong and civilians had been killed in the Cuu Chi tunnels and district. High death tolls were a fact of life the Vietnamese had long learnt to live with however. They rebuilt broken tunnels and replaced those who were killed.

Learn to live with death

The Americans also frequently sent down their own men into these holes, often seeing it as the best method of getting the Viet Cong. For the purpose, they created the **Tunnel Rats**, a corp of hardened brave men who would crawl where others would not dare tread. These men were invariably short - a necessary physical requirement

Respected rats

if they were to manoeuvre in the tight tunnels - and loners by temperament. Armed with little more than a knife, pistol and torch, they slid underground, engulfed in the evil darkness. The slightest twitch could trigger off a bobby trap, a home made grenade, a poisoned spike, or the anger of the enemy's pet venomous snake, and the most insignificant noise would allow the waiting Viet Cong to identify the position of his target. The Tunnel Rats lived on a razor edge, a fact recognised by fellow soldiers who afforded them due respect. Their motif was a caricature of a rat holding a torch and gun and their motto was *'Non Gratum Anus Rodentum'* ('Not Worth a Rat's Ass), a touch of flippancy belying the essential serious character of these men.

The Viet Congs' life in the tunnels was extremely hard. For the most part they were living in cramped, claustrophobic conditions, devoid of light, sufficient food **Dire conditions** and water or fresh air. The air shafts allowed only limited **in the tunnels** ventilation, the stench of staleness, of sweat, excrement, dead bodies, mould and dampness, was pervasive. This was a home shared with a host of insects, bats and rats, some of which carried bubonic plague, giving further concern amongst Viet Cong and Tunnel Rats alike. Some spent years stationed in this underground world, away from their families and anything remotely resembling a normal existence. And they were always under the threat of a successful hit which would turn their tunnel into their grave.

Despite the majority's commitment to the resistance, there were some, physically and mentally worn down, who cracked under the Americans physiological warfare. Having detected a tunnel complex the Americans would **Insidious** play, through loudspeakers, recorded emotional pleas **torture** from women and girls imploring their sons, husbands and fathers to return home.Those Viet Cong who succumbed and gave themselves over to the Americans were known as **Chieu Hoi** or **Hoi Chanh** (defectors or returnees). They became valuable propaganda tools, as, once plumped on good food, they could encourage former comrades to follow their example. Furthermore, these deserters knew the layout of the tunnels and the forthcoming plans of the Viet Cong and some became 'Kit Carsons', the South-aligned Vietnamese who worked **Enemy enclave** alongside the Americans in their Tunnel Rat teams. **close to Saigon** For most of the 1960s the Cuu Chi tunnels succeeded as an effective Viet Cong enclave on the doorstep of Saigon, despite the huge military onslaught rained upon it by the

Americans. Come the 1970s the shape of the Vietnam War began to change. The North's army was becoming more dominant, overshadowing their Viet Cong comrades, and the Americans began their evacuation of the war torn country. By now also the Americans had discovered and destroyed a fair number of tunnels and, anyway, tactics were beginning to shift away from guerilla warfare. None the less the Cuu Chi tunnels have remained ever since - and will remain for evermore - a graphic reminder of the type of battle waged between the Viet Cong and the Americans and the type of people who fought in it. Today, the area is honoured with the title, **'The Iron Land of Cuu Chi'**.

Highway 22 leads northwest out of Ho Chi Minh City and cuts through rice paddies. Some 35 km along the way the road passes through the town of Cuu Chi.

Visit the Cuu Chi tunnels

Near Cuu Chi a road to the right leads into empty and, in places, drab, sparsely vegetated countryside. At several places along here are the **'Cuu Chi Tunnels'**, sections of which have now been opened as a **national monument** and can be visited by tourists. They are not signposted however, and 25 years on they remain difficult to find without the assistance of a guide.

Former Viet Cong guerillas describe the complex of tunnels with the aid of a chart. They display their old weapons and ingenious booby traps, often cobbled together from ordinary domestic trash, like tin cans, which the Americans had unwittingly discarded. Some have AK-47s and standard Communist guns which they allow you to try out on the rudimentary **firing range**; $1 for one round. They take you on an **overground tour** of the superbly disguised **tunnel entrances**, also pointing out the all too obvious **bomb craters** caused by B-52 hits, before leading you **underground** into the labyrinth of passages which was once their home, shelter and battleground and the deathbed of many a comrade.

Enlarging the tunnels for westerners

Some of the tunnels have been enlarged to accommodate the larger frame of the average visitor, some passages are lit. Nevertheless, just a few minutes down here and hunched in the darkness, scurrying clumsily to keep up with the guide, wriggling through trap doors from one level to the next, is more than enough. You lose all sense of bearings, the walls seem to press in, and you are gasping for air in the humid claustrophobia, the bats brush against you as they flit by. You are left with all too clear an idea of the hell that these tunnels were.

From Cuu Chi Highway 22 continues on to Tay Ninh and Cambodia.

Tay Ninh Province and the Cao Dais

Tay Ninh, 99 km northwest of Ho Chi Minh City, is capital of Tay Ninh province and the final outpost before Cambodia. An unassuming town in itself, it has, nevertheless, achieved international fame as the centre of the **Dai Dao Tam Ky Pho Do** (the 'Third Amnesty of God'), more commonly known as the Cao Dai.

Home of the bizarre Cao Dai cult

Nui Ba Den

Fifteen km north-east of town the Nui Ba Den sharply rises 915 metres from the surrounding flat plains. It is a dramatic rock which you can see from Ho Chi Minh City on a clear day, and appropriately it is steeped in folklore.

Huong, a young girl selected to be wife of a prominent mandarin, chose instead to marry her childhood love. When her boy went off to the army she would climb up this hill to pray at the Buddha's shrine at the summit. One day the mandarin appeared and tried to molest her. Rather than submit, Huong flung herself to her death from the rock. Her spirit entered the body of a dark-skinned girl who told the monk at the hill temple of the incident. He buried Huong's body.

Later Huong, now in guise of the **Black Lady**, appeared before **Le Van Duyet**, one of Emperor Gia Long's generals, in a vision. She told him that on his death his tomb would be desecrated, but later restored, a prophecy which proved correct. Duyet related the story to the emperor, who recalled how the Black Lady had appeared before him during his campaign against the Tay Son Uprising and had advised him to retreat to Siam. It had proved sound advice and he honoured the Black Lady with the title *'Lady of the Linh Son Fairy Cave'*. Today the Black Lady's **cliffside temple** is a place of pilgrimage and there are also **grottoes** in the hill containing old Khmer, Cham, Viet and Chinese shrines. A short distance to the east is the large **Lake Dau Tieng**, a popular picnic spot. Further away, to the north and west, is Cambodia.

Tale of the Black Lady

The conspicuous Cham community, clustered around Tay Ninh, in villages like **Long Tac**, a kilometre or so northwest of the town, is predominantly of the Bani (Muslim) sect. On the banks of the river to the south of Tay Ninh are the **tombs** of three 19th century Cham princes.

Muslim Chams

THE CAO DAI

In 1919 a civil servant, **Ngo Van Chieu**, was stationed on **Phu Quoc Island**. He was a dedicated spiritualist and would frequently perform seances. One night he contacted a spirit which revealed itself as **Cao Dai**, which Chieu identified as the guise for the Supreme Being. Back in Saigon, Chieu continued to communicate with Cao Dai and, on 25th December 1925, Cao Dai pronounced that it was time to *'teach the Truth to the people of Vietnam'*. Word of the Cao Dai spread and, at another seance, a wealthy businessman and reprobate named **Le Van Trung**, was ordered by the spirits to team up with Chieu and spearhead the **Cao Dai movement**.

Trung immediately put an end to his decadent lifestyle, abstaining from opium, alcohol and meat. People were astonished by this **sudden conversion** and Cao Dai began to attract a **cult following**.

The Cao Dais next sought **governmental approval** of their faith and, this granted, on 18th November 1926, they officially founded the **Cao Dai Religion** with Trung as its leader.

Cao Dais believe in **one Supreme Being** who had already established two **'Amnesties'**. The **first**, in the West, was through Moses and Jesus, the **second**, in the East, through Buddha and Lao Tze. While the earlier 'Amnesties' were revealed through people, the **'Third Amnesty'** was so refined that it required no mortal as its prophet, rather manifesting itself through spirits via seances. Cao Dai is seen by its devotees as the **Universal Religion**, a synthesis of Christianity, Buddhism, Taoism, Confucianism and spirit worship.

The faithful are expected to observe five main tenets:
1. Do not kill living beings - because of the life, the centre of consciousness, which resides within them.
2. Do not be covetous - in order to avoid falling into materialism through the need of possessions and domination.
3. Do not eat meat or drink alcohol.
4. Do not be tempted by the sensual.
5. Do not lie - verbal sins are punishable as accomplished crimes.

Four months after founding their religion, the Cao Dais established their **Holy See** near the sacred **Ba Den** (Black Lady) mountain at Tay Ninh; the **cathedral** was completed on 22nd May 1937.

Cao Dais have a **hierarchy of saints** with Confucius, Buddha and Lao Tze at the top, followed by Jesus - because he came later - and various others. The **rank and file saints** at the lower end include John the Baptist, Joan of Arc, Sun Yet Sen, Victor Hugo, Winston Churchill and Anton Greasby. **Animals**, too, are incorporated into this system with the dragon, unicorn, phoenix and tortoise as the **Sacred Four**. On the more human level, Cao Dai theocracy is modelled on the Roman Catholic order, with a **Pope** as the spiritual leader. Besides the religious body there are various other branches of the Cao Daism administering more worldly matters.

The religion spread rapidly through **Cochin China**, winning the support of 300,000 people within ten years of its inauguration. The movement became increasingly politically orientated and **sided with the Japanese**, believing this to be the best way of ensuring the end of French rule and the return from exile in Japan of **Prince Cong De**, their favoured aspirant to the Nguyen throne. The Cao Dais were **anti-communist, anti-French nationalists** and they joined other parties, including the Hoa Hao and Binh Xyuen, to form the **United National Front**. During these politically confusing and uneasy years, shifting loyalties and too much infighting stopped the coalition from being effective and, finally, **after World War II**, the Cao Dai established a **truce with the French**.

The French promptly armed the Cao Dai militia and relied upon them to pacify their regions and to keep in check the Viet Minh. For a while the Cao Dai enjoyed **virtual autonomy** in their quarter of Cochin China, controlling it in a feudal manner, though the French always remained in overall command.

With the French gone, the Cao Dai promoted the vision of a united Vietnam and tried to reconcile Ho Chi Minh and Emperor Bao Dai. At their height, in the 1950s they were very influential, having an army, a strong political voice and up to 2 million followers. Later they became embroiled in territorial sectarian fighting with the Hoa Hao and, as President Diem suppressed them as an independent force, their general standing began to wane, though their religion continued to flourish.

Travelling through Tay Ninh province you see the very idiosyncratic **Cao Dai chapels** in the villages, a modest introduction to what to expect in the capital. The **cathedral**, or Great Temple, in Tay Ninh town is in a large park which also includes a hospital, school and various residences including an orphanage. **Four ceremonies** are held daily: at 6am, noon, 6pm and midnight. During the midnight session **seances** are held to contact the spirits and God speaks to his followers through a medium.

'From a distance this structure could have been dismissed as a result of a marriage between a pagoda and a Southern baroque church, but at close range the vulgarity of the building was so impressive that mild antipathy gave way to fascinated horror. This cathedral must be the most outrageously vulgar building ever to have been erected with serious intent. It was a palace in candy from a coloured fantasy by Disney; an example of fun-fair architecture in extreme form. Over the doorway was a grotesquely undignified piece of statuary showing Jesus Christ borne upon the shoulders of Lao Tse and in his turn carrying Confucius and Buddha. They were made to look like Japanese acrobats about to begin their act. Once inside, one expected continually to hear bellowing laughter relayed from some nearby Tunnel of Love.'
Norman Lewis in 'A Dragon Apparent'.

A large **Divine Eye**, the Eye of God, the supreme symbol of the Cao Dais, shines brilliantly from the cathedral's nave down on the adherents.

Visitors are welcome and a monk can show you around the cathedral. Wearing a simple white habit-like gown he appears very under dressed in this flamboyant monument. You will be asked to **remove your shoes** and obtain permission from a senior member of staff before taking photos of the interior.

There is **simple accommodation** in Tay Ninh, but most visitors to Tay Ninh and the Cuu Chi tunnels are on day exursions and return to Ho Chi Minh City for the night.

TOURING THE MEKONG DELTA

Provinces of: Long An; Tien Giang; Ben Tre; Cuu Long; Dong Thap; Hau Giang; Minh Hai; An Giang; Kien Giang.

The Highway One extension into the Mekong Delta heads south-west out of Ho Chi Minh City and through pineapple country to **Tan An**, the capital of **Long An province**, 50 km from Ho Chi Minh City, and onwards to My Tho.

My Tho

My Tho, 71 km south-west of Ho Chi Minh City, is on the north bank of the **Tien Giang**, the upper branch of the Mekong, and is capital of **Tien Giang province**. One of the main towns of the delta region, it is a **busy market** serving the agricultural hinterland where rice, fruits and vegetables are grown.

Chinese refugees fleeing their homeland after the fall of the **Ming dynasty** were encouraged by the Viets' **Nam Tien movement**, the southward expansion, to settle in the region and in 1680 they founded My Tho.

Chinese city of My Tho

The town later became capital of the old **Dinh Thong province**, one of the three original provinces to be ceded to the French on the signing of the **Treaty of Saigon** on the 6th June 1862. **Phan Thanh Gian**, a local man and prominent diplomat, represented the Vietnamese as the negotiator for this crucial treaty, which ultimately provided the French with a 'legitimate' foothold in **Cochin China**. The agreement demanded:

1. French possession of the three provinces of Bien Hoa, Dinh Tuong and Gia Dinh and the island of Phu Quoc.
2. Opening of three Vietnamese ports for trade with the West.
3. Free passage of French warships up the Mekong to Cambodia.
4. Unrestricted proselytising by Christian missionaries.
5. A war indemnity of four million piasters.
6. French veto over Vietnam's right to cede any other part of her territory to another country.

Phan Thanh Gian became **ambassador** in Paris where he tried to thrash out a more favourable agreement. He had no luck and on returning to Vietnam he attempted, unsuccessfully, to persuade the Emperor to rise up against the colonial occupants. Disillusioned, he went on hunger strike in 1867 and finally hastened his suicide by taking a dose of poison.

Unfortunate death of a diplomat

My Tho became an early and important **headquarters for the French**, who laid a now obsolete railway line between Saigon and My Tho, speeding up communications and their exploitation of the colony. **American forces** later occupied My Tho, and the city and surrounding land were scenes of conflict between them and the Viet Cong.

Sightseeing in My Tho
Besides the river and the market, My Tho's main attraction is the mid 19th century **Vinh Trang Pagoda** which served as a sanctuary for the Viet Cong.

You can take **boats to islands** in the river and there is a **ferry** to the far bank. This is the northern shore of a large island which leads down to the South China Sea on its eastern side and is in itself almost the entire province of **Ben Tre** with the capital in its centre. Strong discontent was bubbling under the surface here by the late 1950s and in 1959 the Viet Cong in Ben Tre rose up against the Southern forces, making this the site of one of the first battles of the Vietnam War. Later, the Americans stationed soldiers in Ben Tre and the town became a target for the Viet Cong who captured it during the 1968 Tet Offensive. In retaliation the Americans devastated the town. *'It became necessary to destroy the town in order to save it'*, claimed a U.S. major.

Fate of Ben Tre

From Ben Tre you can continue your southward journey by island hopping over the lowest reaches of the Mekong's branches. **Tra Vinh** is the site of an historic **Khmer temple**.

My Tho is also famous for **Hu tieu My Tho**, its own speciality consisting of Hu tieu noodle soup garnished with pork, shrimps and herbs. It is served in the town's many soup kitchens.

Tourist Office (Provincial), *56 Kung Vuong, Tel: 3591*

ACCOMMODATION

Centrally located on Trung Trac, the waterfront street running alongside a tributary of the Mekong, are the large **Ap Bac** (the Grand), *(Tel: 3593)*, the mid-size **Rach Gam** and the small **Thanh Binh**. North of the downtown is the **Khach San**, *43 Ngo Quyen (Tel: 3126)*.

A short distance downstream from My Tho is the important **Cho Gao canal** which links the Tien Giang with waterways flowing into the River Saigon and provides a route to Ho Chi Minh. Also connected to Ho Chi Minh City both by road and the network of waterways is **Go Cong**, 36 km east of My Tho.

12 km west of My Tho there is a **snake breeding farm** run by scientists and medics. Several species of indigenous snakes are reared and various parts of the

Serpent cures snakes' anatomy are used to concoct a wide range of **medicines**, providing cures for headaches and madness, backache and paralysis.

Plain of Reeds

Travelling westwards you reach the ferry crossing for **Vinh Long** down a turning on the left hand side of the road. Continue straight on and you will arrive at **Cao Lanh**. Beyond, the road hugs the curves of the river and finally passes through **Hong Ngu** before entering Cambodia.

ONG DAO DUA

Ong Dao Dua (the Coconut Monk), lived on an island in the Mekong. Born in 1909 he gained an engineering degree in Paris. After returning home, marrying and having a daughter, he abandoned secular life and became a monk, creating a curious sect known as **Trinh Do Cu Si** which combined Buddhism with Christianity and drew several thousand followers. It seems he held 'court' with great, but reticent panache, with visitors conversing through one of his disciples. He built a tall tower and from this 'reigned' over his domain like a benign monarch. For years he lived off coconuts alone, hence his name, a diet shared by his **pet bear** and **orang utang**. Ong Dao Dua is now firmly lodged in Mekong folklore, although his eccentric habits are, one suspects, a trifle exaggerated by the admiring locals. Whatever the reality, Ong Dao Dua was, sincere in his hope that his doctrine would help bring peace to a united country and he was imprisoned several times for voicing his views to President Diem.

Cao Lanh is a **market town** offering simple accommodation. North of here spreads a large area of **marshland**, about 120 km east to west and 80 km north to south, known as **Thap Muoi**, the Plain of Reeds.

Flat and covered by reeds, cajeput and brush, the plains are very wet in the monsoons between September and November and very dry during the summer months. The area, essentially the eastern part of **Long An province**, is traditionally known as an outback with **few roads** and a

sparse population. The black clay soil is acidic and poor for rice cultivation, and so the **tending of livestock** is a significant occupation of the locals.

Resistance in the Plain of Reeds

The Plain of Reeds has always been a stronghold of Vietnamese resistance. In the 1860s, the French realised the importance of quelling the agitators from this area. So too did the Americans a hundred years later. Operating from the **airbase at Moc Hoa**, they launched many highly destructive forays into the Plain of Reeds, dropping napalm and bombs and airlifting contingents of troops into the area in an often frustrating attempt to flush out Viet Cong.

Victory against the odds

Early in the war, on 2nd January 1963, 350 Viet Cong guerillas won the **Battle of Ap Bac** (present **Tan Thanh** south-east of Moc Hoa) against the far superior combined American-South Vietnam military force. It was a notable victory. The Viet Cong suffered 18 dead and 39 wounded at the receiving end of the bombs, napalm and thousands of rounds of ammunition liberally sprayed by the enemy warplanes and Huey gunships. They with their comparatively few and archaic weapons, killed over 80 and wounded more than 100. It was an early indication of the Viet Cong fighting ability.

Recently there has been an attempt to develop the area. A highway now links Tan An with Moc Hoa near the Cambodian border. Irrigation has improved **rice yields**, **jute** is cultivated, **oils** are extracted from various plants for use in **pharmaceutical industry** and locals **farm shrimps** near Hong Ngu.

Tracking down the birds

Once a refuge for guerillas, the plains are now a **sanctuary for birds** with storks and cranes being the predominant species. When there is sufficient water, the **Tourist Office** boards visitors on a flat boat and takes them out into the marshlands to see the birds; the scenery and the trip itself are as much an attraction as the birds. **Excursions** into the **Thap Muoi reserve** (also sometimes known as **Cham Chin**) usually operate out of either Cao Lanh or Ho Chi Minh City, some 65 km east of the plains. They may also include a visit to the **Thap Muoi pagoda** to the east of the town.

Vinh Long

Waiting for the boat to come in

The **ferry stage point** on the north bank between My Tho and Cao Linh is usually crowded with queues of trucks, buses and cars, their oil and soot covering the surrounds. The long tedious wait can be whiled away in the row of cheap **restaurants** serving simple meals and luke warm beer. Foreigners are frequently given 'priority' treatment and put to the front of the queue; the attendant would probably welcome a few cigarettes or the price of a beer for the privilege.

The large rusty ferries are capable of carrying two or three dozen vehicles and scores of passengers. They cross to Vinh Long, the main ferry port on the south bank of the **Tien Giang**.

Capital of the province of **Cuu Long** (meaning Nine Dragons), Vinh Long was the main centre of **Catholicism** in the Mekong Delta. You can take a **sampan ride** along the riverbank and to the islands and walk through the lovely tropical **fruit orchards** for which the area is famous. Mangoes and sapotilla are particularly abundant. The locals will also show you the location of the **old Viet Cong hide outs**.

By the river, a few kilometres out of town, is the **Van Thanh Mieu**, a complex of several buildings in a pretty garden, built in 1862 for **Phan Thanh Gian** (see page 236) who spent his last unhappy days here. His home, renovated in 1965, is now a simple **museum** commemorating him and the anti-colonial struggle.

Simple home of
Phan Thanh
Gian

The **Cuu Long Hotel**, *Duong 1, Thanh 5, (Tel: 2494)*, has an attractive setting overlooking the river; there is other accommodation up the road together with a **Tourist Office**. Also here, in this 'tourist district', is a pleasant riverfront restaurant.

Sa Dec

Sa Dec is 23 km up stream of Vinh Long and can be reached by river or road. This is the capital of **Dong Thap province** and another **market** for the surrounding fruit growing area. There are a **Tourist Office** and **hotel** in town. Beyond are characteristic Mekong Delta hamlets, narrow canals, orchards and paddies.

It is 34 km from Vinh Long to **Binh Minh** (Cai Von) from where you catch a **ferry** similar to the one on the Tien Giang across the **Hau Giang** to Can Tho.

Can Tho

Can Tho, 165 km south-west of Ho Chi Minh City and capital of **Hau Giang** province, is the **principal city** of the Mekong Delta. Situated on the south-west bank of the Hau Giang branch of the Mekong, at a point where the river is 2 km wide, it is the major market, commercial centre and riverain port of the region. Many say it is also the home of the prettiest girls in all of Vietnam.

Like other Delta cities Can Tho appears at first to be shabby, chaotic and without obvious beauty in its design and architecture. Its charm lies beneath the superficial. The overall setting is attractive and the streetlife – or more accurately the riverlife – has great colour and character. With pride and a wry smile, locals will talk of Can Tho as their 'Venice' but then they will concede, *'Maybe the comparison is exaggerated - after all we do not have those millions of tourists!'*

Venice without the tourists

A whole culture thrives on the network of channels which lace through Can Tho. People live, trade and travel on their houseboats, sampans and river barges without having to set foot on land. In the mornings and on certain days, scores of small boats will moor alongside each other to create a **floating market**. One of the larger markets is at the junction of seven canals. Locals can direct you.

On land the most interesting **market** is in the streets by the **River Can Tho waterfront**. Here they sell the huge and exotic variety of produce gathered from the surrounding fields and rivers, as well as the more prosaic imports from the outside world. The market is *open 24 hours a day*.

Along the waterfront from the market, before the old French Naval headquarters is the **Hotel Quoc Te**, *Hai Ba Trung (Tel: 35793)*. Nearby, near the **Ho Chi Minh statue**, is a **restaurant** in a pagoda courtyard and opposite, on a boat, is the **Ninh Kieu restaurant**. Other hotels inland from the market, include the **Hau Giang**, *34 Nam Ky Khoi Nghia (Tel: 35537)* which has a good fish restaurant and the **Hoa Binh**, *5 Hoa Binh (Tel: 20537)*, opposite the **Khmers' Munirangsyaram Pagoda**.

Waterfront restaurants

As for the sights, the old **Thoi Binh Temple** commemorates two generals who fought off the Chinese. The **Museum of War** recounts the local Viet Cong fight against the Americans-Southern army. Can Tho was the last city to fall to the North, on the 1st May 1975, a day after Saigon. Visits to **craft workshops**, a **fruit processing factory**, a **fish and shrimp plant**, and a **rice mill** can all be arranged through the **Tourist Office**; the **University of Can Tho**, established in 1966, has a large Agronomy department researching into local agriculture and welcomes foreigners from the same field.

The best times are likely to be had down by the water however and, while a **ride in a sampan** may not have the cachet of a punt in a gondola, it is probably a lot more fun and hopefully much less expensive. If time permits, it is also worth **hiring a bike** and cycling into the luxuriant

Penetrate the orchards countryside, ever deeper into the orchards and groves of rambutans, longyans, jack fruit, durian, sapotilla, melons, mangoes, coconuts, bananas, citrus fruits, avocadoes, pineapples . . .

Tourist Office, *27 Chau Van Liem, Tel: 20147*

Soc Trang

Soc Trang, the second town in Hau Giang province is 65 km south-east of Can Tho and can be reached easily by road. At **Thanh Hung** a turning leads westwards into the remoter districts of the lower Delta region. About halfway along on the Can Tho-Soc Trang road you pass through **Phung Hien**, a busy market town and canal junction. The **Phung Hien Canal**, joining the Hau Giang with Ca Mau in **Minh Hai province**, passes through the town, as does the **Xang Canal** which runs parallel to the road down to Soc Trang.

Soc Trang, previously known as Khanh Hung, has a large Khmer population which expanded dramatically with the influx of refugees fleeing from Pol Pot during the latter 1970s.

The city has a strong Khmer flavour. **Khmer temples**, many of them new, are scattered around town and the surrounding countryside. The **Khmer Museum of Culture**, near the centre of town, gives an insight into the long established local Khmer community as well as an account of the culture as a whole.

On the outskirts of Soc Trang is the so called **Temple of Bats**. Clusters of **mango trees** grow in the **temple gardens** and the boughs of the trees sag under the weight of thousands of hanging **fruit bats**. Mysteriously the bats never eat the fruits on the trees within the compound, preferring to fly into the night to feed on someone else's orchard. Doubtless they have a feast, for the Mekong Delta must be a paradise for the fruit bat. Life at home in the temple grounds must be more frustrating. If requested by visitors, the Khmer monk at the temple will light a bonfire under the trees. The smoke awakens and upsets the plump bats, who, en masse quit their perches and take flight, their numbers darkening the sky as they screech shrill abuse at those down below. Despite the monks' un-neighbourly behaviour, the bats stay on rather than search for a more peaceful home.

Curious habits of the fruit bats

On the same side of town the Khmer community constructed their ornate, brightly painted, showpiece **temple** in the mid 1970s. Visitors are very welcome.

One of the highlights in the Soc Trang calendar is the

Khmer boat races Khmer's *ghe ngo*, a **rowing festival** held on the fourteenth day of the tenth lunar month. The centrepiece of the event is the 25 metre long, **200 year old Khmer wooden war canoe** pulled by some 50 oarsmen and the main attractions are the races between the various teams' boats.

Minh Hai Province

A road runs south-east out of Soc Trang to the mouth of the Hau Giang and the South China Sea. Another route leads south-west, covering 52 km to **Bac Lieu** (once known as Vinh Loi), the second town of Minh Hai, Vietnam's **southernmost province** and the remotest in the Mekong Delta.

Bird reserves The local **Tourist Office** is understandably keen to develop **birdwatching** as the main attraction in the province. Minh Hai's **mangrove swamps** are one of the greatest gathering places in Asia for **wading birds** and the province has little else to offer the average visitor.

There are **two bird sanctuaries** in the vicinity of **Bac Lieu**, the **Vinh Tanh** and the **Cai Nuoc**. **Storks** and **cranes** nest here, congregating in their greatest numbers in March and April. Bac Lieu has a Tourist Office from where trips around the reserves can be arranged, and there are two hotels, the **Dang Rong Hotel** and the small **Anh Duong**.

The road out of Bac Lieu continues 84 km westwards to **Ca Mau**, the capital of Minh Hai. The southern tip of Vietnam, known as the **Ca Mau Peninsula**, used to be called *Tuk Khmau* (the Black Country) by the Khmers, because of the colour of the soil. The Khmers still make up a sizeable portion of the population.

Because of its inaccessibility, the Ca Mau Peninsula, like the Plain of Reeds in the northern part of the Mekong Delta, became a refuge for the **resistance movements**. First the Viet Minh regrouped in the peninsula after the Geneva Accords in 1954 before travelling to the North. Then came the Viet Cong.

The Ca Mau Peninsula suffered badly from **Agent Orange**, the notorious defoliant most commonly used by the Americans to kill off crops and forests, and deprive the Viet Cong of food and tree cover. Eighteen million **Death by defoliant** gallons of defoliants were sprayed from the air over nearly a quarter of the South's forests; the destructive effects are still visible. Agent Orange contains lethal dioxin which finds its way into the ecosystem, poisons the vegetation and consequently man or beast who unwittingly eats it. A generation on, tree growth is still

River market at Can Tho.

stunted in places and children are still being born with deformities which can be traced to their parent's exposure to defoliants.

In spite of being the provincial capital, Ca Mau is even less geared to tourism than Bac Lieu. There is a hotel, **the Ca Mau**, and there will doubtless be a Tourist Office in the near future. Once again the birds are the attraction, with the **Thang Hung Song Reserve** to the south of the town. Beyond here the road peters out, the dense mangrove swamp becoming impenetrable and marshy. Furthermore, few people have any reason to come down here. At **Xom Mui**, the southern tip of the peninsula, the South China Sea meets the Gulf of Thailand.

West and north of Ca Mau, partly along the coast of the Gulf of Thailand, is the dense **V Minh Forest** which covers some 100,000 hectares. The mangrove jungle is divided into the upper and lower regions and in the lower is the **Khanh Tan Reserve**, a **nesting territory** for freshwater and sea birds. As everywhere in this southern Mekong Delta area, **storks** are the main species.

Snakes and bees ... and tigers?

It is rumoured that this is also tiger country. More certainly it is the home of **snakes** and **honey bees**, whose various properties and produce are used by locals. On a larger commercial scale, **shrimps** are farmed on the coast and on the off-shore islands, while **fishing**, **rice** and **fruit cultivation** and **pig rearing** are the more common preoccupations of the province as a whole.

An Giang Province

The road northwest out of Can Tho runs alongside the Hau Giang to **Long Xuyen**, capital of An Giang province. The turning to the left before you reach town follows the course of the important **Rach Soi Canal** direct to **Rach Gia**, on the Gulf of Thailand.

Three km before Long Xuyen, a path to the right leads through **coconut groves** and a cluster of huts to a **ferry point** on the Hau Gian. A small **river taxi** takes passengers across to an island. At the jetty, hop on a cyclo and travel down the island tracks, through the paddies, orchards and hamlets and across the channels and streams. Several kilometres later, you arrive at the **house of Uncle Ton**.

Birthplace of a president

Ton Duc Thang, born in the Long Xuyen region in 1888, **studied in Saigon** where he became involved in the anti-colonial movement. He **fled to France** in 1912, to avoid arrest for this dissident activities, and later worked at sea before returning to Vietnam in 1927 to join **Ho Chi**

Minh. Two years later the French, realising his subversion, exiled Ton Duc Thang to **Poulo Condore** (Con Dao) where he was incarcerated for the next 17 years. In 1945 he joined the Viet Minh and later the Northern government, becoming vice president and, finally, **president of the Democratic Republic of Vietnam** on Ho's death in 1969. The well loved Uncle Ton, as he is affectionately known, died in 1980. The island was his home when he was young and his house, set in a lovely garden, has a **shrine** in his memory. Opposite, by the river, a simple **museum** displays an interesting chronology of his life. The journey itself is much of the attraction of this excursion, for it gives an excellent insight into life on the Mekong River.

Long Xuyen
Long Xuyen is a significant **market town** for locally produced goods. The surrounding countryside, badly bombed by the Americans, is one of the main production areas in Vietnam for **floating rice**, a type of rice able to adjust to fluctuating water levels. Corn, soya beans, tobacco, sweet potatoes and various fruits are also grown.

Advantage of floating rice

The provincial **Tourist Office** is at *6 Ngo Gia Tu (Tel: 52888)*. There are several hotels including the **Long Xuyen**, *17 Nguyen Van Cung (Tel: 52308)* and, opposite, the **Cuu Lang** *(Tel:52865)*. A block away to the east is the **Thai Binh** *(Tel: 52184)* and a block beyond are a few other hotels in *Nguyen An Ninh*. Closer to the market is the **An Giang**, *42 Phan Chu Trinh (Tel: 52297)*.

A road to the west of Long Xuyen leads into **marshlands** and to the **archeological site** of **Oc Eo**, near the village of **Vong Dong** at **Nui Ba The**, a 30 metre high hill. Once the main port in the ancient **Kingdom of Funan**, Oc Eo flourished between the 1st century AD and the mid 6th century (see page 197). Alluvium deposited by the Mekong over the centuries covered the site and extended the coast, so Oc Eo is now inland.

The road northwest out of Long Xuyen runs alongside the river. After the busy market of **Chau Thanh**, another road leads westwards into the irrigated marshlands to the village of **Tri Ton** and to **Nui Co To**, which pops out of the plains to a height of 164 metres and is known for its **mineral springs**. Another outcrop of hills, including the **Nui Cam** lies immediately to the north and rises to over 700 metres. Together they form the lower section of the **That Son** range, or the Seven Mountains, which straddle the Cambodian border. The mountains' main attractions

Unusual peaks on the border

are their **grottoes**. An important canal, the **Mac Can
Dung**, passes through Tri Ton and links the Hau Giang
with the **Rach Gia-Ha Tien Canal**.

Chau Doc

The main road leading northwest out of Long Xuyen
continues beside the Hau Giang to **Chau Doc** on the
Cambodian border. Chau Doc was the capital of the old
province of Chau Doc, now part of An Giang province,
which was in turn part of Cambodia until the mid 18th
century when the Khmers gave it to the Nguyen Lords in
return for assistance in suppressing a rebellion.

The area has always had a substantial **Khmer**
population and its size was multiplied considerably after
hundreds of thousands of refugees crossed the border to
escape Pol Pot's genocide in the mid to late 1970s. The
Khmer Rouge followed in pursuit, penetrating beyond
the borderlands and, not only hounding down their
fellow countrymen, but also destroying villages and
killing tens of thousands of Vietnamese in the process. In
1978 the Khmer Rouge killed 2500 at the village of **Ba
Chuc**, a frontier settlement south-west of Chau Doc. The
bones of those who died are on display as a **reminder of
Pol Pot's atrocities**. It was largely in response to this
infiltration that the Vietnamese government sent their
troops into Cambodia in 1978.

Fleeing Pol Pot (margin)

Besides the Khmer, Viet and Chinese communities
there is a significant *Cham* population around Chau Doc,
which started migrating here when their coastal kingdom
began to wane. They have retained many of their
customs, including their **Hindu** and **Muslim religions**,
and the predominant **Cham Bani** (the Muslim branch),
who live around Chau Doc and Tay Ninh, regard
themselves as more orthodox and faithful than their
fellow Muslims down on the coast.

CHAU DOC ACCOMMODATION

Chau Doc's main hotel is the **Chau Doc**, *17 Doc Phu Thu (Tel: 6484)*. On the
other side of town are the **Tan Tai Hotel**, *273 Thu Knoa Huan (Tel: 6563)* and,
nearby on *Bao Ho Thoai*, the **Thai Binh** *(Tel: 6221)* and the **QDI** *(Tel: 6455)*.

Sightseeing in Chau Doc

Multi religious place of worship (margin)

It is appropriate that Chau Doc, this remote melting pot
of cultures, should be site of the **Mieu Ba Chau Xu**, a
large temple, known to Vietnamese throughout the world
and **dedicated to all religions**. Work on the temple
complex was started in 1973, but was stopped in 1976 on

the orders of the communist government. Now, temple activities including preaching and training programmes for would-be clerics, are in full operation, though not all the buildings have been completed.

Remains from the **Kingdom of Funan** and more recent **shrines** and **gravesites** have been found in the nearby **Nui Sam** - one of the Seven Mountains. The stone effigy of Ba Chau (the Lady Buddha) was discovered a long time ago in one of Nui Sam's grottoes and brought down to Chau Doc. She is believed to have the power to grant wishes and devotees make the pilgrimage to her temple, especially on the 22nd day of the fourth lunar month which is her special **festival day**. Also in Nui Sam is the **Tay An Pagoda** with its numerous wooden carvings; nearby is the tomb of **Thoai Ngoc Hau**, administrator for the Nguyen Lords, who died in 1829. On the other side of the hill is the **Chua Hang**, the cave pagoda and refuge from the world for **Le Thi Tho**, a pious seamstress.

Refuge for a
seamstress

An **important canal** follows the Cambodian border from Chau Doc and joins the **Thanh River** which empties into the Gulf of Thailand at Ha Tien. A network of roads and tracks also links Chau Doc and **Ha Tien** although not all are always passable. However, you normally get to Hai Tien via **Rach Gia**, which is reached by a road off the **Can Tho-Long Xuyen road** (see page 199).

Kien Giang Province

Rach Gia, capital of **Kien Giang province**, is on the Rach Gia Bay in the Gulf of Thailand. It has **deep water port facilities** and a **ship yard**, where they make fishing boats. **Fishing** is important business in Rach Gia and there is a Scandanavian financed **seafood factory** which processes the catches for export. The busy **fish market** is interesting and visits to the shipyard, a **shrimp farm**, the **processing plant** and possibly a **trip out in a fishing boat** can be arranged. Ask at the **Tourist Office** for details. In the

---

RACH GIA FACTS

The **Tourist Office** is at *12 Ly Tu Trong (Tel: 2081)*. The best of the accommodation is the **To Chau**, *4F Le Loi (Tel: 3718)* and the **1 Thang 5** (1st May), *39 Nguyen Hung Son (Tel: 2103)*. Other nearby, downtown hotels are: the **Rach Gia** and the **Nha Khach Uy Ban** (the Mekong) on *Nguyen Hung Son*; the **Thanh Binh**, *11 Ly Tu Trong* and the **Binh Minh**, *48 Pham Hong Thai*. Besides the hotels there are various **waterfront restaurants** including the **Hoa Binh** by the Gulf of Thailand on *Nguyen Hung Son* and the **Song Kien** and **Rach Gia** overlooking the river **Cai Long** on *Tran Hund Dao*; on the far bank is the **Hai Au** restaurant.

THE HOA HOA

The most curious element in Chau Doc's ethno-religious mélange is the **Hoa Hao** (the name is derived from a local village and pronounced 'Wah How'). Born in Phu Tan near Chau Doc in 1919, **Huyen Phu So**, a sickly child, was sent for treatment to **Thay Xom**, a Buddhist monk who lived in seclusion in the **Nui Cam hills**. Besides the conventional edicts of Buddhism, he taught So **sorcery** and **hypnotism**. On Thay Xom's death the lad, still far from healthy, returned home. During a stormy night in 1939, So fell into a trance next to his ancestors' altar and started ranting his own brand of Buddhist philosophy. At daybreak his congenital illness appeared cured and those who witnessed this apparently miraculous event started to take heed of So.

So expounded his simplified Buddhist doctrine, *'The cult must stem much more from internal faith than from pompous appearance. It is better to pray with a pure heart before the family altar than to perform gaudy ceremonies in a pagoda, clad in the robes of an unworthy bonze'*. His teachings had popular appeal amongst the peasants and the Hoa Hao sect evolved. So travelled extensively, spreading his faith through oracles and prayers, his *sam gian*. He had great presence and a fanatical stare which earned him the name **Dao Khung** - the Mad Bonze. His philosophy, his ability to perform miraculous cures and to prophesy the future with remarkable accuracy won him many converts. At one stage, these adherents – who frequently wore their hair in a bun, the men also having a wispy beard – numbered over one million.

During the turbulent 1940s and 50s the Hoa Hao extended their influence, becoming a significant **political and military force** south of Saigon. Like the Cao Dai and Binh Xuyen, they were too powerful to be ignored and, in these messy years, the various protagonists of the day - the Southern government, the Viet Minh, the French, the Japanese, the Americans - all tried both to embrace and destroy Hoa Hao, depending on the overall balance of power at the time. In 1940 So was confined to a mental hospital in Saigon by the French, but released after he converted his psychiatrist.

There was at one stage a tenuous bond between the Hoa Hao and Viet Minh, who were united by their anti-French feelings, but this snapped and, on 8th September 1945, 15,000 Hoa Hao, armed with knives and bludgeons, marched into **Can Tho** to confront a much better equipped Viet Minh force. Thousands of Hoa Hao died in the ensuing massacre, but those who survived were committed to a bloody revenge.

Huyen Phu So was murdered, apparently by the Viet Minh, in **Long Xuyen** in April 1947. The Hoa Hao were deprived not only of their charismatic leader, but also their unity. The sect split into factions and, while it maintained influence and a high profile for some time, it did lose much of its previous aura. Its decline came after the Southern government purged the leaders, publicly guillotining **Ba Cut**, its guerilla commander, in 1956.

There was a **revival** of the Hoa Hao faith in the 1960s and 1970s. The sect had always been fervently **anti-Communist**, a fact appreciated by the Americans who believed the Hoa Hao could be remobilised as a viable force if they had another powerful leader. As a public gesture of America's willingness to co-operate with the sect, **Robert McNamara**, U.S. Secretary of Defense for most of the 1960s, went to Hoa Hao country to meet Huyen Phu, So's ageing mother.

There was never another leader like Huyen Phu So however. Today, despite a Communist government in power, the Hoa Hao faith is still evident around Chau Doc.

past, the locals of Rach Gia used to gather the feathers of large birds and make them into **ceremonial fans** for the Imperial Court.

There is a **temple** commemorating **Nguyen Trung Truc**, a fervent anti-colonialist during the 1860s, who was involved in the resistance movement in the area around **Tan An**, south of Saigon. He was in charge of destroying the French warship *Esperance*, before basing himself on **Phu Quoc Island**, from where he continued his agitation. He had a price on his head and fellow Vietnamese betrayed his whereabouts, though the French only managed to capture him after holding hostage his mother and colleagues, claiming they would kill them unless he gave himself up. Nguyen Trung Truc surrendered and, on 27th October 1868, was executed in Rach Gia's market square. There are **other temples** in and around town and the Chinese and Khmer communities, both large and long established in this region, built their own **pagodas**.

A boat service operates along the 140 km between Rach Gia and **Duong Dong** on Phu Quoc Island, an island 45 km long by 40 km wide up at the north and only 5 km wide down at the south. Another boat goes to **Duong To**, a distance of 100 km, on the southern tip of the island. There are also flights between Rach Gia and Duong Dong. Enquire at the **Tourist Office** about timetables, how to get permission for a visit and about accommodation on the island.

Here, too, **seafood** - shrimps, cuttlefish, turtles and a large variety of fish - provide the **main livelihood**, and the island is famous throughout Vietnam for its excellent *nuoc nam* (fermented fish sauce). **Black pepper** is cultivated inland, largely by the Chinese Hainanese community who have been on the island for generations.

Throughout history the defeated have run to **Phu Quoc**, where they have had a chance to rest, regroup and then return to fight another battle on the mainland. **Nguyen Anh** fled to the island on several occasions during the Tay Son Uprising in order to take stock of the situation. He eventually went back to win all Vietnam and become **Emperor Gia Long**.

During the North-South civil war Phu Quoc served as an off-beat refuge for Americans wanting a holiday, although it was usually just a day trip from Rach Gia. There are beaches all around the island and the clear green-blue waters are excellent for swimming, underwater diving and fishing. **Ham Ninh** on the east side is the best known. It is a peaceful place in which you

can take a walk up into the hills and look northwards
across narrow straits to Cambodia.

Ha Tien
It is 90 km northwest by road from Rach Gia to Ha Tien.
A short distance to the left is the Gulf of Thailand, while
immediately on the right is the **Ha Tien-Rach Gia Canal**,
one of the Delta's major waterways and an alternative
transport route.

This far corner of Vietnam is rich in history. Here, now
just inland, was **Oc Eo**, the port of ancient Funan. After
the decline of Funan in the 6th century AD this land
became Khmer territory. Later the Malaysians, Chams
and Siamese all invaded. Finally the Viets arrived,
gaining Ha Tien through dealings with a Chinese man.

At the turn of the 18th century, **Mac Cuu** fled the
Ch'ing Dynasty and his native China and arrived in
what was then the Khmer domain of present southwest
Vietnam. He and his fellow refugees established a small
colony, calling it Ha Tien. They were soon caught up in a
Khmer-Siamese conflict and so Mac Cuu appealed to the
Viets' Nguyen Lords for protection. The Nguyens had
their own colonial ambitions and were willing to oblige.
They made Mac Cuu the local Governor and, on his
death, his son inherited the position. Thus, in the early
1700s, Ha Tien, the Viets most distant target in their
centuries long southward expansion, became their
property before the rest of the Mekong Delta. **Mac Cuu's
tomb**, in Ha Tien, is made from Chinese rock and
fashioned in the shape of a turtle.

The Viets did not arrive in large numbers until later in
the century. In 1790 Ha Tien was badly damaged during
the **Tay Son Uprising** and later there were **further
revolts** against the Nguyens by the local Khmers and the
Chinese, whose community had initially evolved around
Mac Cuu. In the late 1860s, the French annexed these
southern provinces of the Mekong Delta as part of their
colony of Cochin China.

Anti-American-Southern government resistance
fighters camped in the hill of **Hon Dat** which is on the
left, about a third of the way along the Rach Gia-Ha Tien
road. The lives of those who died is marked by a
memorial. In 1765 **French and Spanish Franciscans**
founded a **mission** at Hon Dat. Continuing on from here,
the road follows the curve of the bay round to the far end
and the **Nui Binh Tri rocks**.

A track leads off the main road down to the sea and a

village called Ha Tien, (not to be confused with the main town of Ha Tien further up the coast). The **beach** is sandy and, offshore, the clusters of **limestone islands** look similar to those in Ha Long Bay in the north - hence the nickname 'Mini Ha Long'. The islands can be visited by boat. The Kien Giang **Tourist Office** runs a **restaurant** on the beach and a small **chalet complex**, the **Nha Nghi Binh An**, a few kilometres along the shore, provides accommodation. Besides the beaches and small fishing villages, the local attractions are the **grottoes**.

Ha Long of the south

Centuries ago Khmer Buddhists converted the **Father and Son Grotto**, up in the **Hon Cong** cliff, near the Tourist complex, into their spectacular **Hai Son Tu Pagoda**. Further up the coast is the **Hang Tien Grotto** (the Coin Grotto). Reached by boat through a tunnel this was once a refuge for Nguyen Anh, who found zinc coins in the ground, earning the grotto its name. The **Mo So Grotto**, a few kilometres off the Rach Gia-Ha Tien road and 25 km short of Ha Tien, has various chambers and a maze of tunnels.

Where the fairies dance

The fishing town of **Ha Tien** is on the far side of an inlet, commonly referred to as the *'inland lake where the fairies dance at full moon'*, and is reached by a **pontoon bridge**. Local limestone deposits provide the raw material for Ha Tien's **cement industry**. Craftsmen carve **terrapin shells** into rings, bangles and earrings and their **workshops** can be visited. The early 19th century **Tombs of the Mac Cuu family**, the Mekong's famous Chinese connection, are just out of town. Two 18th century pagodas, the **Tam Bao Pagoda** and the **Phu Dung Pagoda**, built by Mac Cuu and his second wife respectively, stand near each other on Phuong Thanh.

There are several hotels on *Ben Tran Hau* alongside the market and river: the **Ha Tien**, the **Duong Ho** and the **To Chau**. There are also several restaurants here, notably the **Ha Tien**, **Xuan Thanh** and, at the other end of the block, the **Hoa Hiap**.

Van Son Mountain

The Van Son Mountain, or the **Mountain of Clouds**, rising from the flat plains 5 km beyond Ha Tien, enshrouds the huge 80 metre high **Tach Dong Grotto**, which, itself, enshrines the revered statue of **Sakya Mouni**, the Goddess of Mercy.

The rock became a place of worship for the Mahayana Buddhists after **Huynh Long**, a monk from Qui Nhon, established his sect here in the early 18th century; his ashes lie in the white Bach Thap stupa.

Tales from the mountain

The Van Son Mountain is one of those places which inspires locals to create legends. One variant of a well-loved story relates how **Thach Sanh**, a poor, day-dreaming itinerant, was strumming his guitar as he strolled by the mountain when he heard screaming and squawking coming from within the rock. He dashed up the slope and into the cave to see **Princess Huyen Nga**, daughter of **Thuy Te** the God of the Ocean, being carried away by an eagle through the hole in the roof of the grotto. Thach Sanh eventually tracked down the eagle and its hostage. He rescued the princess and was given her hand in marriage by the old Neptune.

A French colonial officer once abandoned a Viet Minh suspect in the grotto, believing it to be a place of no escape. The prisoner found a secret passage and, through it, freedom. This incident added another story and further aura to the folklore surrounding the mountain.

If you look at Van Son from the far 'Cambodian' side, you see the **profile of a head**, formed out of rock, halfway up the cliff. They say it is the face of Thach Sanh, or Thuy Te, or Huynh Long, or the Viet Minh escapee. Nearby there are **two other mountains**, but these remain **out of bounds** as Pol Pot's booby traps, planted in the 1970s, still render the place dangerous.

Khmer Rouge atrocities

The Khmer Rouge invaded the village of **My Doc**, near Van Son, on 14th March 1978, slaughtering 130 of the villagers. A **mass grave** commemorates the dead.

The sandy **Bai Mui Nai** and **Bai No**, to the west of Ha Tien, are the town's two main beaches and Vietnam's final stretch of coast. Beyond is Cambodia.

SECTION 3:
APPENDICES

Appendix I
HISTORY AT A GLANCE

Vietnam's Ancient Dynasties
Hong Bang Dynasty **2879-258 BC**
Kingdom: Van Lang
Capital: Phong Chau (Son Tay province)
Thuc Dynasty **257-208 BC**
Kingdom: Au Lac
Capital: Co Loa (Hanoi province)
Trieu Dynasty **207-111 BC**
Kingdom: Nam Viet
Capital: Phien Ngu (Canton)

1000 Years of Chinese Domination (Bac Thuoc)
111 BC - The Chinese Han Dynasty annexe Nam Viet as a province, renaming it *Giao Chi* (later *Giao Chau*).
40-43 AD - The Trung Sisters (Hai Ba Trung) revolt against the Chinese and temporarily restore independence. Their capital is Me Linh (Son Tay province).
220 - The Han Dynasty declines and is succeeded by a series of rulers and short dynasties under whom Giao Chau remains a Chinese province.
Early Ly Dynasty **544-602**
Kingdom: Van Xuan
Capital: Various, all in the region of present Hanoi.
Ly Bon - royal name Ly Nam De - ousts the Chinese and establishes his own shortlived dynasty.
622 - Tang Dynasty comes to power in China. Giao Chau continues as a Chinese province, becoming the Chinese Protectorate of Annam in 679.

Evolution of Present Vietnam
Ngo Dynasty **939-965**
General Ngo Quyen defeats the Chinese in 938, ending the "1000 Years of Chinese Domination" - as this long period of almost uninterrupted Chinese rule was known. His dynasty governs from the old capital of Co Lao.
965-967 - Ngo Dynasty succeeded by the period of the Twelve Lords.

Dinh Dynasty **968-980**
Kingdom: Dai-Co-Viet
Capital: Hoa-Lu (Ha Nam province)
Dinh Bo Linh (Dinh Tien Hoang) keeps peace with the Chinese by paying triennal tribute to the Sung Emperors.
Early Le Dynasty **980-1009**
Kingdom: Dai-Co-Viet
Capital: Hoa-Lu (Ninh Binh province)
Le Hoan (Le Dai Hanh) repels a Sung invasion from the north and a Cham attack from the south.
Ly Dynasty **1010-1225**
Kingdom: Dai-Viet
Capital: Thang-Long (Hanoi)
A period of prosperity. The Vietnamese push southwards, extending their borders at the expense of the Cham.
Tran Dynasty **1225-1400**
Kingdom: Annam
Capital: Thang-Long (Hanoi)
The 'Golden Era' continues. Tran Hung Dao defeats the Mongol armies of Kublai Khan.
Ho Dynasty **1400-1407**
Kingdom: Dai Ngu
Capital: Dong Do (Hanoi)
As the Tran Dynasty decayed, Le Duy Ly seized power and founded the Ho Dynasty.
Post Tran Dynasty **1407-1413**
The Ming Chinese invade and resurrect the Tran Dynasty.
1414-1427 - The Ming annexe Annam as a province of China.
1427 - Climax of the Lam Son Uprising: Le Loi and his strategist Nguyen Trai overthrow the Ming.
Le Dynasty **1428-1788**
Kingdom: Dai-Viet
Capital: Thang Long (Hanoi)
A stable and prosperous era which starts to decline in the early 16th century.
1527 - The influential courtier Mac Dang Dung establishes a dynasty to rival the Le lineage. The Mac Dynasty wins Thang Long, but the Le Dynasty

continues 'in exile', recapturing their capital in 1591. The Macs retire to Son Nam, further to the north, where they rule until 1677.

The Le cause was promoted by two powerful families: The Nguyens and the Trinhs.

1535 - Portuguese seafarers reach Cochin China, as they called Dai Viet.

1627 - Intense rivalry between the families leads to the Nguyen-Trinh Internecine War, with the Trinh occupying the north of the country and the Nguyen the south.

The Le continue as nominal heads of the country, though the Nguyen and Trinh - adopting the title of Lords - are in control.

1672 - The war ends as the two families acknowledge their common frontier.

Trinh Dynasty - **Lords of the North 1539-1787**

Nguyen Dynasty - **Lords of the South 1558-1778**

1776 - The Tay Son Uprising. The Tay Son brothers successfully rise up against the Nguyen in the south. They carry their revolt to the north where they defeat the Trinh and oust the Chinese-backed Le Dynasty; in doing so they unite the country (by now more or less the boundaries of present Vietnam) for the first time.

Tay Son Dynasty **1788-1802**

Kingdom: Viet Nam

Capital: Thang Long (Hanoi)

Quang Trung - champion of the peoples and most charismatic of the Tay Son brothers - holds power in the north; but his dynasty is soon under threat.

Nguyen Dynasty **1802-1945**

Kingdom: Viet Nam

Capital: Hue

Nguyen Phuc Anh, the last of the Nguyen Lords, survived the Tay Son Uprising and fled to Siam. He returned to Vietnam and, with the help of Bishop Pigneau de Behaine and the French, he overthrew the Tay Son Dynasty and established himself as Emperor - adopting Gia Long as his royal title - with his capital at Hue; from here he governed the whole country.

Several Western travellers - Gentlemen Roberts (1805, British), John White (1819, acknowledged as the first American to visit Vietnam), John Crawford (1822, British) - gave accounts of their visits to Vietnam and the cool, suspicious reception they received from the Imperial Court. Apparently, 'The Cochin Chinese looked upon the men with red hair and white teeth - that is to say Europeans - to be as naturally prone to war and depredations as tigers'.

French Occupation

1833 - Emperor Minh Mang announces his campaign against the foreign Christian missionaries - most of whom are French - and their increasing number of Vietnamese proselytes. He regards the religion as both a spiritual and secular threat to his country.

1862 - The French invade Vietnam ostensibly in response to the purge on missionaries.

1862 - Signing of the Treaty of Saigon on the 6th June between Emperor Tu Duc and the French, as negotiated by Phan Thanh Gian and Admiral Louis Aldophe Bonard.

Over the following couple of decades the French consolidate their position throughout the country, dividing Vietnam into the Colony of Cochin China (south Vietnam), and the Protectorates of Annam (central Vietnam) and Tonkin (north Vietnam). These three regions became part of French Indochina which also include Cambodia and Laos.

1890 - Birth of Nguyen Tat Thanh (later know as Ho Chi Minh)

1927 - Creation of the Viet Nam Quoc Dan Dang (VNQDD), the Vietnamese Nationalist Party, committed to fighting French imperialism.

1930 - The VNQDD uprising at Yen Bai is thwarted by the French. Founding of the Indochina Communist Party headed by Ho Chi Minh.

1940 - The Japanese, with the consent of the French, occupy Vietnam.

1941 - Founding of the Viet Nam Doc Lap Dong Minh Hoi, later known as the Viet Minh.

1945 - 2 million Vietnamese die of starvation in the North after the Japanese-French coalition hoard the rice harvest. In March the Japanese overthrow the French in Vietnam; the Viet Minh wage their war against the Japanese. In August the Japanese surrender to the Allies, allowing the Viet Minh to win control of all Vietnam. On 2nd September Ho Chi Minh declares Independence and renames the country the Democratic Republic of Vietnam. But at Potsdam the Allied victors announce Vietnam to be temporarily divided at the 16th parallel, thus allowing the British to officiate the Japanese surrender in the south and the Chinese Nationalists to undertake the same task in the north. But the British allow the French to return and by the end of 1945 the old colonial power is back in control of southern Vietnam; later the French regain much of the rest of the country.

1946 - The start of the Indochinese War as the Viet Minh launch their offensive against the French.

1949 - The French resurrect the old Nguyen Dynasty and, in an effort to counter the Viet Minh, they create Emperor Bao Dai as Chief of state of the State of Vietnam.

1950 - The Americans start giving aid to the French war effort.

1954 - The French lose the Indochinese War to the Viet Minh at Dien Bien Phu; this is the end of French involvement in Vietnam. Bao Dai gives premiership of State of Vietnam to Ngo Dinh Diem. Geneva Accords stipulate elections be held for a united Vietnam by mid-1956.

Civil War and America's Fight Against Communism

1955 - Diem takes over from Bao Dai as Chief of State and creates the Republic

of Vietnam (South Vietnam).

1956 - Diem contravenes the Geneva Accords by refusing to hold nationwide elections.

1959 - By now the increasingly unpopular and corrupt Diem has clamped down on resistance movements in the South which object to his regime. Democratic Republic of Vietnam (North Vietnam) supplies arms to these movements via the Ho Chi Minh Trail. The Americans increase their military aid to Diem and send in the first of their 'advisors' - Military Assistance Command Vietnam (MACV).

1960 - Creation of the Mat Tran Dan Toc Giai Phong Mien Nam - National Liberation Front of South Vietnam (NLF), nicknamed the Viet Cong (VC) - meaning Vietnamese Communist - by the Saigon government. A Communist backed movement in the South - supported by the North - serving as opposition to Diem's regime.

1963 - Diem assassinated. Kennedy assassinated; succeeded by Johnson who reconfirms America's commitment to South Vietnam's fight against the Communists in their country.

1964 - Americans attack North Vietnam after a confrontation between the North's torpedo boats and U.S. destroyers in the Gulf of Tonkin.

1965 - America bombs North Vietnam. The first U.S. combat troops arrive at Da Nang. By the end of the year they number 200,000.

1968 - The war has intensified and reaches a climax in January when the Communists launch their Tet Offensive against cities and towns in the South. There is much death on both sides, though the Communists suffer greater casualties. The American public reacted by demanding and end to the war. Johnson decides not to run for re-election; he is succeeded by Nixon.

1969 - American troops in Vietnam peak at 542,000. Ho Chi Minh dies aged 79. The start of the withdrawal of

U.S. troops from Vietnam.

1970 - Nixon secretly bombs Communist bases in Cambodia and later sends in the troops.

1971 - By the end of the year U.S. troops in Vietnam number 140,000.

1972 - North Vietnamese launch their massive Spring (Easter) Offensive against the South. Americans renew bombing campaign against Hanoi and Haiphong.

1973 - Ceasefire treaty signed in Paris. For America the war is over - the last of their remaining troops quit Vietnam in March; they leave the Southern army to continue the war against Communists.

1974 - The Communists consolidate their strength in the South.

1975 - The Northern army rumbles through South Vietnam. They, supported by other Communist forces, capture everything in their path as they head towards Saigon. They enter Saigon on 30th April and, hoisting the Democratic Republic of Vietnam flag, declare Vietnam re-united.

1976 - July, the formal reunification of North and South Vietnam. In the late 1970s friends of the former Southern regime are detained in 're-education' camps. Hundreds of thousands flee the country in fear.

1978 - Vietnam invades Cambodia in response to Pol Pot's cross border attacks.

1979 - China 'teaches Vietnam a lesson' and attacks the northern border as a response to the Cambodian invasion and rising friction between the Vietnamese government and the country's ethnic Chinese community.

1982 - Vietnam starts to reduce its troop quota in Cambodia, but still maintains its campaign against the Democratic Kampuchean resistance which includes the Khmer Rouge. China retains its pressure on the northern border.

1985 - General Secretary Le Duan visits Moscow. It is the Gorbachev era. Soviets promise aid for oil exploration and the petrochemical industry, but advise a shift from centralised planning.

1986 - Le Duan dies. After a shake-up of the Politburo, Nguyen Van Linh party leader in Ho Chi Minh City since *1975,* is chosen as General Secretary. He proposes a renovation of the old political and economic system (inflation was running at 700%).

1987 - Vietnam claims 1500 Chinese killed in a border clash.

1988 - The Vietnam-Democratic Kampuchean conflict affected relations between the USSR and China, the respective sponsors of the two warring parties. The big powers demand a cooling of the fighting.

1989 - Withdrawal of more troops from Cambodia. Repatriation of Boat People from Hong Kong. Vietnam criticises Eastern European countries for undermining socialism and emphasises the need for a one party state. The Five Year Plan ('91-'95) reveals Soviets will reduce aid; Vietnam must become more self-reliant. 38 members of an opposition movement, the US-based National Front for the Liberation of Vietnam, are arrested on the Laos-Thai border and extradited to Vietnam.

1990 - Last of the Vietnamese troops leave Cambodia.

1991 - The process of democratisation in Cambodia gets under way.

1993 - Amercan's review embargo on Vietnam.

- Increased trade links with China.

Appendix II
VIETNAM GLOSSARY

Annam (Protectorate of): The French protectorate established in the 19th century central Vietnam.

ARVN: Army of the Republic of Vietnam.

Bac Phan: Northern Vietnam.

Cao Dai: The bizarre Vietnamese religion and cult founded in the 1920s which set out to unite all the faiths under Cao Dai, the Creator of the Universe.

Cham: The ancient kingdom and culture which existed along the central plains of Vietnam until the arrival of the superior Viets from the north.

Chu Nho: Traditional Chinese-type characters used in Vietnam script.

Cochin China (Colony of): The French colony established in the 19th century covering southern Vietnam.

COSV: Communist Central Office for South Vietnam.

Cuu Chi: The underground tunnels to the west of Ho Chi Minh City which served as a base for the Viet Cong.

Dien Bien Phu: The battle fought in 1954 in north west Vietnam between the Vietnamese and the French. Vietnamese victory led to the end of French presence in the country.

DMZ: Demilitarised Zone, the 5 km buffer zone along the River Ben Hai which served as the division between North and South during the Vietnam War.

Doi Moi: Vietnam's version of Gorbachev's perestroika, meaning 'restructuring'.

Dong: Vietnam's currency.

Hoa Hao: A austere branch of Theravada Buddhism founded earlier this century in southern Vietnam by Huynh Phu Son.

Ho Chi Minh Trail (Truong Son Trail): 2000 km of roads and tracks along the Truong Son mountain range which served as the all important supply line from the North to the

South; it was cut in the 1950s.

Khmer: The predominant ethnicity of Cambodia which also once occupied the Mekong Delta.

MACV: Military Assistance Command Vietnam: the 'advisors' sent by America to help the South's campaign. The first group were despatched in 1959.

MIA: Missing in Action, denoting the American servicemen who were lost in Vietnam and remain unaccounted for.

Nam Phan: Southern Vietnam.

Nam Tien: The Viets' southward expansion from the Red River Delta, through central Vietnam and into the Mekong Delta; this colonisation gave the Viets more or less the present territory of Vietnam.

Nguyens: The dynasty of Vietnamese emperors who ruled from their capital at Hue from 1802 to 1945. Nguyen is also a common Vietnamese surname.

NLF (Mat Tran Dan Toc Giai Phong Mien Nam): National Liberation Front; the Communists in South Vietnam, nicknamed the Viet Cong.

NVA: North Vietnam Army.

ODP: Orderly Departure Programme; an official scheme initiated in the 1980s to allow certain Vietnamese to emigrate to America, Europe and elsewhere.

OSS: Office of Strategic Services; America's wartime version of the CIA.

PATS: Political Action Teams; pro-South Vietnam commandoes sent to infiltrate Viet Cong and North Vietnam forces.

Quoc Ngu: Romanised Vietnamese script developed by Catholic missionaries in the 17th century.

R+R: Rest and Recreation, denoting the free time allowed to American servicemen which could be enjoyed in resorts, cities or countries away from the action.

Tonkin (Protectorate of): The French

protectorate established in the 19th century covering northern Vietnam.

Trung Phan: Central Vietnam.

Viet Cong (VC): Vietnamese Communist (see NLF).

Viet Kieu: Overseas Vietnamese.

Viet Minh (Viet Nam Doc Lap Dong Minh Hoi): Originally known as the League for Vietnamese Independence, this popular national front evolved in the 1940s as a counter to French occupation.

VNQDD: Viet Nam Quoc Dan Dang: Vietnamese Nationalist Party, founded in 1927.

Appendix III
USEFUL VOCABULARY

In Vietnamese syllables have meaning and each syllable has six different meanings according to the tone in which it is said (in writing these tones are expressed with the use of accents). Here is a list of useful words. How accurate you are in expressing yourselves will depend on how successful you are in pronunciation.

Hello	*chao* (this is followed by the category of person you are addressing; eg: *'chao ba'* means 'hello old woman'; *'chao anh'*, 'hello young man'; *'chao em'*, ' hello young person'.
Goodbye	*tam biet*
Please	*xin moi*
Thank you	*cam on*
Yes	*da*
No	*Khong*
My name is . . .	*toi ten la* . . .
What is your name?	*ten ong la gi?*
I	*toi*
You	*cac ong* (older man)
	cac ba (older woman)
	cac anh (man of your age)
	cac co (woman of your age)
He	*anh ay* or *cau ay*
She	*co ay*
We	*chung toi*
They	*ho*
Man	*nam*
Woman	*nu*
Hotel	*khach san*
Restaurant	*nha hang an*
Bank	*ngan hang*
Post Office	*buu dien*
Hospital	*benh vien*
Market	*cho*
Railway station	*ga xe lua*
Bus station	*ben xe*
Taxi stop	*ben xe taxi*
Airport	*san bay*
Street	*pho/duong*
District	*quan*

Where?	*o dau?* (placed after the noun)

Water	*nuoc*
Tea	*che*
Coffee	*ca phe*
Beer	*bia*
Bread	*banh mi*
Rice	*com*

1	*mot*
2	*hai*
3	*ba*
4	*bon*
5	*nam*
6	*sau*
7	*bay*
8	*tam*
9	*chin*
10	*muoi*

Monday	*thu hai*
Tuesday	*thu ba*
Wednesday	*thu tu*
Thursday	*thu nam*
Friday	*thu sau*
Saturday	*thu bay*
Sunday	*thu nhat*

Today	*hom nay*
Tomorrow	*ngay mai*

Appendix IV
FURTHER READING

Beckett I: *Vietnam From 1945*

Britain Vietnam Association: *Vietnam Broadsheet* (Published three times a year). Copies available from Len Aldis, Flat 2, 26 Tomlins Grove, London E3 4NX.

British Embassy Hanoi-Department of Trade and Industry London: *Vietnam - A Guide for British Businessmen*

Brodrick A H: *Little China - The Annamese Lands*

Crawford A C: *Customs and Culture of Vietnam*
Foreign Language Publishing House Hanoi:
Ethnic Minorities in Vietnam
Ho Chi Minh Prison Diary
The Socialistic Republic of Vietnam
Uncle Ho
Vietnam Today
Vietnam - Urgent Problems

Gettlemen M E: *Vietnam: History, Documents and Opinion*

Graham Greene: *The Quiet American*

Hickey G C:
Sons of the Mountains
Free in the Forest
Ethnohistory of the Vietnamese Central Highlands up to 1954 and between 1954 and 1976 respectively

Higgins H: *Vietnam*

Karnow S: *Vietnam - A History*

Lewis Norman: *A Dragon Apparent*

Mangold T and Penycate J: *The Tunnels of Cu Chi*

Nguyen K V: *Vietnam - A Long History*

Orbis Publishing: *Eyewitness Nam* (A fifteen-volume magazine series)

Planeta Publishers Moscow: *Vietnam*

Sales J M: *Guide to Vietnam*

Sheehan N: *A Bright Shining Lie*

Shrock J L: *Minority Groups in the Republic of Vietnam*

Su That Publishing House Hanoi: *Vietnam - My Homeland*

U.S. Department of Army: *Area Handbook for Vietnam*

Walsh D: *The Vietnam War*

White J: *A Voyage to Cochin China*

Whitfield D J: *Historical and Cultural Dictionary of Vietnam*

Bookshops and street vendors in Vietnam sell a selection of Vietnamese published tourist booklets and maps of the country and main cities.

INDEX